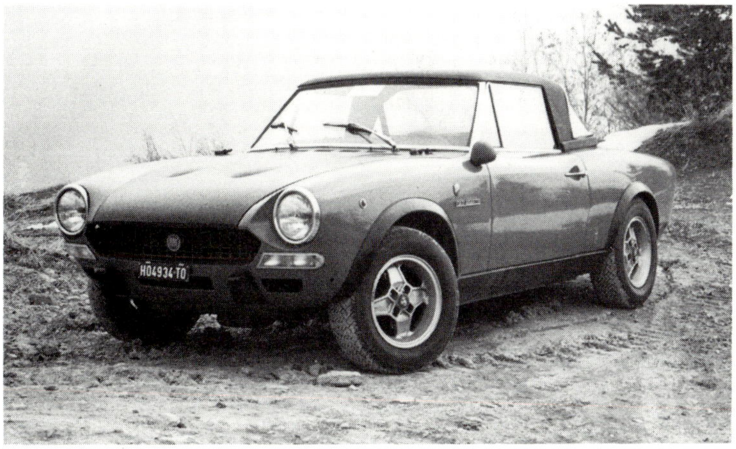

Graham Robson

FIAT SPORTS CARS

From 1945 to the X1/9

OSPREY

First published in 1984 by Osprey Publishing Limited,
12–14 Long Acre, London WC2E 9LP
Member company of the George Philip Group

© Copyright Graham Robson 1984

This book is copyrighted under the Berne Convention. All rights reserved. Apart from any fair dealing for the purpose of private study, research, criticism or review, as permitted under the Copyright Act, 1956, no part of this publication may be reproduced, stored in a retrieval system, or transmitted in any form or by any means, electronic, electrical, chemical, mechanical, optical, photocopying, recording, or otherwise, without prior written permission. All enquiries should be addressed to the publishers.

British Library Cataloguing in Publication Data

Robson, Graham
   Fiat sports cars.
   1. Fiat automobile
   I. Title
   629.2'222   TL215.F5
ISBN 0-85045-558-8

Editor Tim Parker
Design Gwyn Lewis

Filmset by Tameside Filmsetting Ltd
Ashton-under-Lyne, Lancashire
Printed and bound by Butler & Tanner Ltd
Frome, Somerset

HALF TITLE *Perhaps Fiat's most successful postwar sports car was the 124 Spider shown here in its fastest guise—the Abarth Rallye*

TITLE PAGE *Surely an outstanding sports car by any measure. Some feel the lines are strange although from this view the Fiat Dino Spider looks as well as it goes*

In only their second season, Lancia (or Fiat) won the World Rally Championship for makes with a team of Lancia Rallye cars. In this particular car, Walter Rohrl won the Acropolis Rally, with Markku Alen's sister car in second place, close behind him

Contents

Acknowledgements 6

Introduction 7

1 1100S and *Trasformabile* 8
2 8V—the engineer's toy 22
3 1200 and Osca 29
4 2300S Coupé 47
5 850 Coupé and spider 57
6 124 Spider and coupé 72
7 Dino—the Maranello connection 95
8 128—front drive 113
9 130 Coupé—speed with dignity 122
10 X1/9—mid-engined elegance 133

APPENDICES

1 124 Abarth Rallye 152
2 Ferrari and Fiat co-operation 160
3 Lancia in the 1970s 162
4 Stratos 177
5 Turbine car project 185

Index 189

Acknowledgements

It was not easy collecting the material for this book. In an ideal world, Fiat of Turin would have opened up their files, and flooded me with statistics and memorabilia—but it didn't happen like that. Fiat in the 1980s is a forward-looking concern, one which is larger, no less complex and—at times—just as troubled as BL; accordingly they have had to side-track their heritage to some extent. This, I hope, excuses the fact that some of the production figures quoted in these pages are either approximate, suspect, or even non-existent.

Even so, I would like to thank Fiat—both the parent company in Italy, and its British subsidiary, Fiat Auto (UK) Ltd, for the very generous help they gave me during 1982 and 1983. It must have been difficult for them to organize facilities for a British writer speaking little Italian, but they did it with true Latin charm. My principal thanks, therefore, should go to Mike Thorold-Palmer (Fiat Auto [UK]), and to Richard Vitale (Fiat Turin) for setting up the visits, and the interviews.

It was through them that I was able to visit the fascinating Centro Storico building (which supplied many of the photographs used in these pages), to meet Signor Gian Beppe Panico at Bertone, and Fredi Valentini at Pininfarina. Paola Gandolfo provided a very exciting Fiat Ritmo 125TC Abarth for me to use while in Italy, while Graham Gauld (Britain's own Fiat historical expert) helped guide me through the morass of names and places.

I'm grateful to my good friend Richard Langworth, of New Hampshire, USA, for his work on my behalf across the Atlantic, and to my colleague Jeremy Walton for breaking ground at Bertone well ahead of me. (His research into the Fiat X1/9 has now been published as an Osprey *AutoHistory* title.)

Fiat-Lancia's competitions chief, Cesare Fiorio, took time out from preparing for an important World Championship sports car race at Brands Hatch to reminisce about Fiat's rallying activities in the 1970s, and about the birth of the Lancia Stratos. Karl Ludvigsen told me about his experience of Fiat cars, and the Fiat company, in North America.

One personality I could not see was Dr Dante Giacosa, the brilliant engineer who directed Fiat's design activities from the 1940s to the early 1970s, but I acknowledge his genius in any case. Without him, and his most noted lieutenants, I doubt very much if there would have been any successful sporting Fiats for me to write about.

Finally, of course, I acknowledge the Italian spirit, and the Italians' love of fast cars, for without them there would have been no inspiration, nor any demand, for Fiat to make sports cars. At the moment, Fiat's sports cars have all died away, but the Italian *brio* has not. It gives me hope for the future.

Photographic credits

Finding fresh material with which to illustrate this book is a hard task. Such is the power of Fiat's press office that we live in danger of never finding a photograph of one of their cars which has not been spread around the world for every enthusiast or otherwise to see. But new material we undoubtedly have, at least, in great part. Nevertheless our first consideration must still go to Fiat through their Centro Storico in Turin. Linked with them we must thank their Fiat and Lancia press offices in the UK. Also we must group both Pininfarina and Bertone with Fiat for their considerable help.

Yet we must not forget all those freelancers, both photographers and agencies, who on this occasion to a man (and woman) have come up trumps. In alphabetical order: *Autocar*, Hugh Bishop, Graham Gauld, Geoffrey Goddard, Martin Holmes, LAT (*Motor Sport*), Moncalvo Fotographie, Karl Ludvigsen, *Motor*, Dr Eberhard Seifert, Alessandro Stefanini, Jerry Sloniger, Colin Taylor Productions and *Thoroughbred & Classic Cars*.

Introduction

When I started preparing to write this book in 1981, I meant it to be a celebration. In 1984, it has turned into something of a requiem. Even in 1981, Fiat were making fine sporting cars but, now, in 1984, it is all over. The massive Italian company, which has produced exciting sports cars like the Dinos, best-selling machines like the 124 Sport Coupé, and amazingly-advanced little mid-engined machines like the X1/9s, is now out of the sports car business for good.

Even so, I am at least able to relate a complete story of the sporting Fiats—open or closed, two-seat or four-seat, down-market or frankly exclusive—which have been sold since 1945. It is a story in which one man—Dr Dante Giacosa, Fiat's distinguished technical chief for so many years—figures very strongly, and in which the Italian genius for breathing character and excitement into the most unpromising *looking* material appears again and again.

Not only have I been able to unravel the complex way in which one model was developed from another (how many people realized, for instance, that the Dino's front suspension was that of a very ordinary Fiat family saloon?), but to puzzle out how it was often made possible from modest beginnings, and to impossible timetables.

I happen to be one of those unconventional people who think that sporting Fiats have meant more to more people than have the sporting Alfas, and I also believe that their real merits are still, in many cases, misunderstood. In the past, too many people have suggested to me that the best-selling Fiat sports cars have really been no more than rebodied saloons, and the same people have become amazingly hostile when I suggested that there have been many famous MGs, Triumphs and—yes—even Alfa Romeos which evolved in exactly the same way.

This, then, is a near-40 year old story of how a war-shattered Italian colossus not only recovered and became prosperous, and built many millions of useful family cars along the way, but found enough time, and inspiration, to produce a whole series of sporting cars as well. I am a great admirer of the way the Italians enjoy their motoring, if not of the way they cast aside their heritage, and I believe the story of Fiat's modern sporting machinery is at least as important as any book about MG, Jaguar, or Ferrari.

I only wish that I could look forward to driving a new-style, 1980s, Fiat sports car. Ah, well—this book, at least, should demonstrate the Fiat genius of the past.

Graham Robson

Fiat Sports Cars

1   1100S and *Trasformabile*
The first faltering steps—1940s and 1950s

Fiat's first postwar sports car was really conceived, not in 1945, when the shooting and the bombing had stopped, but in 1932, when the original Type 508 Balilla was announced. Not only was the Balilla the first under-one-litre Fiat for some years, but it was also the model which saw the first use of a new generation of engines. At first this unit was a 995 cc side-valve unit, distinguished by the 75 mm cylinder stroke 'trade mark' which was to persist at Fiat until the end of the 1960s.

The original Balilla, admittedly, was a very ordinary car, but each development of the basic design was better than before. In 1933 the 508S Balilla Sport two-seater was announced, and a year later the 508CS came along, complete with an overhead valve version of the engine, and a four-speed gearbox. From 1937, the Balilla became the Type 508C, complete with an enlarged (68 mm bore) 1089 cc overhead valve engine, a four-speed gearbox with synchromesh on third and top gears, a new long-wheelbase chassis frame, and coil spring independent front suspension.

So far, so good, but the direct, and obvious, ancestor of the first postwar Fiat sports car, was the Type 508C MM model of 1938, which was specifically developed for the Mille Miglia race. (MM, of course, denoted Mille Miglia, in the model title.) The power of the 1089 cc engine was boosted to 42 bhp, and top speed was at least 87 mph. Apart from its instant success in the Mille Miglia race (a 508C MM won its class, and averaged 69.59 mph over the 1000 mile race), the car was notable for being the first-ever Fiat with full-width or all-enveloping bodywork.

The latest car's engine was developed by Dr Dante Giacosa, who was later to become Fiat's technical chief; at the time, Giacosa has written, he also designed an in-line six-cylinder engine with the same engine capacity, and prepared a chassis with four-wheel independent suspension, but both were abandoned at the development stage.

Even so, the 508C MM was a real trail-blazer for Fiat, indeed for the sporting world, because of its body style, which was evolved for Fiat by Carrozzeria Savio. With its full-width lines, and the smooth contours, it might have been an early 1950s machine instead of one first shaped in 1937. There

LEFT *Ancestor of all modern Fiat sports cars was the 508C MM of 1937–38, with styling which influenced cars until the 1950s. It was the first-ever Fiat with full-width panelling, and was really intended for sports car racing*

RIGHT *Dr Dante Giacosa, the designer of so many famous Fiats between the 1930s and early 1970s*

Fiat Sports Cars

was a conventional 1100/1500 type radiator grille up front, and the rear wheels were covered by spats, while the roof swept only gradually downwards towards the tail and, in later types, almost came to a rounded point above the rear number plate.

All this, of course, was in the 1930s, when Fiat was the dominant Italian car-maker, when it actively competed in races and rallies, and when Mussolini's Italy thought itself an important force in world politics. For Italy, however, the tragedy of World War 2 got under way in 1940, capitulation to the Allies came in 1943, and there was bitter fighting over the countryside for the next two years. Once the Anglo-American war machine had properly swung into action, invasion forces moved inexorably northwards, past Rome and up towards the Turin-Milan axis, and all the time the industrial centres were persistently being bombed by British and American planes. By May 1945, Mussolini had been overthrown, and murdered, the German Armies had been pushed back on to the Plains of Lombardy, and the older Fiat factory at Lingotto had been almost destroyed by bombing, even though the newer Mirafiori factory had escaped comparatively lightly.

Italy, as a nation, was in chaos, but Fiat recovered quicker than most industrial concerns. Within weeks the first postwar trucks were being assembled, and within months the first postwar cars (of 1940-specification, 500, 1100 and 1500 types) were being made. The time was certainly not ripe for Fiat to indulge themselves in the building of limited-production sports cars (and, in any case, there were precious few opportunities for customers to use them properly, on the road, or on race tracks), as survival, physical and economic was vitally important. However, once Vittorio Valletta returned to Fiat as president and managing director, in April 1946 (having been removed by the Allied Military Government in 1945 as a suspected Fascist sympathiser . . .), postwar planning could once again begin in earnest. At the same time, Dante Giacosa became director of Fiat's design office, which covered cars and trucks; under Giacosa, Oscar Montabone was in charge of the motor vehicle design department.

Whatever brand-new model, to be produced out of the debris of postwar Italy, was going to be a major undertaking, and it came as no surprise that the first such car, the 1.4-litre Fiat 1400, did not appear until 1950. As Giacosa has said: 'It was inevitable in 1946 that the production programmes should arouse some uncertainty on the part of the top management. After years of war, when the whole commercial effort had been suspended, in a

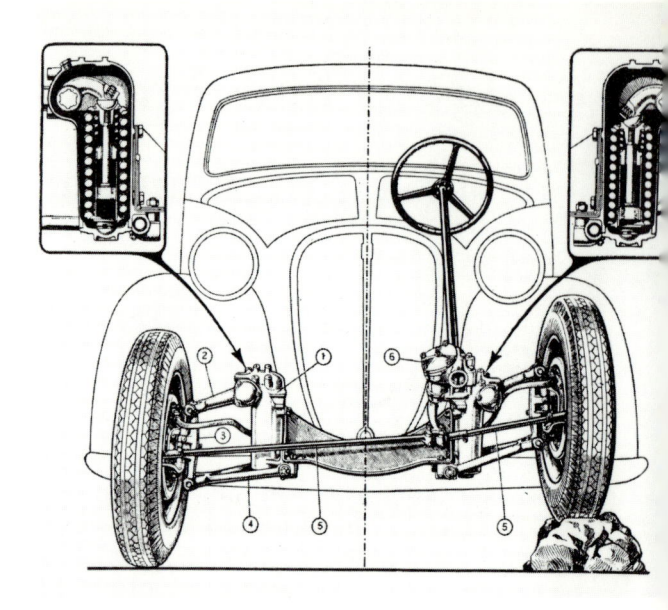

ABOVE *This was Fiat's first independent suspension for the Balilla of 1937, also used on the 1100S of 1947–50, the 8V Coupé of 1952–54; and the gas-turbine powered prototype. It featured coil springs enclosed in an oil bath, and telescopic dampers*

RIGHT *The 508C Balilla chassis of 1937, with independent front suspension, was that which formed the base of the pre-war 508C MM, and the postwar 1100S sports coupés*

situation full of problems caused by shortages of primary materials, it was natural that there should be doubts about which new model should be launched first on the market'.

One way, however, to cheer up the staff of Fiat, while they were toiling away at new bread-and-butter models for the 1950s, was to bring back some sporting interest, and this is precisely what was done. In Giacosa's words: 'The project for the 1100S, the sports model of the 1100 and a direct descendant of the 508C MM built for the Mille Miglia races in 1938 and 1939, helped to galvanise the atmosphere. Fiat could not keep out of the 14th Mille Miglia, to be held in 1947: this was a competition that mobilized auto manufacturers and aroused interest the world over; it marked the revival of the automobile industry after the war years. It was decided to go all out to build a coupé capable of putting up a good show in the race, but also adapted to use as a tourer by a sporting clientele.'

Thus it was that the 1100S, Fiat's first postwar sports car, came to be developed, more by a process of inspired expediency than by one of deep and devoted study of the market place. Nevertheless, it was a car which had great appeal to the Italians, at a time when there was a huge demand for *any* kind of new car, and especially for cars with a special or sporting character.

Giacosa, in the meantime, had spent some time working for Piero Dusio, designing the single-seater Fiat-engined Cisitalias, and the two-seater sports car of the same name, so he now knew more about the tuning limits of the robust 1089 cc Fiat engine. Perhaps it was no coincidence that the first coupé Cisitalias looked very much like the 508C MM of 1938, and that the first 1100S models of 1947 looked rather like the Cisitalias which were just coming along?

The chassis and running gear of the new 1100S was that of the 1100 saloon, which is to say that it had channel-section side-members, liberally pierced to minimize weight, it had cruciform stiffening to add to the torsional rigidity, it was upswept over the live rear axle, and it supported independent Dubonnet front suspension units, in which the coil springs were enclosed in an oil bath. The wheelbase, front and rear tracks, steering, tyres, wheels and brakes were all like those of the 1100 saloon, for the main novelties were in the engine tune itself, and in the shape of the body shell.

More detailed engine tuning, and downdraught Weber carburation helped boost the power output to 51 bhp at 5200 rpm—60 per cent more than the 32 bhp rating of the 1100 saloon, and 9 bhp more than produced for the 508C MM of 1938—enough to ensure a top speed of 93 mph. The bodyshell of the new 1100S, like that of the 508C MM, was styled and built by Savio, and had similar, but not identical, lines. The whole car was 10 in. shorter than the 508C MM, mainly because the tail was more abbreviated than before, and in place of a traditional-shape radiator grille there was something of a 'waterfall' style, not unlike that of the original Allards. For this, the production car, there actually was a tail window in the fastback roof, whereas the 508C MM racing car had had none, and the interior of the cabin was so narrow that the seats were staggered. That of the right hand (passenger) occupant was set back several inches, so that the driver had more elbow room for wheel movements, and for changing gear.

The 1100S was a splendid little car, but it was not at all refined, and it certainly was not cheap. The original 1947 price was 2,150,000 lire (£1075 at the then current rate of exchange). The very first prototype was shown at a hillclimb competition from Sassi to Superga in May 1947, when driven by factory test driver Carlo Salamano, while the very first production models, complete with their Savio fastback coupé bodies, were delivered in time to compete in the Mille Miglia race itself.

It was a triumphant debut. Naturally the cars could not be expected to win, for outright victory went to Clemente Biondetti's 2.9-litre Alfa Romeo and second went to Tazio Nuvolari's Giacosa-designed Cisitalia 1100. Two more Cisitalia's took third and fourth places, but the new Fiat 1100S sports cars took fifth, sixth, seventh and eighth overall, with Capelli driving the highest-placed example. A year later, the remarkable little cars did even better, for Biondetti's V12 Ferrari won the

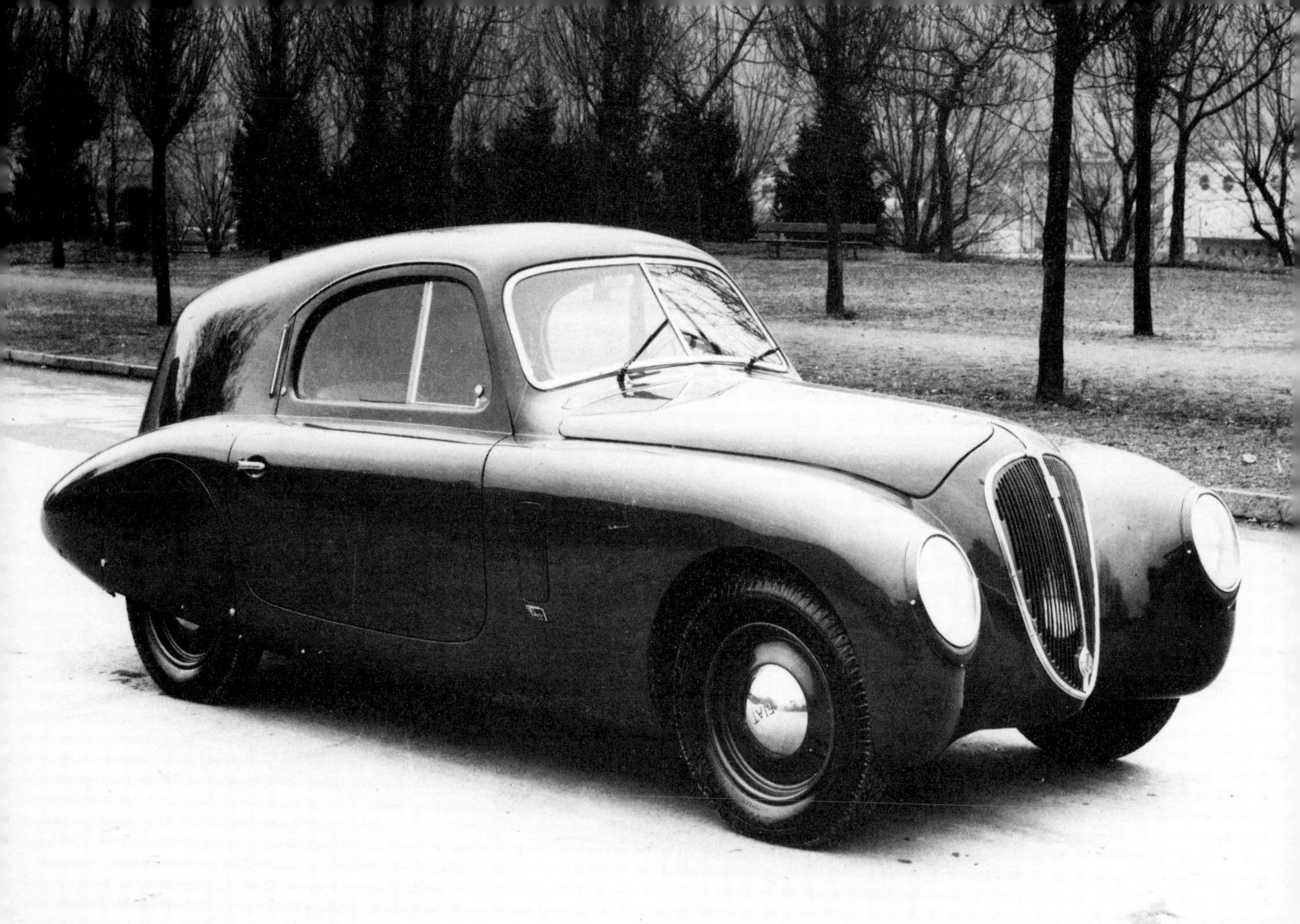

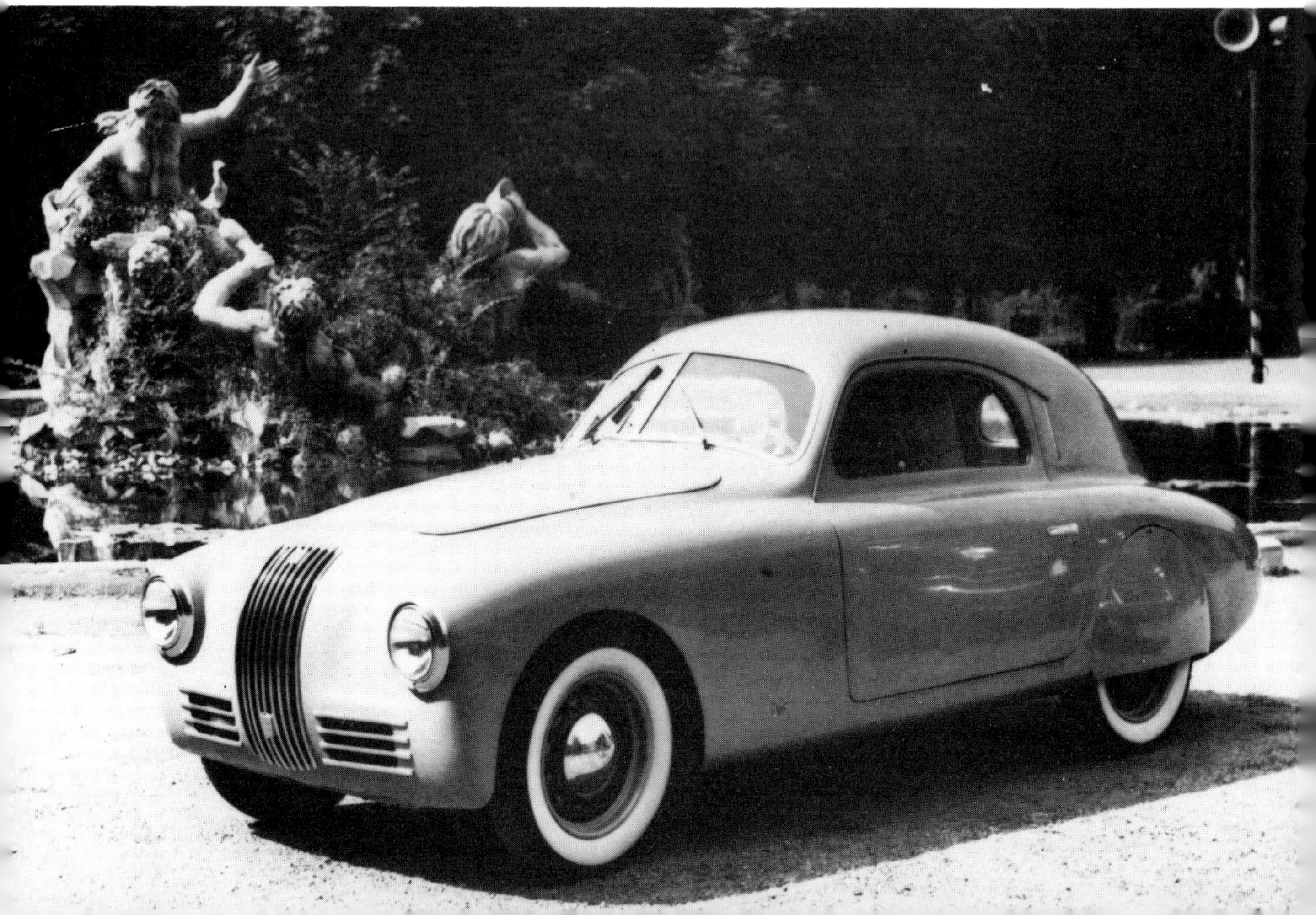

LEFT *The 508C MM of 1937 pioneered the basic body style adopted for the 1100S in 1947. In this original guise it completely lacked a rear window. The rear wheels were covered, to improve the aerodynamics*

BELOW LEFT *The first postwar sporting Fiat was the 1100S of 1947–50, a car directly descended from the 508C MM of 1937. The chassis and running gear were based on that of the 1100 saloons, while the style was an updated version of the 508C MM, this time with a proper rear window! Only 401 of these cars were built, all with special light-alloy bodies*

ABOVE RIGHT *The 51 bhp engine of the 1100S of 1947, still of prewar design, but most efficient. Note the drum hand brake on the transmission at the tail of the gearbox*

CENTRE RIGHT *In 1950, the 1100S was replaced by the more practical 1100ES, with extra interior space, and more modern styling by Pininfarina, though with no major chassis changes. It was an important 'prototype' of the later Lancia style*

BELOW RIGHT *This, of course, is not a Fiat, but the famous Lancia Aurelia GT coupé by Pininfarina. I need hardly point out the close similarity in looks to the Fiat 1100ES, which preceded it by a year or so*

13

Fiat Sports Cars

event, a Fiat-engined 'special' took second place, and true 1100S types took third and fourth places overall. The third-place car was driven by the Apruzzis and averaged 67.25 mph, compared with 75.8 mph for the winning Ferrari.

Although the 1100S cars only sold in limited numbers (a mere 401 examples were built between 1947 and 1950) they set a standard that all future Fiat models would have to beat. While using mainly standard components from a Fiat saloon model, the 1100S was given a more sporting character with the help of a tuned engine, higher gearing, and special coachwork. Such an approach was to be duplicated on later Fiat sports cars, in the 1950s, 1960s and 1970s.

Fiat, however, recognized that the original 1100S was only a stop-gap model, and they set out to improve on this by announcing, at the Geneva Motor Show in 1949, an alternative body style by Pininfarina on the same 7 ft 11.2 in. wheelbase and chassis frame. Not only was the Pininfarina style an

TOP *Pininfarina was the important cornerstone in the development of Italian sporting styles in the late 1940s—this was the famous Giacosa-chassis'd Cisitalia 1100 of 1947. Not only was the Fiat 1100ES evolved from it, but the Lancia Aurelia GT coupé as well. The car, though not a Fiat, was powered by a Fiat 1100 engine, and had Fiat transmission*

ABOVE *One of Pininfarina's early offerings on the basis of the 1100/103 saloon's floor pan, a fixed-head coupé built in 1953...*

RIGHT *... Facia styles had not yet been made to look particularly attractive*

14

even more shapely offering than before, but it offered close-coupled four-seater accommodation. According to styling experts, and noted Pininfarina-watchers, the Fiat 1100ES, as it became known when it finally went into small-scale production in June 1950, was a natural evolution from the lines of the famous Cisitalia coupé, and there is no doubt whatsoever that there is also a definite 'family' resemblance to the legendary Lancia Aurelia coupé which followed it in 1951. The 1949 prototype, incidentally, had a vestigial centre grille to recall the old model, but the production car of 1950 had lost all trace of this.

Compared with the original 1100S, however, the Pininfarina 1100ES was heavier, more bulky, and unavoidably slower. When fully laden it weighed at least 500 lb more, and needed a lower (4.55:1) final drive ratio to help produce a top speed of 87 mph; the original 1100S, don't forget, had been capable of at least 93 mph. The Pininfarina car, too, was inflicted with a steering column gear change.

However, the 1100ES is important to Fiat's sporting heritage, if only because it was the first production machine to be fitted with Pininfarina coachwork. The Turin-based company, up to this point, had been used to producing one-off bodies, but here was a big order—by its own standards—for 50 such cars were eventually built in about a year. It was one of Pininfarina's first steps along the way to becoming a larger, and commercially more important, concern.

By the beginning of the 1950s, however, Fiat had really lost interest in the separate-chassis 1100s, which dated from 1937 after all, and a new unit-construction 1100 was being developed. However, there was something of a time lapse before any thought could be given to sporting versions of this new car.

In the interim period, with the company up to its neck in the design of other new saloon cars like the 1400s, 1900s, and the tiny rear-engined 600s, they also allowed themselves to be diverted by the hand-built 8V Coupé, but this is such a fascinating little episode that I must give the car a chapter all to itself. It meant, however, that there was little 'play time' to devote to other projects, and in effect the next series-production Fiat sports car was not to be started until the 8V project was dead.

Fiat's first all-new postwar car was the 1400, which was first revealed at Geneva in March 1950. It was not a car with any sporting pretensions, though its unit construction four-door bodyshell, its independent front suspension, and its 1395 cc four-cylinder engine were all new. The 1900 which followed in 1952, complete with long-stroke 1901 cc engine, was merely a more up-market version of the same design. No-one who drove those cars was ever heard to suggest that there was the bare bones of a sports car locked somewhere inside.

The 'new 1100', the 1100/103, which followed in 1953, was a very different proposition. The only connection with the obsolete 1100E saloon, which was dropped to make way for it, was that the bare bones of the old 68 mm × 75 mm, 1089 cc overhead valve engine had been retained, although the new engine was a completely redesigned version of the

Fiat Sports Cars

1100S and Trasformabile

ABOVE *Perhaps the happiest view of the 103E Trasformabile is from overhead. There were, of course, only two seats, and this car actually has safety belts fitted*

TOP LEFT *To give this car its full title—the Fiat 1100/103TV Trasformabile—the first series production Pininfarina car built on the basis of the 1100TV saloon's underpan, suspension and running gear. Introduced in 1955, there was total production of several hundred, and the styling could best be described as 'controversial'; that wrap-round windscreen was clearly aimed at the North American market*

LEFT *Recognition points of the 103E Trasformabile were the snouted bonnet panel, the twin-nostril grille/air intake, and the chrome stripe behind the doors. Those are indicators on the crown of the front wings*

old. The new 1100 was everything which the 1400/1900s were not—light, compact, sprightly, and with excellent handling for the period.

Starting in 1946, Giacosa had laid down a new system of numbering for new vehicle projects at Fiat, and since a great deal of reference to these will be made in this book, I ought to explain what it was all about. In Dr Giacosa's own written words: 'To get some order into the numbering of the models and designs, I had laid down that new models should be designated by a three-digit number, of which the first should be 1 for automobiles, 2 for trucks, 3 for long-distance coaches, 4 for town buses. Later on, 5 was used for tractors and 6 for engines for special purposes. This explains the reasoning behind the designation of automobiles in the project stage: "100", "101", "102" etc.' It was a numbering system which survived intact until the late 1970s, progressing as far as Type 140, and it involved not only complete cars, but major engine projects as well.

Project 100 eventually matured as the rear-engined 600 saloon (and we shall meet this again, in connection with the 850 Coupés and Spiders of the 1960s, in a later chapter), while Type 101 was the big new 1400 saloon of 1950. Project 102 concerned front-wheel-drive cars derived from the brilliant and well-thought-of Grégoire design, whereas the Type 103 was always meant to have an orthodox layout, and be a last-minute alternative to the 102s if they were ever cancelled.

Type 103, therefore, referred to a front-engine/rear-drive four-seater saloon, which was first noted late in 1946, but which was not even started, as a plaster mock-up until 1948. By 1949 the Type 103 was a firm project, while the more advanced 102s were not dropped until 1951. At first Dr Giacosa thought it should have a new engine, and had a variety of straight four-cylinder and 60-degree vee-4 units were built and tested. There were suggestions that the car should have front-wheel-drive, or at the very least that it should have rear-wheel-drive and independent rear suspension, but by the autumn of 1951 the style, and the layout,

Fiat Sports Cars

had been rationalized, and agreed. The new 1100/103 had a front-mounted engine, really a much redesigned version of the existing unit, the four-speed gearbox and steering column gearchange from the 1400 saloon, and a conventional hypoid bevel rear axle. It was a short and stubby, but attractive little four-door saloon, styled by Fiat themselves, and with a 36 bhp power output it was capable of 72 mph. It was announced at Geneva in March 1953, and was joined, only months later at the Paris Show in October, by the 50 bhp 1100/103TV ('TV' stood for 'Turismo Veloce'), which was a real little sports saloon, with a top speed of nearly 85 mph, extremely creditable for its day, particularly for a full four-door saloon of small-medium size.

In the meantime, a new sporting two-seater was on the way, and eventually made its bow at the Geneva Show of March 1955. The minor mystery is not as to the number eventually built (though that *is* a mystery, as I will shortly explain), but as to the exact origins of the style. According to Dr Giacosa, in his autobiography, it was a style evolved by Luigi Fabio Rapi (of Fiat) 'with my assiduous help', but it was also a car built for Fiat by Pininfarina, and bearing a close relationship in looks to a Lancia from that Torinese specialist!

The chronology is as follows:

The new two-seater open sports Fiat, which eventually rejoiced in the title of 1100/103TV Trasformabile, was evolved in 1954, and launched in March 1955 at Geneva, where it was to be found on the Pininfarina stand. In the meantime, however, Pininfarina had styled a striking two-seater spider for Lancia, on the basis of the Aurelia GT, and this car was revealed during 1954, several months before the Fiat made its bow; this style featured a wrap-round windscreen, a dip in the waist-line as it passed the seats, and the Fiat which followed it looked remarkably similar.

At this range of nearly 30 years, no archivist can tell me precisely who designed what—I am inclined to call this the 'Pininfarina' car, a title by which it is normally identified, especially as the bodyshells were all built for Fiat by Pininfarina. I am also tempted to conclude that Signors Giacosa and Rapi were involved in the shaping of their Fiat, but saw the prototype Lancia before they completed their job.

This rather artificially posed picture establishes the chassis 'base' of the Trasformabile, which was that of the stubby but remarkably nippy 1100TV saloon

1100S *and* Trasformabile

The fact is that the Trasformabile was announced in March 1955, and was based on the unmodified underpan of the 1100TV saloon, complete with its saloon-car suspension, and the steering column gearchange, but with a special new bodyshell and stress-bearing superstructure. Naturally the wrap-round screen was one recognition point, but the divided 'twin-nostril' grille and the vertical bumper overriders were others.

It was not a car which was going to win many beauty contests, thought its claimed top speed of 88 mph made it attractive enough. Pininfarina set about building the car in numbers—small numbers by Fiat's Mirafiori and Lingotto standards, but large enough for their own expanding business. But how many did they build? Who really knows. Fiat's own publication, *Tutte le Fiat* claims 571 cars in two years to the autumn of 1957, but figures supplied especially for this book mention 1030 cars. Pininfarina, for their part, say they built 780 bodies. There will be much confusion of this type throughout this book....

In 1957, the 1100/103 saloon was considerably modified, not only with revised styling, but with a large engine. The new more crisply-styled model had a 72 × 75 mm, 1221 cc, 55 bhp engine and was called the 1200 Gran Luce. Although it did not replace the existing 1100 saloons, the new engine did replace the original one in the two-seater, which therefore became the 1200 Spider, and was identified by slightly different bumpers, and other details. The wrap-round windscreen was retained unchanged, as were the swivelling seats which could be turned towards the doors, to make for easier entry and exit from the car. On this model, too, there was a central gearchange, which made the car seem altogether more sports-car like.

In spite of its rather stubby looks, and what must have been a rather appalling drag coefficient, the 1200 Spider was a lively, if not blindingly fast, two seater. *Road & Track* tested a Spider in October 1958, and reported a top speed of 89 mph.

Comparatively speaking, the 1200 was more successful than the 1100 Trasformabile, for according to the latest Fiat claims, a total of 2363 cars were built before the model was dropped in favour of the smooth new cabriolet of 1959. In North America, where the car might have been expected to be popular, the 1200 Spider seems to have sold well in spite of a certain amount of 'neglect' from the Fiat concessionaires, and what (in 1958) was the rather high price of $2621. The 'neglect' was caused because the importers were far more interesting in marketing the new 600 and 1100 saloons, and because they provided no press demonstrator—*Road*

Pininfarina was never slow to persist with the development of a theme thought to be successful. The Lancia Aurelia Spider (sometimes called the 'America') had much in common with the Fiat 1100/103E Trasformabile, but the longer wheelbase makes the lines more harmonious. From this angle, there are obvious similarities in shape, the Lancia's grille, however, is quite unmistakeable

& *Track* had to borrow a privately-owned machine.

No-one could blame Fiat of Turin by neglecting the little 'ugly duckling' in 1958, for they had more important new sports cars to consider. Not only did they have a new body style on the way, but a brand-new twin-cam engine to power it. It was an exciting time for Fiat, and the events of the 1960s would prove that this time their instincts were right.

1100S and 1100ES Coupés

PRODUCED May 1947 to mid-1951
NUMBER BUILT 401 1100S, 50 1100ES Pininfarina
GENERAL LAYOUT Front-engined two-seater or two-plus-two seater coupés, with separate chassis frame. Four-cylinder engine at front, driving rear wheels, with independent front suspension. Direct descendant of 1937–1939 Type 508CM 1100.
ENGINE Tuned version of long-running 1089 cc unit, as used in many Fiat models in 1930s to 1950s. Four-cylinder layout, in line, with three crankshaft main bearings. Cast iron cylinder block, and light-alloy cylinder head. Two valves per cylinder, overhead mounted, operated by pushrods and rockers from single camshaft mounted in side of cylinder block, driven by chain. Bore, stroke and capacity 68 × 75 mm, 1089 cc (2.68 × 2.95 in., 66.5 cu. in.). CR 7.5:1. One downdraught Weber carburettor. Maximum power 51 bhp at 5200 rpm
TRANSMISSION In unit with engine, four-speed manual gearbox, with synchromesh on top and third gears. Final drive ratio 4.1:1. Overall gear ratios 4.1, 5.98, 9.14, and 15.12:1
CHASSIS AND SUSPENSION Front engine, rear drive. Separate chassis frame, with drilled channel section side members, like that of other 1100 Type 508 models. Independent front suspension by oil

bath enclosed coil springs, wishbones, and anti-roll bar. Worm and sector steering. Suspension of rear live axle by half-elliptic leaf springs, and anti-roll bar. Front drum brakes, rear drum brakes, with transmission hand brake. 5.00–15 in. cross-ply tyres, on 3.0 in. wide wheel rims.
BODYWORK Separate coachbuilt light-alloy bodyshell by Savio. Two-door, two-seater, fastback sports coupé body style. Length 12 ft 10.8 in.; width 4 ft 10.25 in.; height 4 ft 5.1 in. Wheelbase 7 ft 11.25 in.; front track 4 ft 0.5 in.; rear track 4 ft 0.25 in. Unladen weight 1818 lb
PERFORMANCE SUMMARY Top speed 93 mph. Typical fuel consumption 22 mpg
NOTE From 1950, the 1100S became the 1100ES, with Pininfarina styling, and the following changes:
TRANSMISSION Steering column gear change. Final drive ratio 4.55:1. Overall gear ratios 4.55, 6.64, 10.14, and 16.78:1
BODYWORK Separate coachbuilt bodyshell by Pininfarina. Two-door, 2+2 fastback sports coupé body style. Length 13 ft 5 in.; width 5 ft 1.5 in; height 4 ft 5 in.

1100TV Trasformabile (Roadster)

PRODUCED May 1955 to Autumn 1957
NUMBER BUILT 1030
GENERAL LAYOUT Front-engined two-seater sports roadster, with pressed-steel unit construction body/chassis unit. Four-cylinder engine driving rear wheels, with independent front suspension.
ENGINE Version of long-running 1100 saloon design, in TV (Turismo Veloce) form. Four-cylinder in-line unit, with cast iron cylinder block, and light-alloy cylinder head. Three crankshaft main bearings. Two valves per cylinder, overhead mounted, and operated by pushrods and rockers from single camshaft in side of cylinder block, driven by chain. Bore, stroke and capacity 68 × 75 mm, 1089 cc (2.68 × 2.95 in., 66.5 cu. in.). CR 7.6:1. One downdraught dual-choke Weber carburettor. Maximum power 50 bhp (net) at 5400 rpm. Peak torque 52 lb ft at 3200 rpm
TRANSMISSION In unit with engine, four-speed manual gearbox, no synchromesh on first gear. Final drive ratio 4.3:1. Overall gear ratios 4.3, 6.75, 10.23, 16.59, reverse 16.59:1. 15.8 mph/1000

From 1957, when the 1100TV gave way to the larger-engined 1200 Gran Luce, the Trasformabile was similarly up-engined. The only important style change was to the bumpers. I thought you'd also like to see the fashion of the period as well...

rpm in top gear. Steering column gear change
CHASSIS AND SUSPENSION Front engine, rear drive. Unit construction pressed-steel body/chassis unit, using underframe of Fiat 1100 saloon. Independent front suspension by coil springs, wishbones, and anti-roll bar. Worm and roller steering. Suspension of rear live axle by half-elliptic leaf springs and anti-roll bar. 9.9 × 1.4 in. front drum brakes, 9.9 × 1.4 in. rear drum brakes, plus transmission drum hand brake. 5.20-14 in. cross-ply tyres on 3.5 in. wide wheel rims. Bolt-on pressed-steel disc road wheels
BODYWORK Pressed-steel shell, in unit with 'chassis', produced for Fiat by Pininfarina, on basis of standard Fiat 1100TV underframe and some inner panels. Two-door, two-seater, open spider style. Length 12 ft 6.3 in.; width 4 ft 9.8 in.; height 4 ft 2.1 in. Wheelbase 7 ft 8.1 in.; front track 4 ft 0.4 in.; rear track 3 ft 11.8 in. Unladen weight 1875 lb

1200 Convertible

PRODUCED Autumn 1957 to Spring 1959
NUMBER BUILT 2363
GENERAL LAYOUT Same basic car as the 1100TV Trasformabile, with enlarged engine, and other new details. Changes as follows:
ENGINE Bore, stroke and capacity 72 × 75 mm, 1221 cc (2.83 × 2.95 in., 74.5 cu. in.). CR 8.0:1. Maximum power 55 bhp (net) at 5300 rpm. Peak torque 60 lb ft at 3000 rpm
TRANSMISSION Remote control floor gear change
PERFORMANCE SUMMARY (*Road & Track*, October 1958) Maximum speed 89 mph, 0–60 mph 18.8 sec., standing start ½ mile 21.0 sec., overall fuel consumption 40 mpg (Imperial)

2 8V—the engineer's toy
Fiat's designers indulging themselves

At the Geneva Show of March 1952, Fiat surprised everyone, by announcing a brand-new sports coupé, which they christened 8V or *Otto Vu*. It was a surprise, not only because it had not been leaked in advance, but because it was new from end to end. Even then, sports cars usually picked up many components from mass-production cars, but there was virtually nothing in the new 8V that anyone could recognize from other Fiat models. Most exciting of all, for the pundits and analysis, was that it was equipped with an entirely new 2.0-litre vee-8 engine.

However, there was more—and less—to this car than met the eye at first. It was not the completely engineered and developed racing sports car that it might have been, nor was it to be built in large numbers at a bargain price. In many ways it was that rare project of modern times—an engineer's toy. That eminent motoring historian and Fiat-watcher, the late Michael Sedgwick, described the 8V as 'technicians thinking aloud', though in fact they had been thinking of something else when the engine was first designed.

The story really started in the late 1940s, when Giacosa was evolving a new range of postwar Fiats for Vittorio Valletta. I have already mentioned how the *nuova* 1100 came into being in 1953, but this car had already been preceded by the rather lumpy 1400

ABOVE RIGHT *There were several coachbuilders' styles for the 8V, but this was Fiat's own, and the shape in which the car was first revealed in 1952. It is posed on the cobbled banking of Fiat's famous test track*

BELOW RIGHT *The smooth rear aspect of the 1952 Fiat 8V, showing the 'fast' back and the central position of the fuel filler cap*

BELOW *The Fiat 8V of 1952–54 has been described as 'Fiat engineers thinking aloud', for it was a strictly limited-production (114 cars built) machine with an advanced chassis and a 70 degree vee-8 2-litre engine. There were only two seats, and the car had front and rear independent suspension*

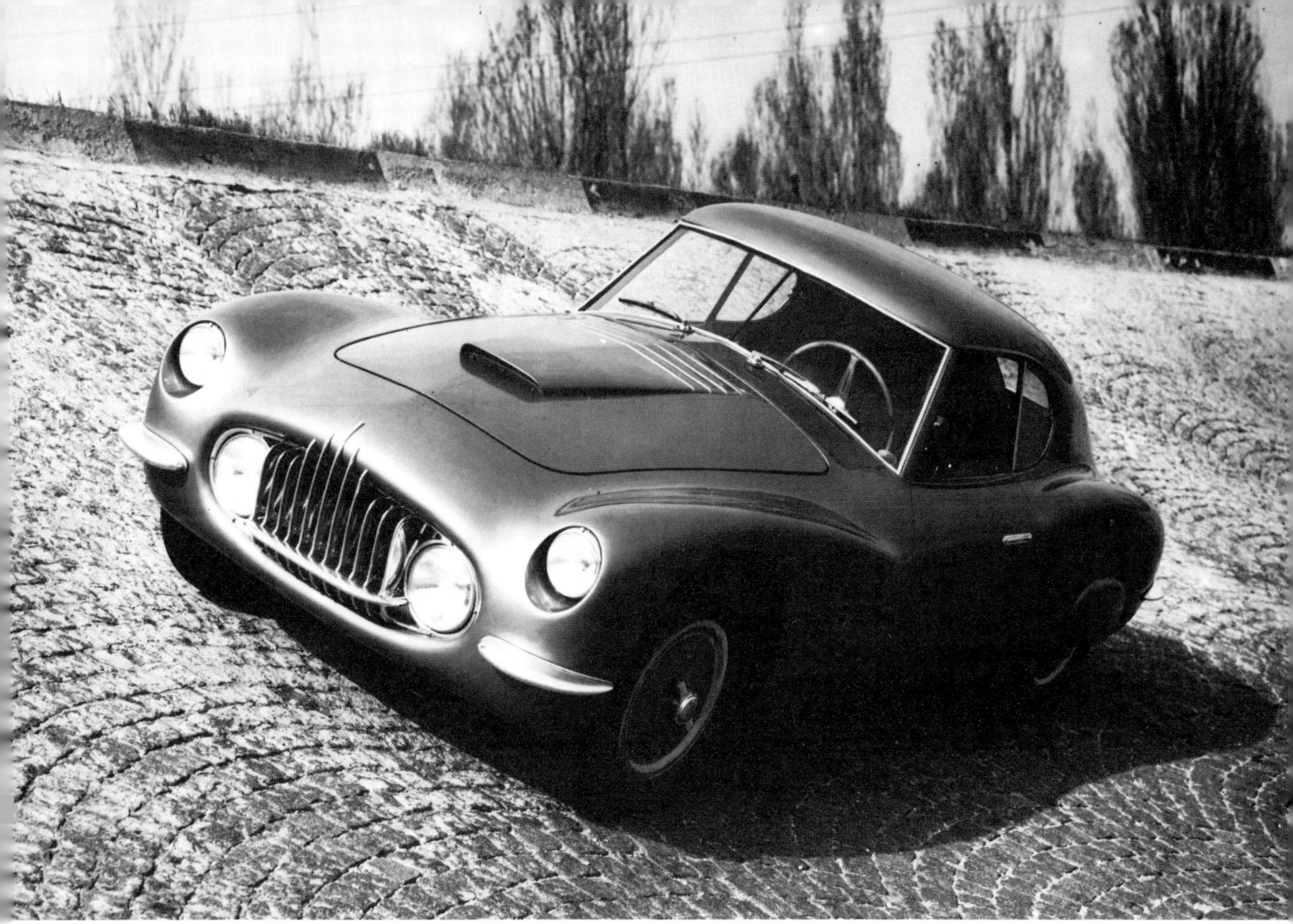

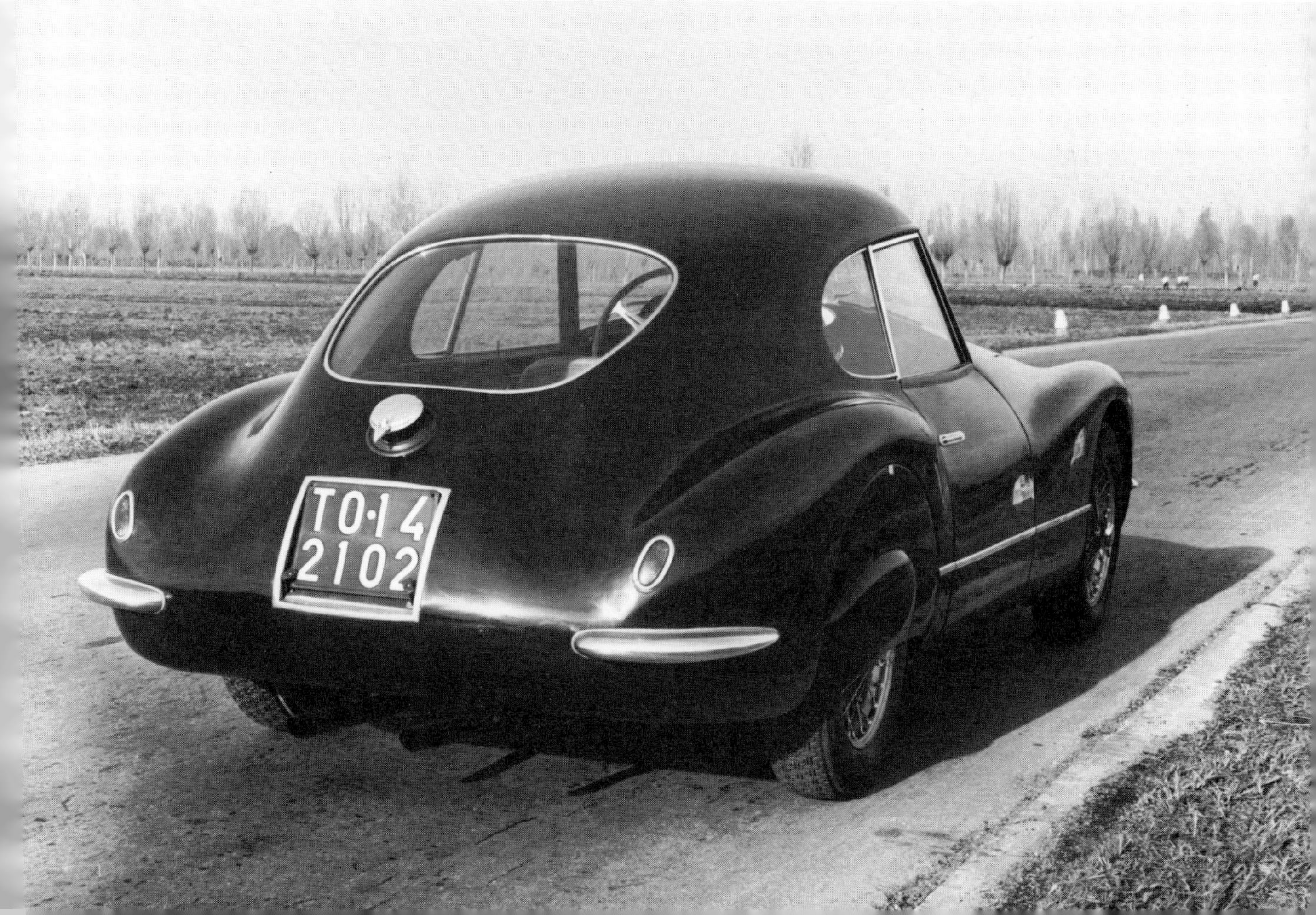
TO·14
2102

Fiat Sports Cars

ABOVE *The nose of the 8V was carefully thought out, with a minimum-size grille, and four headlamps arranged slant-style*

ABOVE RIGHT *A rare picture of the 8V's engine and gearbox taken from a Fiat publication. The 70 degree vee angle was not ideal for balance purposes, but was chosen to minimise the width of the unit inside the confines of an engine bay; this also explains the odd shape of the exhaust manifolds*

of 1950. Believe it or not, the engine used in the 8V coupé was connected with that project.

Project 101 was the first all-new Fiat of the late 1940s, and as the 1400 it went into production with a 1395 cc, 44 bhp, four-cylinder engine. However, well before launch, when the car was no more than an experimental mock-up, Fiat management had visited the 1948 Geneva Show, were apparently horrified by the progress exhibited by their rivals, and set about upgrading the specification of Project 101. Not only was the existing design of engine to be enlarged, but space was to be found under the bonnet for a narrow-angle vee-6 engine to be installed, so that a faster and more luxuriously trimmed limousine could be evolved.

Giacosa, when consulted, was not at all impressed by this, and made a counter proposal that a narrow-angled vee-8 should be designed instead. In the meantime, the Type 101's engine was eventually enlarged to 1395 cc, and even before any type of vee-engine could be designed, a long-stroke 1901 cc unit for use in the same unit consutruction body/chassis unit, and also to power Fiat's new Jeep-like four-wheel-drive Campagnola cross-country vehicle, was produced.

In 1949, however, Project 104, which was actually an engine only, and not a complete car, got under way. Giacosa's brief was to be sure that the new unit would fit an existing engine bay and, having discarded the narrow-angle vee-6 request, he set about the design of a narrow-angle vee-8. The ideal vee-angle, of course, is 90 degrees, but there was no space for this, or for conventional exhaust pipe systems, so the resulting design was a 70 degree layout (I do not believe this angle has ever been used by any other company), and the exhaust ports were led out at the top of the cylinder heads to slim down the engine's profile even further.

By 1950 the engine was running, and in the same year Fiat supplied a lengthened underframe to Pininfarina for a new limousine style to be evolved. As it happens, the prototype they produced was too heavy, and not striking in its looks, so the long-wheelbase project was cancelled. Fiat, however, were left with a fine little vee-8 engine, and Giacosa soon gained permission to build a sports car prototype for assessment.

The result was the 8V coupé, an amazing little car which established several 'if only' records for Fiat, and remains unique to this day. It is the only Fiat ever to have been sold with a vee-8 engine, the only 'production' car to have been build on a hand-to-mouth basis in the experimental workshops, and the first-ever Fiat to be sold with all-independent suspension.

As with so many other Fiats of the period, it was Giacosa as the engineer, and Rapi as the stylist, who were mainly responsible for the new car which, incidentally, was Type 106, using the Type 104 engine. (The Project 105, by the way, was the 1.9-litre four-cylinder engine already mentioned, and nothing to do with this project.)

8V—the engineer's toy

The basis of the car was a simple two-tube frame running lengthways, (oval section on the first six cars, round thereafter), which really formed only the connection between front and rear suspension systems, as the car's steel floor, the structure, and the skin panels were all welded together, and to the frame itself, on assembly. In a much-less advanced way (but a more simply devised way) than the 1400s and 1100/103s, the 8V had unit-construction body/chassis construction.

The independent front suspension was 'conventional-Fiat', of the type first launched on the Balilla 1100 in 1937, which is to say that there was a double wishbone geometry, and a vertical coil spring and hydraulic damper unit all encased in an oil bath, mounted inboard and operated by a rocker arm from the top wishbone itself. (The world of Grand Prix racing thought they had invented rocker arm suspension in the 1960s, but Fiat had beaten them to it....) At the rear, too, there was independent suspension, of almost exactly the same type, except that there was an additional telescopic damper to each wheel, and of course there was accommodation for drive shafts, and no need for steering. To accommodate this, it was necessary to have a chassis-mounted differential, which was most conveniently available on the new four-wheel-drive Campagnola. In fact, just to make it all more interesting (for the Campagnola had a rigid rear axle), the *rear* suspension drive shafts and the differential unit were effectively those of the *front* wheel transmission of the cross-country vehicle. To complete the suspension and chassis layout, there were front and rear anti-roll bars, and the latest saloon-type worm and roller steering was chosen—all cars, naturally, having left hand drive.

To back the 72 × 61.3 mm, 1995 cc vee-8 engine, which produced 105 bhp in 8V standard form, and which was not at all related to any other Fiat engine, before or since, there was the new four-speed gearbox of the 1400.

The original body style was by Rapi, with input gleefully provided by the enthusiastic Giacosa, and this was partly influenced by the need to make the combined body/chassis unit as rigid as possible and as light as possible, and that it could nevertheless be built by hand in Fiat's own workshops. It was streamlined, and quite unmistakeable, in the modern idiom, with a fixed steel fastback roof and wind-up windows. There was a vee-screen having a

Worm's-eye view of the rear of the 8V's chassis, showing the tubular frame construction, and the mounting of the differential on the chassis. Parts of this transmission were 'borrowed' from the Fiat Compagnola four-wheel-drive cross-country machine

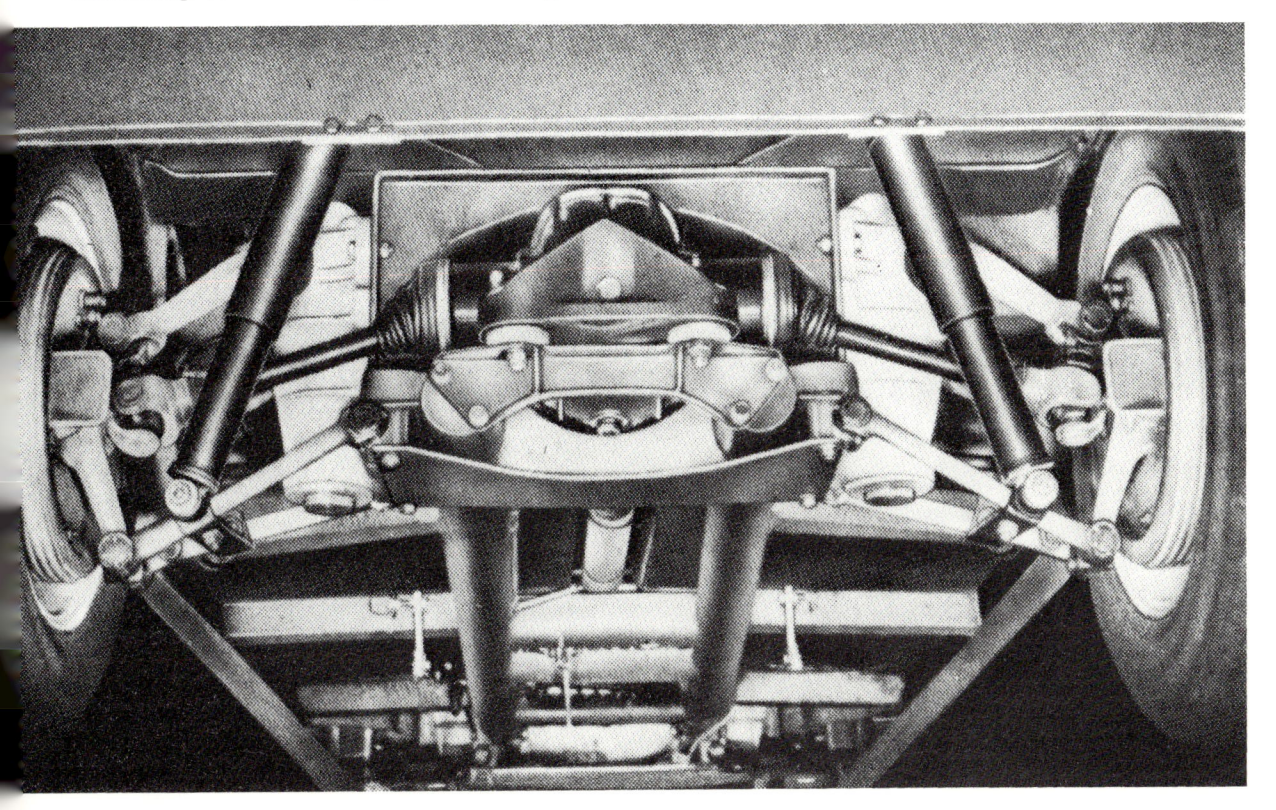

Fiat Sports Cars

ABOVE One of the very last 8Vs built by Fiat featured a fibreglass bodyshell, seen here in a rather eerie part-finished state; only one car was built

RIGHT At rest in Fiat's Centro Storico in Turin, is one of the special Fiat-Abarth record cars (built in 1956), and an 8V two-seater sports coupé

26

very slim central pillar, and at the front there were not only headlamps built into the crown of the wings, but another pair mounted at each side of the oval grille. To improve the aerodynamics (said to have been partly developed in Fiat's wind tunnel) there were wheelarch covers at the rear. On the very first cars the centre lock wire wheels had rather plain and ugly disc covers.

The 8V, as revealed at Geneva in 1952, was not yet completely developed, and much of the intensive road work was carried out for Giacosa by Carlo Salamano, a racing driver of distinction who had made new-model development his other profession. No doubt Salamano was one of those who liked the two-seater coupé's layout, where the passenger seat was set back by several inches from that of the driver so that in the narrow confines of the cockpit he could have plenty of room to thrash his elbows about at high speed—this car might not have been a Ferrari-beater in the Mille Miglia, but clearly there were minds at work who wished that it could be so.

Naturally it was the engine which most analysts found most interesting. Even though it was clearly not a specially-designed racing unit (if it was, it would have had a five-bearing crankshaft instead of three bearings, a 90 degree vee-angle for ideal balancing, and far better cylinder head breathing with horizontal exhaust ports) it was still remarkable enough. The standard engine breathed through two downdraught dual-choke Weber carburettors (Weber, of course, was already owned by Fiat), and although it peaked at 6000 rpm, it had very little usable torque below about 3000 rpm.

At a time when there were still very few powerful engines of this size which could be race-tuned, and which did not cost a King's ransom, the Type 104 8V engine was bound to be popular among Italian enthusiasts. Soon after the car was revealed, Fiat began to supply engines to Siata, and it was with their help that engines were later tuned to give 115 bhp at 6000 rpm, and finally 126 bhp at 6600 rpm.

Potentially the 8V was a very quick car. As Gordon Wilkins commented in *The Autocar* when testing an early car which had been prepared for the Mille Miglia in 1952: 'There is a big central gear lever and some noise is apparent from the box. There is also a deep roar from the engine, but it is smooth up to over 6000 rpm. The normal axle ratio is 3.9:1, but for the Mille Miglia an axle of 4.1:1 had been installed, giving the following useful speeds at 6000 rpm: first gear 53 mph, second 70 mph, third 96 mph, and top 125 mph. But *quickly*!

'On changing from third to top the backrest is still pressing firmly against the back, and the results are seen in a time for the standing kilometre said to have been covered in 30.9 seconds. I timed the car over a flying kilometre in 19 seconds (118 mph) and the revs were still rising at the end, so the claimed maximum of 128 mph would not appear to be greatly optimistic with suitable gearing.

'Handling and road behaviour leave an impression of a thoroughbred with stability, liveliness and immense power. There is general slight understeer. The steering is high geared, and the car goes into a four-wheel-drift with all tyres squealing and the throttle wide open in a way which expert drivers will find greatly reassuring.'

In other words, by the standard of the day it was a very fast car indeed, and the aerodynamics must have been outstanding. After all, the 160 bhp Jaguar XK120 of 1952, which had a 3442 cc engine, could go no faster, and accelerate no faster than this.

It was not, however, a car which Fiat could ever hope to sell in large numbers, especially as it was priced at 2.85m lire (well over twice that of the 1400 saloon, for instance, if this comparison is valid), and obviously because it was not tooled even for series production. The engine itself was not a sensible proposition for production in large numbers, and it combined advanced features like a light-alloy cylinder block and crankcase, with wet liners, against 'old-fashioned' details like siamezed inlet ports, inefficient exhaust porting, and pushrod overhead valve gear. The sparking plugs, incidentally, were mounted outboard, and almost in a sideways position, to be combined with an asymmetrically domed piston crown. A second-hand comment quoted by Laurence Pomeroy in *The Motor* suggested: 'you ought to have a piston top shaped so as to hold up the charge where it can see the spark'—having originally been made about the racing MG Magnettes of the 1930s.

Siata of Turin had built the first prototype in 1950/1951, but most of the 114 'production cars' were assembled by Fiat, in their own experimental workshops. However, a significant number of rolling chassis, with part of their under-structure in place, were supplied to famous coachbuilders like Vignale, Pininfarina, and Zagato, for them to design their own coupé derivations. According to the Dutch authority Wim Oude Weernink, about 90 of the cars had Fiat-bodies, the rest being clothed by the coachbuilders. Vignale is thought to have produced five or six 8Vs, Pininfarina one or two, and Zagato about eight (all competition lightweights).

After the first 34 cars had been built by Fiat, the car's style was changed. At the side the wheel 'nave' plates were removed, while the nose was tidied up considerably, with twinned 'Chinese eye' headlamps and a smaller grille.

Fiat Sports Cars

Just for fun! Pininfarina fashioned this special body style for the 8V in the early 1950s. It shows a great deal of contemporary Ferrari influence, including the entire nose/grille/headlamp layout

Even so, after little more than two years, it was nearly all over, and production had never really exceeded one car a week. There were, however, two important one-offs. At the Turin Motor Show in spring 1954, when the 8V had effectively already died, one example was shown with a light-weight fibreglass bodyshell (to the same style as that of the steel-bodied car), and this body only weighed 48 km/106 lb. It may have been the only such car to be completed, and is now in Fiat's Centro Storico in Turin.

Siata also got together with Fiat to produce their own Siata 208, which was a racing sports car with a complete 8V *gruppo mechanici* of engine, transmission and suspensions, but there was a special Siata space frame chassis and coachwork by a variety of Turin's most famous body makers. Siata's main contribution to mechanical development was that they helped to tune the engines themselves, and they also developed a five-speed version of the Fiat gearbox. A total of 56 such Siatas were built, and whereas the last 'official' Fiat 8V was built in 1954, the Siata 208 continued until 1955. 8Vs and 208s were in production at the same time, of course, which sometimes led to confusion as to which precise type of Fiat-powered machine was racing where.

It was as a racing sports car, of course, that the 8V was intended to make its name, but in fact it was only a limited success. Ovidio Capelli won the Stella Alpina in August 1952, the 8V's first success, and Elio Zagato (naturally enough, in a Zagato-bodied 8V) won the 3 Hours of Bari in 1954, and this car eventually won the Italian sports car championship of 1956. In 1957, Ludovico Scarfiotti, later to become a Ferrari Grand Prix driver, used an 8V to set ftd at the Aosta-St Bernard hillclimb.

Even though *The Autocar* carried out a full road test of a second-series 8V (with 'standard' Fiat-built body style) in July 1954, when the model was just going out of production, it remained essentially an Italian phenomenon. But it *was* a phenomenon, and one of which Fiat can still be proud. It was, in all respects, a quick car—much quicker than any other production 2.0-litre of its day, though one has to say that even the standard-bodied car was simply and even rather sparsely trimmed and furnished. But a measure of its performance was that no other Fiat sports car would be able to out-run it until the Ferrari Dino-engined machines of the late 1960s.

How many of these now remain in existence? Very few, I fear, for the engine was never backed by a comprehensive parts service, and must be virtually unknown to all but the most fervent admirers. An 8V in good condition, today, would be a real collector's piece.

8V Coupé

PRODUCED March 1952 to mid-1954
NUMBER BUILT 114 in all
GENERAL LAYOUT Front-engined two-seater coupé, with separate chassis frame, and body welded to it on assembly. V8-cylinder engine driving rear wheels, and all-independent suspension
ENGINE Especially developed for this model. V8-cylinder layout, with 70 degrees between cylinder banks, light alloy cylinder block, and light alloy cylinder heads. Three crankshaft main bearings. Two valves per cylinder, operation by pushrods and rockers from a single camshaft mounted in the cylinder block 'vee', driven by chain. Bore, stroke and capacity 72 × 61.3 mm, 1996 cc (2.83 × 2.41 in., 121.9 cu. in.). CR 8.5:1. Two downdraught dual-choke Weber carburettors. Maximum power 105 bhp or 115 bhp (net) at 6000 rpm. Peak torque 108 lb ft or 107 lb ft at 3600 rpm/4600 rpm respectively
TRANSMISSION In unit with engine, four-speed (or five-speed, in one or two cases) gearboxes, without synchromesh on first gear. Final drive ratio 4.445:1. Overall gear ratios 4.445, 5.59, 7.85, 12.07, reverse 12.07:1. 16.8 mph/1000 rpm in top gear
CHASSIS AND SUSPENSION Front engine, rear drive. Separate steel chassis frame, with tubular side members, welded to body shell on assembly. Independent front suspension by coil springs, wishbones, and anti-roll bar. Worm type steering. Independent rear suspension by coil springs, wishbones, and anti-roll bar. 11.4 in. diameter front drum brakes, 11.4 in. diameter rear drum brakes, no power assistance. 165-400 mm cross-ply tyres. Centre-lock wire-spoke road wheels
BODYWORK Pressed steel shells, welded to chassis frame on initial assembly, in variety of closed coupé styles, by coachbuilders such as Fiat, Ghia, Pininfarina, Vignale, Zagato. Two-door, two-seater styles. Typical dimensions (Fiat original shape)—Length 13 ft 2.6 in.; width 5 ft 1.7 in.; height 4 ft 3.4 in. Wheelbase 7 ft 10.5 in.; front track 4 ft 2.8 in.; rear track 4 ft 2.8 in. Unladen weight 2340 lb
PERFORMANCE SUMMARY (*Autocar*, 9 July 1954) Maximum speed 119 mph, 0–60 mph 12.6 sec., standing-start ¼-mile 21.5 sec., overall fuel consumption 16 mpg (Imperial)

3   1200 and Osca

Grace from Pininfarina, pace from Osca—mass sales for Fiat

By the late 1950s, one of Fiat's ambitions was to start building, and selling, sports cars in real quantity. With the dumpy little Trasformabile they had made a start, but only a start, for compared with the number of saloon cars they were currently building, the numbers sold had been miniscule. The 1200 Trasformabile had received an encouraging reception in North America, and there was evidence that the sports car market, currently dominated by three British marques—Triumph, Austin-Healey and MG—was still expanding. Next time, Fiat were determined to do better.

Unlike the British manufacturers, however, Fiat were not prepared to take a gamble and tool up for a unique chassis, or unit construction body/chassis structure. Any new model, like the previous one, would have to be based on the underpan, and engineering, of another existing Fiat. Furthermore, it would be about the same size as the existing model, for Fiat were not yet ready to consider building a sports car with a small engine (the 948 cc Austin-Healey Sprite, of course, would not appear until mid-1958), or a large-engined car for which the demand would be more limited.

In the meantime, much more exciting possibilities had opened up. I can do no better than to quote Dr Giacosa, who wrote: 'The story began on 11 July 1957, when I welcomed Ernesto Maserati to Mirafiori for the first time. The Maserati brothers had ceded their plant and the name of the company to the Orsi family in 1937. Subsequently they founded a new company called Osca. Finding themselves in financial straits they turned for help to Fiat. . .'.

(Strange how often small companies in trouble turned to Fiat to be rescued. Fiat, Italy's largest industrial concern, seemed to have a paternal soul, and usually felt obliged to help.)

I should explain a little further. Alfieri, Ernesto and Ettore Maserati had started building racing cars, including their own make of engines, in Bologna in 1926. During the next decade these cars became

The new Fiat 1200 Cabriolet of 1959 was an altogether smarter car than the rather dumpy Trasformabile which had struggled for acceptance through the 1950s. The facia and control layout of the 1959 1200 model was smart and efficient

Fiat Sports Cars

ABOVE *An early motor show shot of the 1200 Cabriolet in Germany. The price tag on the screen says DM 10,700*

ABOVE RIGHT *The general facia layout of all 1200/1500 Cabriolets of the early 1960s, with matching speedometer and rev-counter dials, a sturdy steering wheel, and foot pedals sprouting from the floor, rather than from under the scuttle*

ever faster and more famous, but the expense weighed too heavily, and this explains their decision to sell out to the Orsi interests. Alfieri Maserati was already dead, but the two surviving brothers provided consultancy services to Orsi until 1947.

It was on 1 December 1947 that they left Maserati, moved to new premises in Bologna, and set up Officina Specializzata Costruzione Automobili (Osca), where once again they were set on building their sports and racing cars, but this time without their own name on the bonnet badge. Osca was always small, always under-capitalized, and their decision to make new twin-cam four-cylinder engines was always fraught with financial difficulties. A 1453 cc twin-cam was already in existence by 1954, when it was made famous by the outright victory at the Sebring 12 hour race, in a car driven by Stirling Moss and Bill Lloyd. Within a year this engine had reached 1490 cc—and what were to become recognized as the 'classic' bore and stroke dimensions of 78 × 78 mm—with at least 110 bhp available in twin-plug racing guise.

But it was a complex, if sturdy, little engine, and there was no way that the Maserati brothers could afford to have it tooled-up for series production. Instead, each engine had to be laboriously built, and machined, by hand.

Which explains Ernesto Maserati's visit to Turin, to see Fiat. His vision, upheld by a favourable reception at Fiat, was that Fiat should build this engine for him, in larger though not staggering quantities, that Fiat should fit it to a new sporting model of their choice, and that they should also supply engines to Osca for their own use. I ought to explain, if I have not already made it clear, that this twin-cam Osca engine bore no relation to any existing or future Fiat unit. In the past it has been suggested that the 'Osca' twin-cam was no more than a clever conversion of one or other of the medium-sized Fiat pushrod engines. Not so: not one component or casting was of Fiat design.

Ernesto Maserati's visit could not have come at a more opportune moment. Although he did not know it, Fiat were just starting development of a new cabriolet to replace the 1200 (TV) Trasformabile, and it rapidly became clear that his engine could be fitted to the new car. Fiat, too, were receptive to such a new engine, not only because they now had a famous engine designer (Aurelio Lampredi, ex-Ferrari) who knew about such things, nor even because they had noticed how well the twin-cam Alfa Romeo Giuliettas were selling, but because they had also heard rumours of twin-cam engines said to be coming soon for high-price versions of the British MGA and Triumph TR3.

A deal was struck. Fiat would adopt the Osca engine for their own use, install limited tooling in Turin, and put it into production for their own, and for Osca's use.

The search for a new body style had, indeed, begun, and it had taken very little study to decide on the base for the new bodyshell. With a launch date scheduled for 1959, Fiat could see that their mass-production bodies would be the 500s and 600s (too small), the 1100s and 1200 Gran Luces (promising), and the new 1800/2100 models (too large). The design of the 1100/1200 Gran Luce's 'chassis' was relatively new, the 1221 cc engine was to be announced before the end of 1957 for installation in the sharply-styled 1200 Gran Luce, and this family was scheduled to run for some years.

The new car, coded Type 118, whether fitted with twin-cam engine or not, was therefore to be based on the running gear of the Gran Luce, itself a development of the 1100/103TV of 1953. Fiat were not able to consider styling or building the new car themselves, so once again they turned to the only Italian specialist coachbuilder who could take on the job—Pininfarina—and invited them to prepare a new style. In this respect, therefore, the new 1200 Cabriolet was no more than a restyled TV Trasformabile.

But, what a restyle! On this occasion, and for this job, the creative sculptors at Pininfarina really excelled themselves. Gone were the over-decorated and (in the writer's opinion) uncoordinated lines of the original, and in their place was a really smooth, 'international', cabriolet.

Pininfarina's conversion from producing flowing shapes like the Lancia Aurelia Spider, the Alfa Romeo Giulietta Spider, and the TV Trasformabile, had begun in the mid-1950s, with cars like the stunning Lancia Floride show car being the first to show off smooth sides and crisper shapes. For mass-production cars, Pininfarina had also produced surprisingly acceptable results for the British Austin A40 and the series-production Ferrari 250GT of 1958—perhaps, with these cars in mind, we should have known what to expect.

Compared with the Trasformabile, the new Cabriolet was 8.4 in. longer overall, riding on the same wheelbase, and about one inch taller, but so delicately drawn were its lines that it appeared to be a much larger car. From the side view, the wing crown line swept smoothly from headlamp roundels to tail-lamp clusters, with just one tiny, stylized, 'nick' behind the door opening to break it up. The windscreen was no longer severely cranked (such styles were already falling into disrepute in North America), but conventionally swept, while the doors now housed glass winding windows. Like the old car there was still a small air intake in the top of the bonnet panel, and a large grille with a vertical

Neat, compact, and effective power pack for the 1200 Cabriolet of 1959. That is a big rubber mounting at the rear of the gearbox, not a transmission brake. Minor changes were made for the 1200/1500 engine installation in later Cabriolets; for example a new gearbox case was ribbed for extra strength

Fiat Sports Cars

1200 and Osca

ABOVE LEFT *Many Italian coachbuilders tried to improve on the production cabriolets—Here's Moretti's 1959 version as a coupé with Osca engine*

LEFT *The original 1200 Cabriolet of 1959 could be identified by the small-mesh radiator grille. This particular car had an optional steel hardtop, or, as the Italians charmingly describe it, a tettuccio rigido*

ABOVE *Behind this 1500 are some of its Fiat contemporaries—the 1100 saloon, 600 saloon and twin cylinder 500*

RIGHT *Here's the 1500S of 1961 shot in Germany. The cars are rare today*

33

Fiat Sports Cars

ABOVE *Close-up of the 1500S badging shows bizarre graphics of the day*

BELOW *Fiat supplied underpans to Pininfarina, who constructed the Cabriolet bodyshell, painted and trimmed it, then returned it to a Fiat factory for final assembly*

dividing bar, but on the new car these were so nicely detailed as to be almost unrecognizable. The solid chrome bumpers had half over-riders at front and rear, but apart from this there was very little decoration indeed. The wheels and wheel trims were exactly as fitted to the new 1200 Gran Luce saloon, and on this occasion the Pininfarina decals were proudly carried on the flanks of the front wings just ahead of the doors.

(I wonder why they never did this on the original cars?)

The car was to be called a cabriolet, quite obviously, because it was normally to be fitted with a neat fold-away hood, which stowed tidily away under a cover along the rear decking when furled. Because the car was built on the wheelbase of the standard saloon, there was a lot of space in the cockpit. Even though Fiat only required two bucket seats, there was a large flat space (not upholstered as a seat) behind them, into which animals or willing children could certainly be persuaded.

Like the old Trasformabile, Pininfarina made up the bodies by welding on panels produced in their own workshops to a pressed structural underpan supplied by Fiat, and after painting and trimming these body/chassis units were trucked back to the old Lingotto works for final assembly by Fiat. Apart from the badging details on the boot lid, and the difference in the front grille mesh itself, there were no exterior differences between the pushrod and the twin-cam engined cars, except that the twin-cam

1200 and Osca

RIGHT *Apart from minor styling differences, the secret of the original 1500 'Osca' engined Cabriolet was all hidden under the bonnet. The classic twin-cam engine was designed by the Maserati family who owned Osca, and made for them by Fiat*

BELOW *The Osca twin overhead camshaft engine used in 1500S and 1600S Cabriolets was entirely special, and was not a conversion of the normal Fiat pushrod engine, but the transmission was the same*

Fiat Sports Cars

1200 and Osca

car had larger diameter (15 in. instead of 14 in.) road wheels, with radial ply tyres. The series production car, as I have suggested, was a drop-head coupé, but in due course a detachable hardtop was also made as an extra, and Pininfarina also produced a very smart fixed coupé version which they sold direct through their own sales organisation. This coupé retained the normal lines, but had large rear quarter windows, and looked very similar indeed from some angles to the popular Lancia Flavia Coupé, which Pininfarina were to reveal in 1962.

Inside the cockpit, too, the new car looked right, with a neatly cowled display of instruments ahead of the driver (left hand drive only, by the way, which is bad news for British or 'Empire' enthusiasts), inviting seats, and a sturdy looking gear lever on the tunnel between the seats.

The 'chassis'—in other words, the suspensions and the steering, was like that of the superseded TV Trasformabile, and was lifted direct from that of the 1200 Gran Luce, which is to say that there was independent front suspension by coil springs and wishbones, while the worm and roller steering had a very complex linkage running across the car, high up above the clutch bell housing, fixed to the bulkhead in front of the fascia panel; there were many opportunities for this linkage to grow sloppy with age, but new Cabriolets steered remarkably well. At the rear there were half-elliptic leaf springs, not only to suspend, but locate, the hypoid bevel back axle. To trim the handling to sports car standards there were anti-roll bars at front and rear, and on the original cars there were drum brakes all round.

Apart from the attractions of the body style, however, the main interest was in the choice of engines. The basic 1200 Cabriolet, the car which Fiat were already planning even before Ernesto Maserati put in an appearance, was to use the same 1221 cc Type 103G pushrod ohv engine as the old TV Trasformabile model, except that it had a slightly

ABOVE LEFT *A recognition point of the 1600S Cabriolet, announced in 1962, was that there was an offset bonnet intake and a slightly different grille, but the body sheet metal was otherwise unchanged. That air intake pushed clean, cold air, directly to the mouth of the carburettor air cleaners of the twin-cam engine*

LEFT *A special version of the 1500 (twin-cam) Cabriolet was produced by Pininfarina themselves, from the mass-produced bodyshell, with a different grille, blistered bonnet top, and swept back permanent hard top. Later in the 1960s, the same type of body lines were used on Lancia Flavia coupés, but not the same bodyshell, of course*

BELOW *The only way to tell the pushrod and twin-cam Cabriolets apart in 1962 was by reference to bonnet-top air intakes. The blonde girl is leaning on a push-rod engined car with full-width air intake, while the equally striking brunette is guarding the twin-cam Osca-engined car with offset intake*

Fiat Sports Cars

higher (8.25:1) compression ratio, and consequently produced up to 58 bhp, and it had the 1200's four-speed manual gearbox, with synchromesh on the top three ratios. In that form it was expected to be good for about 90 mph.

The Osca-engined car, however, was to be dubbed the 1500 Cabriolet, for it was to have the productionized version of the 1490 cc racing engine, de-tuned and refined, equipped with a single downdraught twin-choke Weber carburettor, and producing a maximum of 80 bhp (DIN) at 6000 rpm. The same gearbox, and final drive ratio (4.3:1) were to be used, for the Osca engine would be a higher-revving unit, and was expected to have a 105 mph maximum speed.

Even while the old-style TV Trasformabile was

ABOVE *Again in 1962, this is Ghia's effort at a 1500 coupé. At least it confirms that the chassis was a sound base for such exercises*

TOP *Is this an improvement on the Fiat/Pininfarina bodyshell? Most would say not—Allemano's 1500 coupé*

still in production, Fiat decided to give their new cabriolet a sneak preview, and they slipped a prototype in to the Pininfarina stand display at the Turin Show of November 1958, fitted with the Osca-derived engine. Quite what they hoped to achieve by this was difficult to understand, for few journalists were fooled. It was, after all, highly unlikely that

1200 and Osca

ABOVE *From spring 1963, the 1500 and 1600S Cabriolets were mildly revised, while the 1200-engined version was dropped. Neither car had bonnet-top air intakes any more, and grilles were widened and simplified. the push-rod engined 1500 had two headlamps and a full-width grille, while the twin-cam Osca-engined car had a four-headlamp layout*

TOP *Fissore's model chose another style with their 1600 coupé. Good looking at the front but spoilt by the rear screen? Wire wheels are novel on this car*

Pininfarina would be building and selling such a car on their own, and just about everyone realised that the Maserati brothers couldn't possibly afford to do the same.

Compared with the production car to come, the prototype had a simple grille shape, using mesh not unlike that used on the Pininfarina-styled Austin A40, had twin 'power bulges' on the bonnet panel, but no air scoop feature, and was shown in the permanent fixed-head coupé guise. *The Autocar* magazine, in reviewing the show, rather sniffily commented that: 'It would appear that Fiat intend to re-enter the high-performance sports car field, for they announce a new coupé on the 1200 chassis, with a twin overhead camshaft engine designed by the Maserati brothers.... Rather strangely, this new Fiat model is not exhibited on the Fiat stand, but is displayed by Pininfarina, who is responsible for the bodywork.'

And that, for the next four months, was that. No

Fiat Sports Cars

more was heard of new cabriolets from Fiat or Pininfarina during the winter, but at the Geneva Show of March 1959, the 1221 cc pushrod-engined version made its world *debut*, an occasion on which it was rather over-shadowed by the new six-cylinder 1800 and 2100 saloons.

The 1200 Cabriolet, in fact, went on sale almost at once, but there was no immediate sign of a production car to back-up that sneak preview from the previous autumn of the Osca-engined car. At this time, incidentally, Fiat must have been mildly apprehensive about the delay, for MG's MGA Twin-Cam, a direct competitor, had now gone into full production, and was shooting at the same sort of targets.

The launch of the 1500, which I will call, slightly inaccurately, the 1500S to avoid confusion with a later derivative of this design, came in the summer, and by the autumn the first production cars were being delivered. The 1500S was never meant to be more than a limited-production machine, for the very minimum of tooling had been installed to make the engines in Turin, and this was in any case assured by the large price differential; the 1200 Cabriolet was priced at 1,420,000 lire, while the 1500S cost no less than 1,800,000 lire. A measure of the 1500S's price level is that it was more costly than the largest Fiat 2100 saloon, and that when small-scale imports of left-hand-drive cars were proposed for Britain in 1960 its price tag of £1843 compared very badly with the £940 asked for an MG MGA 1600, or the £1942 needed to buy a 3.8-litre Jaguar XK150!

Once again, I have to admit that Fiat are unable to give me accurate production figures, for I have no doubt that Dr Giacosa's estimate of 80 1500S cars is too low, and his later estimate of a further 300 1600Ss is also wide of the mark. Not even Pininfarina, so meticulous in respect of other statistics they have sent me, can help, so I must merely hazard a guess of between 1200 and 1500 examples.

The 1200 Cabriolet, however, was a much more successful proposition for Fiat, and it shattered all previous sports car production records. In the four years that it was to run—from March 1959 to March 1963—nearly 12,000 cars were built, and although this was a puny total by Triumph and MG

BELOW RIGHT *1963 and Pininfarina are proud of their bodywork showing off this 1600 Cabriolet at the Frankfurt Motor Show*

BELOW *The 1963 1500 models retained the smart and sleek sheet metal styling of their predecessors*

40

standards, it matched the Alfa Romeo Giulietta Spider production rates, and must have made the Milan-based company sit up and take notice.

The Americans liked the cabriolet, especially in Osca-engined form, though they did not think the basic model was fast enough, for they were now used to more sparkling behaviour by British-made imports. *Road & Track* called the 1200 a 'car for Grand Touring at a leisurely pace' when they tested one in April 1961, and by the tone of the report the testers found it difficult to get excited about its character: 'Driving the Fiat 1200 is pleasant, but rather hard to describe. The car is smooth, willing, and agile, and if it is not the fastest cornering thing in the world, then it at least has no bad habits. . . . What you do get, in a nutshell, is a docile, comfortable touring car, well finished and the equal, in appearance if not in performance, or nearly anything on the road.'

When fitted with the Type 118 Osca engine, however, the car took on a more hairy-chested character altogether, although with a mere 80 bhp under the bonnet it was no more than a match for Alfa Romeo and the British competition. *The Autocar* tested a 1500S in November 1960, finding it slower in most respects than an MGA 1600, but still called the engine 'remarkable', thought that the car performed 'effortlessly or impressively according to the mood of the driver' and found that 'On corners, the Fiat's roadholding is shown to be in keeping with the car's sporting character.'

It was the engine itself, complete with cast-iron cylinder block, impressive-looking light-alloy cylinder head, and the whole range of busy twin-cam valve gear noises, which made the 1500S such an attractive car. It was not that the 80 degree opposed angle of the valves, the heavily domed pistons, or the high-revving capability were particularly modern, but the effect was of an engine with a racing pedigree, and one which, somehow, shouted 'Italian' at anyone ready to listen.

At this stage, of course, the design was only at the start of its development, and before the last of all this family were made in the autumn of 1966 there would be complete engine and gearbox transplants, major braking changes, and a boost to the capability of the Osca engine. It was a complex, and not entirely co-ordinated story, all of which confirms the way that this car had gripped the imagination of Fiat's engineers and managers.

This, then, is a summary of improvements made to the cars in the next six years:

November 1960   Front wheel disc brakes fitted to 1500S
July 1961   Twin-cam car *officially* became 1500S
August 1962   Twin-cam engine enlarged to 1568 cc, and car became known as 1600S

Fiat Sports Cars

LEFT *Even by 1965, the interior facia/instrument styling of the Pininfarina Cabriolets was the same as it had been in 1959. There is a clock between the main dials, and a wood-rimmed steering wheel with aluminium spokes*

RIGHT *A bonnet-full of Osca-type twin cam engine, featuring in the 1600S Cabriolet of 1965*

March 1963	1200 discontinued, replaced by 1500, with new Type 115 (Lampredi) 1481 cc pushrod engine, radial ply tyres, front wheel disc brakes. Bonnet scoop deleted. 1600S got four-wheel disc brakes, and four-headlamp nose. Bonnet scoop deleted.
March 1965	Increased power for pushrod 1500 (75 bhp, was 72 bhp), new five-speed all-synchromesh gearbox for 1500 and 1600S

Fiat had clearly been stung by the rather luke-warm response to the performance of the original 1200s and 1500Ss, and in 1962 and 1963 there were significant revisions. The limited-production Osca-engined car was treated to a larger (80 mm) cylinder bore, which meant a cylinder capacity of 1568 cc, two twin-choke Weber carburettors a 10 bhp increase in peak horsepower, and an even more impressive torque boost from 77 lb ft to 98 lb ft. The new car, called 1600S, was clearly much more flexible, and more broad-shouldered, than before.

There was no way that a simple capacity increase could be carried out on the 1200, which was at the practical limit of stretch, and in any case this would have made the Cabriolet's engine different from those being fitted to the 1200 Gran Luce's saloon body shell. The engineers, therefore, had to carry out an engine transplant.

In place of the 1221 cc engine, with its in-line valves, and an ancestry stretching back to the 1100/103 project of 1953, it was decided to fit the newer Type 115 unit newly developed for the Fiat 1500 Saloon, launched as recently as April 1961.

This four-cylinder unit, with opposed valves, and a bore and stroke of 77 × 79.5 mm, for a capacity of 1482 cc, was designed to be machined on the same transfer lines as the six-cylinder engine of the 1800/2100/2300 models, and shared many common components. The stroke, in fact, was the same as that of the 2300, which meant that the same connecting rods could be used, though the cylinder bore itself was that of the original 2100 which was only built for the first two years of the range's life.

I detail the full story of the development of this family of engines in chapter 4, and at this stage it is only necessary to say that it was designed by Aurelio Lampredi when he moved over from Ferrari during the 1950s. It was an engine used in the cabriolet, renamed 1500 Cabriolet, until 1966, but used on various Italian-built Fiats until 1968, in Spanish Seats until the 1970s, and found, to this day, in the FSO and Polski models (licence-built Fiats) produced in Poland.

The new Type 115 engine was altogether more promising than the old Type 103, if only because it produced 72 bhp at 5200 rpm and 87 lb ft of torque (compared with 58 bhp and 61 lb ft from the final 1221 cc engine). Its fitment, and the concomitant renaming of the car, made it necessary to call the *original* 1500 the 1500S—or considerable confusion would have resulted.

The development and progressive fitment of disc brakes to these cars merely brought them into line with pan-European thinking, and there is no doubt that the four-disc-braked 1600S of 1963–66 was a very sure-footed machine indeed.

42

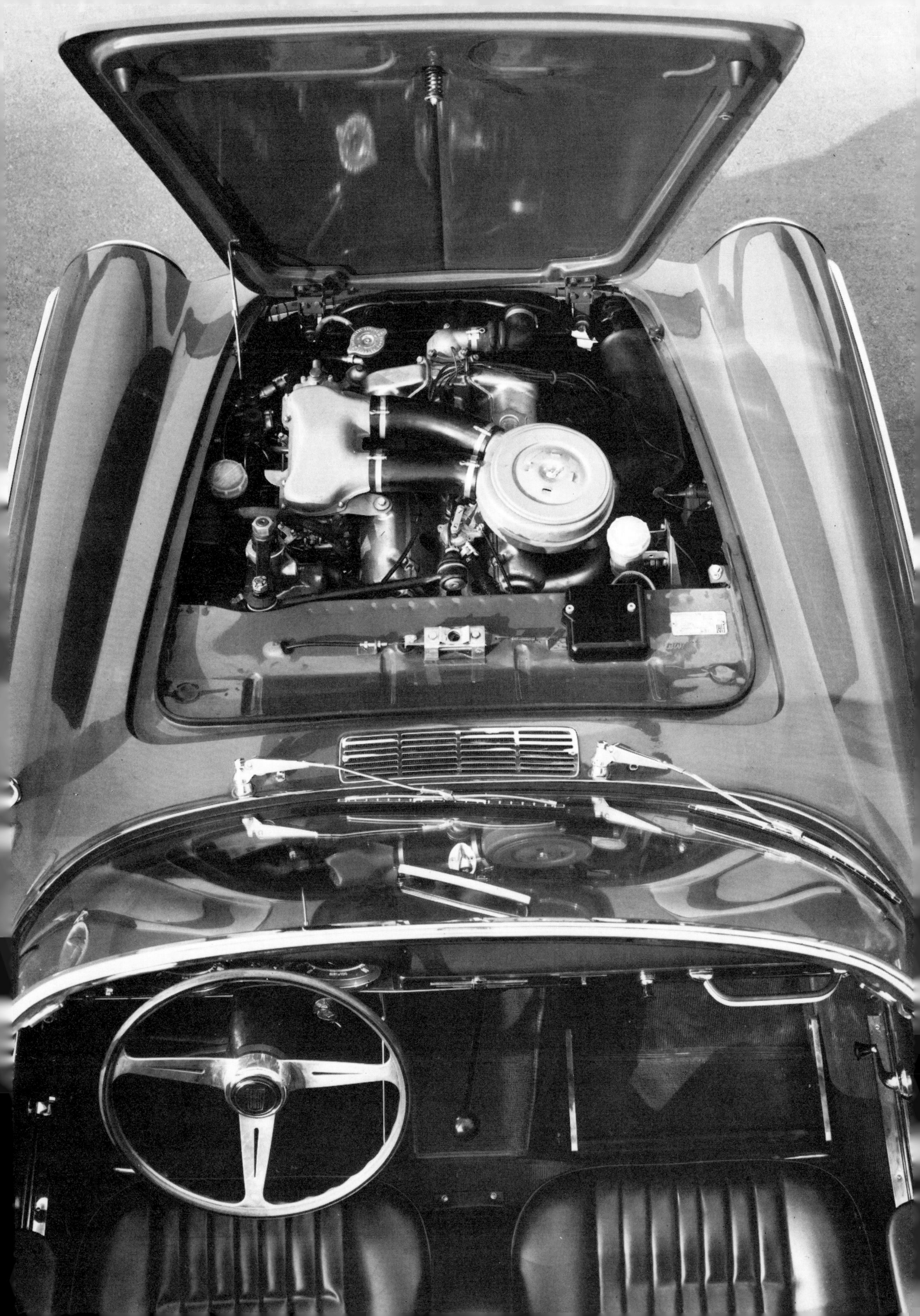

Through all this re-jigging, Fiat and Pininfarina commendably left the smart body style almost entirely alone, the passing of the years being noted only by changes to so-called air-scoops, to grille details, and to headlamp location. The original 1600S of summer 1962 (which did not, in fact, go into production until October) was given an asymmetric bonnet scoop in line with the twin-cam engine's carburettor intake, but from March 1963 both the new 1500, and the 1600S found themselves with smooth bonnet panels and no embellishment of any nature.

From March 1963, too, the divided, trapezoidal, radiator grille style was dropped in favour of a simple full-width style, akin to that originally shown in 1958, and at this point the twin-cam 1600S was given a second auxiliary pair of driving lamps, inboard and below the level of the originals. Finally, in 1965 when the new gearbox was added, the grille of the pushrod-engined cars was widened even further, under and around the headlamps. Certainly at this time Fiat's development engineers were never idle.

I have left consideration of the gearbox situation until last, for the arrival of a five-speed transmission was an event of great importance, out of all proportion to its significance on the Pininfarina-styled Cabriolets. This new gearbox, in fact, was a vital 'building block' to Fiat's future, and is still in large-scale use today.

During the 1960s Fiat gradually introduced a new family of gearboxes to many of their medium-sized cars, gradually replacing the old four-speed, crash-first-gear box used in the 1950s. Motoring archaeologists will want to know that the new design first appeared in the 1300/1500 saloons (Types 116 and 115 respectively), which were launched in April. It was indicative of the flexible way that Fiat were thinking that in this initial application there were four forward gears, and a steering column change. Later on, of course, not only was it built in four-speed and five-speed assemblies, but with direct action *and* remote-control central floor changes.

The casing of the new gearbox was in aluminium, heavily ribbed to strengthen it without adding too much weight, and had a bottom opening, and a flat sump pan, but no removable top cover. All versions were intended to have baulk-ring synchromesh on all forward gears. The main casing was always arranged to house four forward gears, and a variety of separate casings could be bolted up behind this—one version (that of the 1300/1500 saloons, and later 124s) merely housing reverse gear, and another version housing reverse and a geared up 'overdrive' fifth. It was this supplementary casing, too, which allowed access to the selectors, and provided mountings for the steering column, direct floor, or remote control gearchange linkages.

This is a comparison between the internal ratios fitted to the box for the 1300/1500 saloon of 1961, the medium-sized 124 saloon which followed on in 1966, and to the new five-speed derivative for the 1500/1600S Cabriolets:

1300/1500 saloon 3.75, 2.30, 1.49, 1.00, reverse 3.87:1
124 saloon   3.75, 2.30, 1.49, 1.00, reverse 3.87:1
1500/1600S Cab.   3.242, 1.989, 1.41, 1.00, 0.86, reverse 3.34:1

—students of gearbox design will spot that some, but not all, of the intermediate gear wheels were shared between the four-speed and five-speed gearboxes but that the third speed wheels were completely

FAR LEFT *Cabriolet engines of 1963 compared, each with a four-speed gearbox. This is the more mundane overhead valve unit, as originally fitted to the 1500 saloon of 1961, and is not an enlarged version of the 1200, which had an entirely different layout . . .*

LEFT *. . . the Osca-designed twin-cam used a different cylinder block, head, and had all the major components like dynamo and starter in different locations, though the transmissions were the same in each case*

RIGHT *The big advance made by Fiat in 1965, introduced originally on the 1500 and 1600S Cabriolets but intended for later models as well, was an entirely new five-speed all-synchromesh gearbox. In what has now become known as the standard 'Fiat solution', the five gear was carried in an extra casing bolted to the rear of the main gearbox*

different, as were what are known as the 'input' or 'primary' gears.

Thus equipped, the cabriolets had a final fling of rather more than year, and I remained convinced that many lovers of sports cars never realised just how good they really were. Having granted the criticism of the 1600S's price (though this was not, in fact, raised at all in the life of the Osca-engined car, more than six years), I recommend the basic specification of a twin-cam engine, a five-speed all-synchromesh gearbox, four-wheel-disc brakes, and comfortable accommodation inside a Pininfarina-styled bodyshell to anyone. It matched that of the Alfa Romeo Giulia Sprint GT or the older-type spider in all respects except outright performance, even though the final drive ratio had been altered to provide better acceleration (4.44:1 compared with 4.3:1 for the previous 1600S).

Fiat, quite clearly, were pleased with their persistent honing of their design, especially as the 1965 five-speeder also incorporated a revised steering wheel position, helped along by double universal-jointing of the steering column. It was, perhaps, no wonder that they gave the car a new badge, with the Fiat name now circled by laurel leaves. As the brochures emphasized: 'This emblem recalls the Fiat trade mark of the twenties: sports and racing models which triumphed in the hands of the most famous drivers of the day in international races and on circuits in Europe and America, carrying the fame of Fiat to new laurels.'

By this time, however, time was running out for the 1500 and 1600S Cabriolets. The car from which the chassis and underpan of the cabriolets was derived, the 1100, was beginning to look very long in tooth, and although it was not to disappear until 1969, it was due to be overshadowed by the new 124 saloon from 1966. But this was not the real reason for the cabriolet's obsolesence. Fiat were so delighted by the cabriolet's record that they had decided to repeat the exercise, this time on the basis of the 124. Since the 124 Sport Spider was due to have its body/chassis structures built by Pininfarina, and that firm only had the facilities to tackle one mass-production job at a time for Fiat, it had to take over directly.

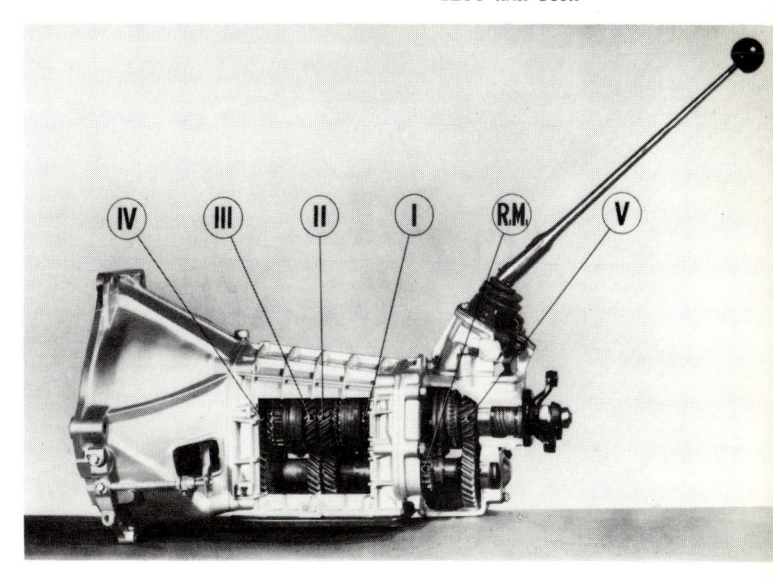

In the summer of 1966, therefore, during the holiday period in Turin, the last of the cabriolets was built, and preparations began to assemble 125 Spiders. The cabriolets had been on the market for more than seven years, and had made many friends. Fiat, of course, were delighted, as well they might have been. A brief summary of production tell us why—the following statistics have been culled from Pininfarina:

CABRIOLET DERIVATIVE	YEARS BUILT	NUMBER PRODUCED
1200	1959–1963	11,851
1500	1963–1966	20,420 and 2210 Coupés (this figure includes 1500S production, estimated at 1200/1500 cars)
1600S	1962–1966	2275 plus 814 Coupés

But should I believe these figures, or those supplied by Fiat, which are:

1200	15,000
1500 and 1500S	37,385
1600S	Not available

—what is a poor author to do?

Fiat Sports Cars

All these figures, however, were about to be dwarfed by the achievements of the next few years. Not only would the best part of half a million sporting cars be built on the basis of the rear-engined 850, but a similar number of sporting 124s would also take shape in the 1960s and 1970s. The next ten years were going to be very exciting.

1200 Cabriolet

PRODUCED March 1959 to March 1963
NUMBER BUILT 11,851
GENERAL LAYOUT Front-engined two-seater convertible (cabriolet), with pressed-steel unit construction body/chassis unit, based on underframe of 1100/1200 saloon car. Four-cylinder engine, driving rear wheels, with independent front suspension
ENGINE Version of long-running 1100/1200 saloon design, in TV form. Four-cylinder in-line unit, with cast iron cylinder block, and light-alloy cylinder head. Three crankshaft main bearings. Two valves per cylinder, overhead mounted, and operated by pushrods and rockers from single camshaft in side of cylinder block, driven by chain. Bore, stroke and capacity 72 × 75 mm, 1221 cc (2.83 × 2.95 in., 74.5 cu. in.). CR 8.25:1. One downdraught dual-choke Weber carb. Maximum power 58 bhp (net) at 5300 rpm. Peak torque 61 lb ft at 3000 rpm
TRANSMISSION In unit with engine, four-speed manual gearbox, no synchromesh on first gear. Final drive ratio 4.3:1. Overall gear ratios 4.3, 5.93, 8.99, 14.53, reverse 14.53:1. 15.8 mph/1000 rpm in top gear
CHASSIS AND SUSPENSION Front engine, rear drive. Unit construction pressed steel body/chassis unit, using underframe of 1100/1200 saloon. Independent front suspension by coil springs, wishbones, and anti-roll bar. Worm and roller steering. Suspension of rear live axle by half-elliptic leaf springs and anti-roll bar. 9.9 × 1.4 in. front drum brakes, 9.9 × 1.4 in. rear drum brakes. 5.20-14 in. cross-ply tyres on 3.5 in. wide wheel rims. Bolt-on pressed-steel disc road wheels.
BODYWORK Pressed-steel shell, in unit with 'chassis', produced for Fiat by Pininfarina, on basis of standard Fiat 1100/1200TV underframe and some inner panels. Two-door, two-seater open cabriolet style, with optional removable hardtop. Length 13 ft 2.7 in.; width 4 ft 11.9 in.; height 4 ft 3.25 in. Wheelbase 7 ft 8.1 in.; front track 4 ft 0.5 in.; rear track 3 ft 11.9 in. Unladen weight 1994 lb.
PERFORMANCE SUMMARY (*Road & Track*, April 1961) Maximum speed 90 mph, 0–60 mph 19.1 sec., standing-start ¼-mile 21.0 sec., typical fuel consumption 35 mpg (Imperial)

1500S Cabriolet

PRODUCED Summer 1959 to October 1962
NUMBER BUILT Figures included in 1500 total
GENERAL LAYOUT Same basic model as 1200 Cabriolet of 1959–63, but with all-new design of Osca twin-cam engine. Compared with 1200 Cabriolet, technical differences as follows:
ENGINE Engine designed by Osca for own use, but series-built by Fiat. Not used in any other Fiat model. Four-cylinder in-line unit, with cast iron cylinder block and aluminium cylinder head. Five crankshaft main bearings. Two valves per cylinder, opposed at 80 degrees in part-spherical combustion chambers. Two overhead camshafts in cylinder head, driven by chain from nose of crankshaft. Bore, stroke and capacity 78 × 78 mm, 1491 cc (3.07 × 3.07 in., 91.0 cu. in.). CR 8.6:1. One downdraught dual-choke Weber carburettor. Maximum power 80 bhp (net) at 6000 rpm.

Peak torque 77 lb ft at 4000 rpm
TRANSMISSION Overall gear ratios 4.3, 5.93, 8.50, 13.27, reverse 13.27:1. 16.0 mph/1000 rpm in top gear
CHASSIS AND SUSPENSION 10.6 × 1.5 in. front drum brakes. 10.6 × 1.5 in. rear drum brakes. 155-15 in. radial ply tyres on 4.5 in. wide wheel rims. Bolt-on pressed-steel road wheels.
BODYWORK Unladen weight 2182 lb
PERFORMANCE SUMMARY (*Road & Track*, April 1960) Maximum speed 105 mph, 0–60 mph 10.6 sec., standing-start ¼-mile 18.5 sec., typical fuel consumption 29 mpg (Imperial).
NOTE Front wheel disc brakes, as late-model 1500 Cabriolets, were standardized in November 1960

1500 Cabriolet (pushrod engine)

PRODUCED March 1963 to summer 1966
NUMBER BUILT 20,420 cabriolet, and 2210 coupé—which includes twin-cam 1500S figures
GENERAL LAYOUT As for original 1200 Cabriolet of 1959–63, except for use of new design of engine from 1300/1500 saloon range, and other details as follows:
ENGINE Version of new 1300/1500 engine design (also a four-cylinder version of six-cylinder design used in 2300/2300S Coupé). Four-cylinder in-line unit, with cast iron cylinder block, and light-alloy cylinder head. Three crankshaft main bearings. Two valves per cylinder, mounted asymmetrically in part-spherical combustion chambers, operation by pushrods and rockers from single camshaft mounted in side of cylinder block, driven by chain. Bore, stroke and capacity 77 × 79.5 mm, 1481 cc (3.03 × 3.13 in., 90.4 cu. in.). CR 8.8:1. One downdraught dual-choke Weber carburettor. Maximum power 72 bhp (DIN) at 5200 rpm. Peak torque 87 lb ft at 3200 rpm
TRANSMISSION As 1200 Cabriolet
CHASSIS AND SUSPENSION 145-14 in. radial ply tyres on 3.5 in. wide wheel rims. 9.8 in. front wheel disc brakes.
BODYWORK Unladen weight 2115 lb
PERFORMANCE SUMMARY (*Motor Trend*, September 1963) Maximum speed 91 mph, 0–60 mph 14.7 sec., standing-start ¼-mile 20.1 sec., typical fuel consumption 30 mpg (Imperial).
NOTE From Spring 1965, the engine was uprated to 75 bhp (net) at 5600 rpm, and a five speed all-synchromesh gearbox was standardized. Final drive ratio 4.1:1. Overall gear ratios 3.74, 4.1, 5.58, 8.61, 14.03, reverse 14.46:1. 18.2 mph/1000 rpm in top gear. Brakes had a vacuum servo

1600S Cabriolet

PRODUCED October 1962 to Summer 1966
NUMBER BUILT 2275 cabriolet, 814 coupé
GENERAL LAYOUT As for 1500S Cabriolet, except for enlarged twin-cam Osca engine, and other details. Technical differences as follows:
ENGINE Bore, stroke and capacity 80 × 78 mm, 1568 cc (3.15 × 3.07 in., 95.7 cu. in.). CR 8.6:1. Two downdraught dual-choke Weber carburettors. Maximum power 90 bhp (DIN) at 6000 rpm. Peak torque 98 lb ft at 4000 rpm
TRANSMISSION As 1500S at first. From March 1965, with 4.44:1 final drive ratio, and new five-speed all-synchromesh manual gearbox. Overall gear ratios 3.82, 4.44, 6.26, 8.83, 14.39, reverse 14.83:1. 17.05 mph/1000 rpm in top gear
CHASSIS From March 1963, 10.6 in. front disc brakes, 10.6 in. rear disc brakes, with vacuum servo assistance
BODYWORK Length 13 ft 4.8 in. Front track 4 ft 0.9 in.; rear track 4 ft 0.4 in. Unladen weight 2281 lb

46

4 2300S Coupé
Silk purse from sow's ear—courtesy of Ghia

By the late 1950s, Fiat was thoroughly buoyant, with a completely dominant position in Italian and even pan-European markets. Four completely new ranges of family car (1400, 1100, 600 and 500), with countless variations on the themes, had been introduced. Now it was time to start all over again.

Because the large 1400/1900 saloons were the oldest models in the line up, Fiat set out to replace them first. Even before the end of 1954, there was mention of a new project—Type 112—which was then supposed to have a 2.3-litre engine, while there was also the Type 111, intended to be a direct replacement for the 1400/1900 saloons. Dr Giacosa recalls that there was some urgency in developing the new car, as Fiat had made a definite commitment to hand over the body dies for the 1400 to Seat in Barcelona in the summer of 1957. (In the event, this transfer was delayed for a year, but the incentive was always there.)

At this time, of course, Fiat were still firmly in control of the engineering destinies of Simca in France, so it was not at all surprising that plaster mock-ups of new Type 111s looked rather the new Simca Aronde. As usual (for not only Giacosa, but Valletta and his subordinates, always loved having new engines around them), the new car might have had a whole variety of power units ranging from a four-cylinder of 1400 type, to six-cylinder units, and even narrow-angle vee-8s of the family developed for the 8V sports coupé.

By 1956, however, Giacosa's engineers had prepared the design of an entirely new in-line six-cylinder engine, the first such layout since the last of the prewar style 1500s had been taken out of production in 1950. Not only was it a modern design, but as it would require entirely new machine tooling to be installed, it was also laid out so that a conventional four-cylinder engine could be built on

The Fiat 2300S Coupé of 1961 was a machine originally developed by Ghia as a private venture. It was based on the underpan, running gear and suspensions of the 1800/2100/2300 saloons first seen in 1959, but only the 2.3-litre 2300 engine was offered with this four-seater fastback body

STUDIO DI STILE
E DI FUNZIONALITA'
PROTESO NEL FUTURO
PER DARE OGGI
LA VETTURA DI DOMANI
MICHELIN X

2300S Coupé

the same lines, and using many of the same components. (This 'four', of course, was the engine already discussed in connection with the Pininfarina-styled 1500 Cabriolet, in the previous chapter.)

A whole series of different body styles were prepared at Turin, and between 1955 and 1957 the preferred shape gradually took on sharper and more squared-up lines, such that the finalized shape was as angular as anything being developed for other concerns by Pininfarina. The new Fiat, however, was all their own work, though Pininfarina were asked for their comments at the last moment, and made certain minor suggestions, which were adopted.

The running gear of the new car, the Type 112, was new from end to end, and it showed the way that Giacosa could now get his way with advanced concepts. The structure, of course, was a conventional pressed-steel monocoque, with four passenger doors and a large boot. Its wheelbase was 8 ft 8.8 in.—the same incidentally, as that of the superseded 1900B (Type 105)—while the tracks were 4 ft 4.8 in. (front), and 4 ft 3.4 in. (rear), all of which gave the car a four-square stance.

At the front there was independent front suspension, by double pressed-steel wishbones, and long longitudinal torsion bars running back to anchorages under the front seats (could Giacosa have been looking at the way Jaguar designed their cars at the time?), and this was allied to conventional worm and roller steering. However, the interesting new type of front suspension was not matched by that of the rear, which was essentially similar to that used on all 1400s and 1900s since 1950, and used many common parts. It was not really a layout compatible with high performance, for the hypoid bevel 'live' back axle was sprung by coil springs above the tubes themselves, and quarter-elliptic leaf springs acting as cantilevers from the floor under the rear seat, while there was a short Panhard rod across the car to provide transverse location. At the front, an anti-roll bar helped to trim the handling, and the drum brakes had vacuum servo assistance.

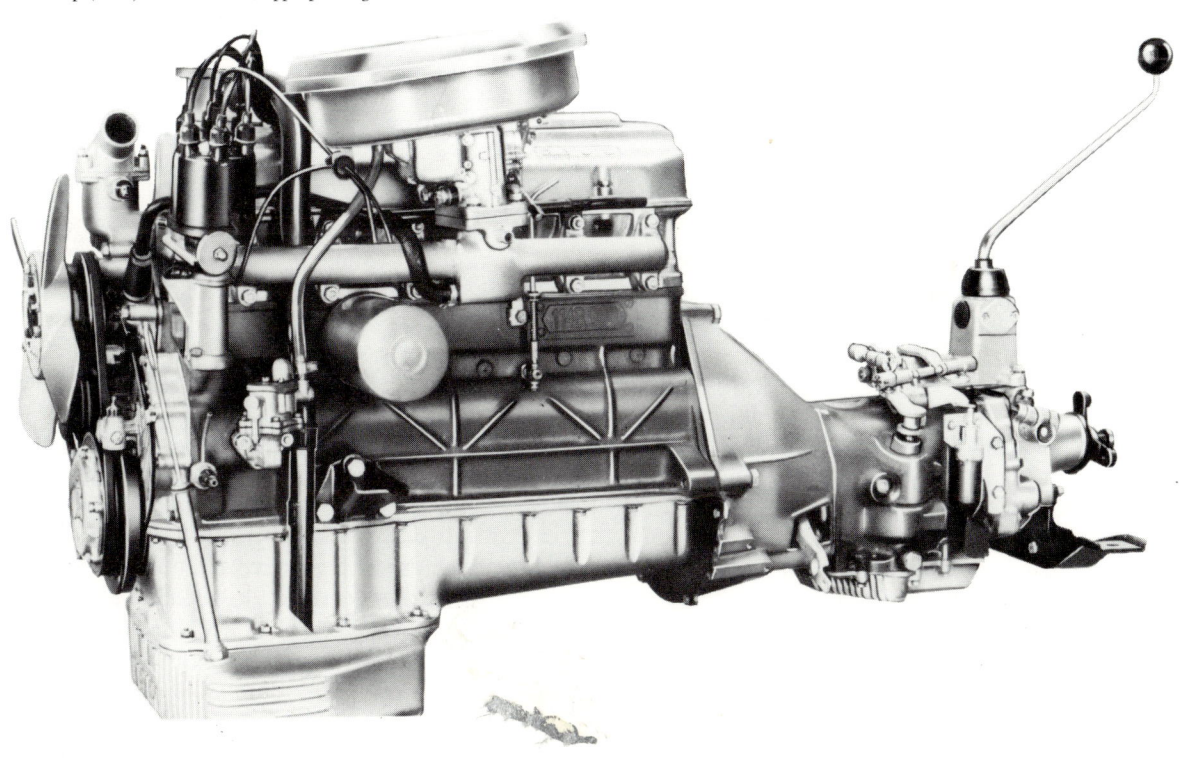

ABOVE LEFT *Here's the 2300 Coupé bodyshell with but 2100 cc under the bonnet in 1961. The car looks strange in a dark colour and would have been no means fast with the smaller engine installed*

BELOW LEFT *'The office' of the 2300S Coupé, with badging in the centre of the facia panel to make the point. There was even a foot bar for the front seat passenger to use, in rally car fashion. Steering wheel by Nardi and strange facia badging*

BELOW *Two tunes of engine were available in the Ghia-styled coupé of the 1960s. The low-powered version was this single-carb 105 bhp (DIN) 2279 cc unit, appropriately called the 2300 . . .*

Fiat Sports Cars

LEFT ... while the more charismatic 2300S had this 136 bhp (DIN)/150 bhp (gross) derivative, which featured two twin-choke carburettors for a six-cylinder engine. Complicated—as was the conversion from steering column to direct-action central gear change

RIGHT The sumptious interior of the Ghia-styled 2300S Coupé of 1961–68, showing full-size four-seater capability, but only two passenger doors. The queue for the favours of the particularly striking model starts behind the author

The major interest for engineers, however, was in a study of the engine. Two models of the Type 112 were announced, the cars being called 1800 and 2100, due to the fact that they had 1795 cc and 2054 cc six-cylinder engines. The most remarkable feature of these units was not that they had part-spherical combustion chambers, and two rows of opposed valves, both operated by long pushrods from a single camshaft in the side of the cylinder block, but that they had been designed for Giacosa by that distinguished engineer, Aurelio Lampredi.

Lampredi, of course, had first made his name with Ferrari, where he had designed the larger of the company's famous vee-12s—the 'long block' 60-degree design which swept the 4½-litre GP cars to victory over Alfa Romeo in 1950 and 1951. Later, he followed this up with the successful 2.0-litre and 2.5-litre four-cylinder GP engines of the early 1950s, and the intimidating straight six-cylinder units used in the sports racing cars. But when Lancia handed over the new Grand Prix cars *and* their legendary designer, Vittorio Jano, to Ferrari, in mid-1955, Lampredi immediately reacted with a 'this place isn't big enough for the two of us' gesture, and walked out. Within 24 hours, Giacosa had heard about this, captured Lampredi, and set him on a Fiat career which embraced the next quarter of a century.

The basic layout—the very basis of the design—was Giacosa's, but the detail was all to the credit of Lampredi. He it was who adopted a complex pushrod valve gear, which included the use of two rocker shafts in the light alloy head rather than one, and had the exhaust valve rather more vertically aligned than that of the inlet. The combustions chambers were not truly part-spherical, but close to this layout. In Dr Giacosa's words: 'We called it "polyspherical" because of its shape, which consisted of three intersecting spherical surfaces.'! In later years both BMW and Renault adopted such refinements, both claiming it as a good idea of their own.

Other features included the use of a downdraught twin-choke Weber carburettor, the relatively high compression ratio of 8.8:1, a four-bearing crankshaft, and a centrifugal oil filter on the nose of the crankshaft in addition to the normal full-flow type.

There were two engine sizes, and two outputs. For the record, these were

1800 72 × 73.5 mm 1795 cc 75 bhp (net) at 5000 rpm
2100 77 × 73.5 mm 2054 cc 82 bhp (net) at 5000 rpm

—both engines used the same basic cast iron block, and aluminium cylinder head, though the 2100 was bored out to 77 mm, and was thus slightly 'oversquare'.

The new engine was backed by a new four-speed, all-synchromesh, manual gearbox, in which the selector mechanism was at the side of the casing, and there was a steering column gear change.

Incidentally, an estate car derivative of the car was also put on sale, and there was also a 2100 'Special' with different front styling, four headlamps, and extra fittings. However, although the new range was politely received (it was, after all, a real advance over the old 1900B), it was not immediately a success in the showrooms, and in fact only 30,000 of this type were produced in just two years.

The Torinese coachbuilders, Ghia, however, were not put off by the lukewarm reception accorded to the new Fiat, for they were sure they could produce something a lot more stylish on their own. In time for display at the Turin Show of November 1960, therefore, where several other coachbuilders also had the same idea, they produced a smart, even understated, two-door coupé, which they called a 2100S special coupé, and they announced that they were planning to put it into small-scale production.

At that time Ghia was still an independent concern (Now, of course, it is wholly owned by Ford, and is really their 'future ideas' office in regard to styling), controlled by Luigi Segre. The young designer who shaped the Ghia 2100S coupé was an American called Tom Tjaarda, who had only joined Ghia in 1958, but who had already shaped the appealing little Innocenti Spider 950 (a rebodied 'frog-eye' Austin-Healey Sprite), and the Karmann-Ghia VW 1500. (In later years he was to be responsible for the Ferrari 330GT 2 × 2 at Pininfarina, the DeTomaso Pantera, the DeTomaso Deauville, and many other show cars.)

Tjaarda used the standard running gear, suspension, and typical Italian floorpan/under panels of the Fiat 2100, which meant that he had plenty of space in the 8 ft 8.8 in. wheelbase both to accommodate four people and to give the car stylish lines *and* real rakish appeal.

The car put on show at Turin was perhaps flag-flying a little for Fiat, for Ghia not only announced that they would start to build up to 15 cars a day in 1961, but they would sell it with a 130 bhp engine; there would be two versions, the luxury version being promised with disc brakes (the Fiat 2100 still only had drums, of course), leather trim in place of cloth, and with electric window lifts.

Perhaps it was as well that Ghia were not able to start selling this new car at once (it is more likely, however, that they never intended to do so, for they must have known what Fiat had in mind), as within months the entire 1800/2100 saloon car range was re-jigged. Dr Giacosa has admitted that the first redesign of the car was already being considered before the car was actually put on sale—it often used to be said of Fiat that the definitive model would not be for sale until about three years after the original announcement of the car! This was the sort of 'development by popular demand' of which BMC and British Leyland were later accused—but Fiat got in first, even if it was nothing to be proud of.

Fiat Sports Cars

TOP LEFT For 1962, Ghia produced a 2300 Cabriolet to tempt Fiat. Fiat didn't buy . . .

CENTRE LEFT . . . nor did they buy Ghia's 2300 estate, or Club, either. They obviously made more than one, for there's another in the background without the roof/rear screen rack

BOTTOM LEFT A year later Ghia tried this swoopy coupé bodyshell on the 2300S chassis, using one of their 'American' efforts as persuasion behind. No one bought

TOP RIGHT Wheels and their trims changed during production as did other minor fittings. Here's a 2300S in Germany

TOP FAR RIGHT The three part rear screen is reminiscent in many European coupé although usually without such a deep centre piece. It's 1964 with the 2300S

RIGHT Pininfarina's effort of 1964 on the 2300S chassis. Strong overtones of one of their Ferrari 365 efforts? No one bought

2300S Coupé

53

Fiat Sports Cars

First of all, however, the new 1300 and 1500 saloons (Types 115 and 116) were launched in April 1961, these cars having the four-cylinder versions of the Lampredi engine, and similar styling though with an entirely different bodyshell. The redesigned large cars followed in June.

Although the basic style, and layout, of the big Fiats had not been changed, the 'chassis' had been thoroughly reworked in detail. Most important was the revision to the rear suspension, where the unsatisfactory 1400/1900-type leaf and coil springs had been abandoned, in favour of conventional half-elliptic leaf springs. There was no other axle location, but a slim anti-roll bar was mounted behind the line of the axle itself. This more compact layout allowed the floorpan to be modified, and the spare wheel to be stowed in a horizontal position (and the luggage volume, therefore, to be increased).

Instead of the drum brakes, servo-assisted Girling disc brakes were now fitted to all four wheels, which was a great advance, and at the same time the front track was slightly increased and the tyre section widened.

To match all this, the larger engine was given a larger bore *and* a longer stroke, which made it slightly undersquare, and increased the capacity to 2279 cc. Other improvements allowed power increases to be offered on both engines, which were now rated as follows:

1800B 72 × 73.5 mm 1795 cc 86 bhp (net) at 5300 rpm
2300B 78 × 79.5 mm 2279 cc 105 bhp (net) at 5300 rpm

(The new long-stroke crank throw for the 2300B was shared with the new four-cylinder 1500, but the bore was, and remained, unique.)

There were no transmission changes for the 1800B, but the new 2300B now offered Laycock DeNormanville overdrive as an optional extra—this only operated on top gear, was engaged by pressing a button on the spokes of the steering wheel, and was automatically disengaged when a change down to third gear was made.

At the same time there were style changes (which included a four-headlamp nose for the 2300B), and a long-wheelbase derivative of the saloon called the 2300 Special.

All this meant that there was a much more suitable mechanical 'chassis' on which to develop a sports coupé, and Ghia were delighted. But that was not all, for Fiat had liked what they saw at Turin in 1960, had speedily got in touch with Ghia, and had officially adopted the new car as a Fiat factory product. The agreement was that Fiat would supply part-built bodies (effectively, these were floor pans with scuttles, and certain structural additions in place) to Ghia, who would complete their own body shell, paint and partly trim the resulting assembly, and truck them back to the old Lingotto plant for final completion on the 1800B/2300B production line.

However, between November 1960, and September 1961, when the first production cars were built, a lot had happened to the concept of the new machine's running gear. From being a 'special 2100S', it had become a choice of 2300 or 2300S coupés. Naturally, the enlarged 2279 cc engine of the 2300B was to be used (there was never any proposal to build a down-market 1800 version, incidentally), but this was offered in two forms. The 2300 Coupé used exactly the same engine as that of the saloon, with a peak power output of 105 bhp, while the 2300S used a much-modified engine which produced a rousing 136 bhp, which made it easily the most powerful Fiat private car of the day.

For the more powerful engine unit, Abarth were contracted to do the job, and provided a new camshaft profile, but more importantly they provided new carburation—the rather strange combination of two horizontal twin-choke 38DCOE Weber carburettors for a six-port, six-cylinder engine. Try working that one out in terms of efficient manifolding!

In addition, to make the car altogether more sporting in character, Fiat also provided a central floor gear change by a shapely but rather willowy lever; because of the specialized side-selector arrangements which existed in this gearbox, a rather complex external linkage, literally round the outside of the box, had to be provided to make this possible.

When all this change was coupled with the use of higher final drive ratios—3.90:1 for the 2300, and 3.63:1 for the 2300S—and the more wind-cheating lines of the coupé, it was clear that the Ghia-styled machine promised to be very fast by any previous Fiat standards. It was no wonder that Harry Mundy, *Autocar*'s distinguished technical editor, tried a car in 1961 and commented that: 'In Italy, this car is already being referred to as the poor man's Ferrari; this is in no way derogatory, for it gives a good assessment of its price in terms of performance.'

The immediate attraction of the 2300/2300S, however, was not in its performance, but in its looks. Ghia made no changes of any nature between showing off the '2100S' prototype in 1960, and building the first production bodies in 1961. When *Motor* tested a car in 1965 they suggested that: 'It is the sort of car you put on like a good suit of clothes...', which was a neat way of summing up its attraction.

The 2300S was three inches lower than the saloon from which it was evolved (though, incidentally, it weighed about the same), and managed to provide very adequate close-coupled four-seater accommodation in spite of having a well-swept coupé roof style. The nose was wickedly individual, with single headlamps at each corner, and with a distinctive grille sweeping out to the side-lamps at each side of the car. There were only two wide doors, and tiny rear quarter windows, while the rear pillar was swept forward at the base, precisely matching the line of the windscreen pillar. This, of course, meant that the rear window was vast, but to keep production problems within bounds it was split into three sections, with slim pillars at the corners of the shell.

All in all, this was an unmistakable body style, with very little decoration—even the vents behind the front wheel arches helped extract air from the engine bay, which got rather hot when the full 136 bhp was being developed.

Inside the cockpit, there were sumptuous leather faced seats, and the front seats reclined completely if necessary, and a full range of instruments on the special fascia, which included a rev-counter and even an oil temperature gauge. The effect, however, was rather spoilt, by the use of an 'umbrella handle' handbrake lever under the scuttle, but this was a carry-over item from the 2300 saloon. All the pedals were pivoted from the floor; this was strange, as pendant pedals were fitted to the 2300 saloons.

It was, of course, a car for the *autostrada* rather than for city streets or narrow and twisty little roads.

There was no power-assisted steering (though this became optional on the 2300 saloon), and most of the controls—such as the feel of the gear change—were for men, and not for women. But it was a quick car, especially in Abarth-tuned 2300S form. The top speed was just over 120 mph (20 mph more than that achieved by the saloon), and it could rush up to 100 mph in little more than half a minute. The bad news, especially these days, for enthusiasts buying and restoring such a car to health, was that the fuel consumption was quite heavy—it would be a pussy-footed 2300S owner who achieved much better than 20 mpg (Imperial).

Fortunately, it was a car which had handling to match its looks, which was something of a relief when the mediocre behaviour of the very first 2100 saloons was considered. Not only was the 2300S based on a better and updated chassis (with British-built disc brakes, and radial ply tyres to add to the security), but it was that bit more squat, and better balanced.

Perhaps *Motor*, in their 1965 test, put the car's entire character into perspective, when they said: 'The 2300S Coupé would be entirely unsuitable as a shopping car. It is long, noisy, not particularly easy to get into, and has rather heavy steering at low speeds. Anyone who buys it should have another car for hack work and enjoy the Fiat for its proper

From May 1965, the 2300S Coupé was slightly revised and updated, with different wheels and side-mouldings, but no mechanical changes. The facia layout was not changed

virtues: very high performance, a chassis which combines stability, comfort and responsive handling at very high speeds, and an interior that can only be described as sumptuous. It is ... for the sort of man who can still contemplate motoring a couple of hundred miles just for the fun of the drive.'

In Italy, at least, the Ghia-styled coupés were good value, if not amazing bargains. Compared with the 2300 saloon's 1,650,000 lire price tag, the 2300 Coupé sold for 2,500,000 lire, and the much faster 2300S for 2,600,000 lire. Translated into sterling, this put the Italian price of the 2300S Coupé at £1490—less than half the price of the cheapest Ferrari, and more than competitive with the Alfa Romeo 2000, which was one of its most obvious rivals.

Incidentally, because there was only 100,000 lire, or about £58 between the price of the two versions, it was surely not surprising that the 'basic' 2300 Coupé attracted little custom. Almost everyone who was in the market for such a car opted for the 2300S—the result was that the 2300 was dropped in 1964.

In April 1963, incidentally, Abarth (which was still an independent concern at the time) took a specially-prepared 2300S Coupé to Monza to attack International Class D (2000–3000 cc) speed records. The car averaged more than 110 mph for three days, to shatter the 1959 record which had been set up by a 'works' Austin-Healey sports car at 97.33 mph. The car looked, and was, almost standard, and even ran with trim and bumpers in place.

Once the car was launched, and Ghia had started supplying bodies, Fiat rather seemed to lose interest in it, just as they seemed to lose interest in the six-cylinder saloons from which the car had been developed. The 2300S was in production until mid-1968, and was only mechanically changed in 1963 to accord with the launch of the 2300 De Luxe saloon, which received an alternator for its engine, the elimination of many regular lubrication points in its chassis, and the power steering and automatic transmission not offered in the coupé. In 1965, too, there were minor style changes, really confined to detail such as the wheel trims, and the decorative side mouldings.

By 1965, in any case, Fiat's enthusiastic designers had turned to other projects, and the 2300S was really living on borrowed time. The 124 Sport Coupé (see Chapter 6) was on the way, and discussions were already taking place with Ferrari over the 'productionizing' of the vee-6 Dino engine. It was the new Fiat Dino Coupé, more than any other car, which made the 2300S Coupé obsolete.

But how many were eventually built? I do not know. Fiat have told me that they cannot separate 2300S figures from those for the 2300 saloons, while Ghia, who might have known, is no longer in the production car business, and has changed hands twice since the mid-1960s. I will not even guess—but I will say that more than 155,000 1800Bs and 2300s were built between 1961 and 1968, and that 2300S production can only have been a very small proportion of this.

In any case, there can be very few 2300S Coupés left for, like many other thoroughbred cars of their period, they suffered from serious rust corrosion as the years passed by. The foremost British magazine involved with such machines, *Thoroughbred & Classic Cars*, acquired a 2300S, and found that they had to spend more than two years, part-time, in getting the bodyshell back to a reasonable state.

For no other reason, however, the 2300S is important to the sporting Fiat saga, as it was the only 'production' body style ever to be supplied by Ghia.

2300 and 2300S Coupés

PRODUCED September 1961 to June 1968
NUMBER BUILT Not known. (See text)
GENERAL LAYOUT Front-engined four-seater coupé, with unit-construction body/chassis unit. Six-cylinder engine driving rear wheels, with independent front suspension
ENGINE Closely related to unit developed for all-new 1800/2100 models of 1959. Six-cylinder in-line layout, with cast iron cylinder block, and light-alloy cylinder head. Four crankshaft main bearings. Two valves per cylinder, mounted asymmetrically in part-spherical combustion chambers, operation by pushrods and rockers from single camshaft mounted in side of cylinder block, driven by chain. Bore, stroke and capacity 78 × 79.5 mm, 2279 cc (3.07 × 3.13 in., 139.1 cu. in.). (2300 type). CR 8.8:1. One downdraught dual-choke Weber carburettor. Maximum power 105 bhp (net) at 5300 rpm. Peak torque 123 lb ft (net) at 2800 rpm. (2300S type) CR 9.5:1. Two horizontal dual-choke Weber carburettors. Maximum power 136 bhp (net) at 5600 rpm. Peak torque 132 lb ft at 4000 rpm
TRANSMISSION In unit with engine, four-speed all-synchromesh manual gearbox. Final drive ratio (2300) 3.90:1, (2300S) 3.63:1. Overall gear ratios (2300) 3.90, 5.47, 7.41, 12.54, reverse 11.70:1, (2300S) 3.63, 5.09, 6.89, 11.67, reverse 10.89:1. (2300) 18.15 mph/1000 rpm in top gear, (2300S) 19.45 mph/1000 rpm in top gear
CHASSIS AND SUSPENSION Front engine, rear drive. Unit construction pressed-steel body/chassis unit. Independent front suspension by torsion bars, wishbones, and anti-roll bar. Worm and wheel steering. Live rear axle, suspended by half-elliptic leaf springs, with anti-roll bar. 11.2 in. front disc brakes, 10.0 in. rear disc brakes, with vacuum servo assistance. 165-15 in. radial ply tyres on 5.0 in. wheel rims. Bolt-on pressed-steel disc road wheels
BODYWORK Pressed-steel shell, in unit with 'chassis', produced for Fiat by Ghia, on basis of standard Fiat 2300 underframe and some inner panels. Two-door, four-seater coupé style. Length 15 ft 1.9 in.; width 5 ft 4.2 in.; height 4 ft 5.7 in. Wheelbase 8 ft 3.3 in.; front track 4 ft 5.1 in.; rear track 4 ft 3.6 in. Unladen weight 2790 lb
PERFORMANCE SUMMARY (*Autocar*, 22 December 1961) Maximum speed 121 mph, 0–60 mph 11.6 sec., standing-start ¼-mile 18.8 sec.

5 850 Coupé and spider
Sports motoring at budget prices– open or closed

It seems amazing now, that Fiat, of all people, took so long to break into the low-price sports car market. After all, they were the largest and most profitable of Europe's car-makers by the mid-1950s, yet they never challenged the British stranglehold on this business. At a time when enthusiasts in North America were rushing to buy the new generation of sports cars from Austin-Healey, MG and Triumph, Fiat were doggedly producing more and more new saloons, and merely dabbling with the relatively expensive Osca and 1200 Cabriolets described in Chapter 3. From time to time, Dr Giacosa and his team played with new ideas, but it was not until the 1960s that they settled on the right formula.

Although the 850 Coupé and 850 Spider were revealed to the world in 1965, the events leading up to their birth originated way back. One of the first postwar projects defined by Giacosa in 1945 was the Type 100, a car intended to take over in due course from the famous *Topolino* 500. Like many such Fiat advanced projects, its basic layout swung from one extreme to the other as a 'paper' design, but serious development work did not begin until 1951, after the layout of the 1100/103 had been finalized.

Even then, consideration was given to front engine/front-wheel-drive or rear engine/rear-wheel-drive cars, and it was not until 1953 that the definitive Type 100, later to be christened the 600, was drawn up. It was a car which had a great deal of influence, not only on other new Fiats, but on new models produced years later by Fiat's competitors. Basically, the 600 saloon, which was launched in 1955, had a four-cylinder water-cooled engine of 633 cc mounted in the extreme tail, driving the rear wheels via a four-speed gearbox mounted ahead of the line of those wheels. It featured four-wheel independent suspension, it was very light, and remarkably spacious considering its very compact outside dimensions. Right from the start, it was an enormous success, and sales simply rocketed away. How successful? I need only say that 600s of one type or another were built until the beginning of the 1970s, not only in Italy but in several other countries, and that up to 2.5-million examples eventually took to the road.

In 1964, Fiat introduced the workaday, rear-engined 850 saloon, really a bigger version of the famous 600, and in 1965 they followed this up with the 850 Spider (styled by Bertone), and the 850 Coupé (styled 'in house' by Fiat)

Fiat Sports Cars

Even so, by the end of the 1950s Fiat were already looking for ways, if not directly to replace the 600, then to complement it, and to widen its appeal in the market place. What followed would make a long and complicated story if told in full (as Dr Giacosa has done in his autobiography), but at this juncture all I need to say is that one project, the Type 122, was eventually handed over to Simca (Fiat's associate company at the time) to be refined and produced as the rear-engined Simca 1000, while another, which had front-wheel-drive and a transverse engine, eventually became the Autobianchi Primula of 1964.

By 1962, as a result of all this, Fiat wanted an additional model to the 600 even more urgently than before, but had absolutely nothing coming along to do the job for them. it was one of those rare occasions in modern Fiat engineering history where a new car needed to be conceived in a great hurry, without time for painstaking development, and where it had to be right, first time.

Thus it was that project 100G was born, and it was not without significance that this type number really indicated that it was in the same family of cars as the original Type 100 (in other words, the 600 family), but that it was larger in most respects (for G stood for *grande*).

Its layout therefore, was to be so boringly obvious from the moment that it was conceived that Giacosa found it all profoundly tedious, and has written: 'The new project did not appeal to me. It was Montabone, recalled to Turin as a junior director with the general management, who took charge of it.'

ABOVE *For the 850 Spider/Coupé installation, Fiat boosted the power output of the 843 cc four-cylinder engine, among other things including a tubular exhaust system and a massive silencer alongside the engine sump*

TOP *The 850 Coupé and spider models shared the same pressed steel body underpan with the 850 saloon, and this was the mechanical package which was hidden away. The engine was behind the line of the rear wheels and the fuel tank was above the transmission, but behind the seats. Rear suspension featured semi-trailing arms, and the electrical battery had to live up front*

RIGHT *The date is 1961 and the car's an 850 Cisitalia Spider based on, presumably, the Fiat 600D chassis. This car must have influenced Bertone's 'real' 850 Spider discussed here*

850 Coupé and spider

The new car, developed at great speed, soon took on the name of '850', because its engine size was 843 cc, and was very closely based on the layout of the 600, even though the design of the smaller car was now nearly ten years old. In fact the only important change was that the fuel tank, which had been in the nose of the 600, found itself squeezed between the engine and the backrest of the rear seat, and the basic style of the car was altered so that there was a small rear 'bustle' at the rear, in place of a smooth sweep over the engine bay.

The new 850, of course, had an entirely new pressed-steel unit-construction two-door saloon bodyshell, looking similar, but rather more smooth, compared with the 600; naturally, its style was the work of Fiat's own styling studios. Compared with the 600, however, its wheelbase was a mere one inch longer, and the rear track was 2.3 in. wider, though the front track, indeed, all the front suspension, remained the same. The whole car, however, was 14.5 in. longer, though little of this extra length went into increasing the size of the passenger compartment.

Like the front suspension, the rear suspension and the steering were all of '600' type. Independent front suspension, therefore, was by a lower transverse leaf spring (which also doubled as a lower wishbone location outboard of its clamps), upper wishbones, and an anti-roll bar to trim the handling, and there was the usual Fiat type of worm and sector steering. At the rear, the independent suspension was by semi-trailing arms (or, in modern parlance, semi-swing axles), coil springs, and an anti-roll bar.

Most of the technical interest, though muted because of the similarity to the long-established 600, was in the engine and transmission. The engine itself was that of the 600, enlarged yet again. Even though it had to live in the very tail of all such cars, where its weight had a considerable influence on the handling, it was a conventional straight four-cylinder unit, with water-cooling, a cast-iron cylinder block and a cast-alloy cylinder head. The crankshaft had three main bearings, there were overhead valves, and centrifugal oil filter incorporated in the crankshaft pulley.

The original 600 had been a 633 cc (60 × 56 mm bore and stroke), 22 bhp unit, while from the summer of 1960 the model had become 600D with 767 cc (62 × 63.5 mm), and 29 bhp. Now, for what many people considered would be the final stretch, the 850 had 843 cc, a bore and stroke of 65 × 63.5 mm, and peak power of 34 or 37 bhp (depending on model) at 5000 rpm.

Looking from the side of the car, and starting from the tail, there was the four-cylinder engine, then the clutch, then the final drive assembly, and in front of it was the four-speed manual gearbox. Drive from the engine was fed over the top of the final drive to the gearbox, which was all-indirect, and back to the final drive from the secondary shaft. For the first time on a Fiat there was Porsche-type synchromesh on all forward gears.

There was nothing exciting about the new 850, and Fiat would have been very surprised if any of the commentators had found it to be so, but there was no doubt that, commercially at least, it was to be a success. And so it was. Before being dropped, in Italy, in the early 1970s, one and a half million cars were built, and it lived on, as the 133, from Seat in Spain for several more years after that.

Well before the dumpy saloon was announced, however, the company had more sporting things in

Fiat Sports Cars

TOP LEFT *The Bertone-styled (and manufactured) 850 Spider body was remarkably sleek, and very distinctive, complete with faired headlamps. It was available like this, with a folding hood, or...*

CENTRE LEFT *... with a detachable steel hardtop as an optional extra. In each case, there were only two seats*

BOTTOM LEFT *The Bertone-styled 850 Spider hid the position of its engine very neatly indeed under what almost looks like a conventional 'boot' lid. No right-hand-drive version of this open car was ever built by Fiat*

TOP RIGHT *Facia layout of the 850 Spider of 1965 and a view of the practical, if not luxurious, rubber-matted floor coverings*

BOTTOM RIGHT *A padded shelf, but certainly no seating accommodation, was behind the two front seats of the 850 Spider*

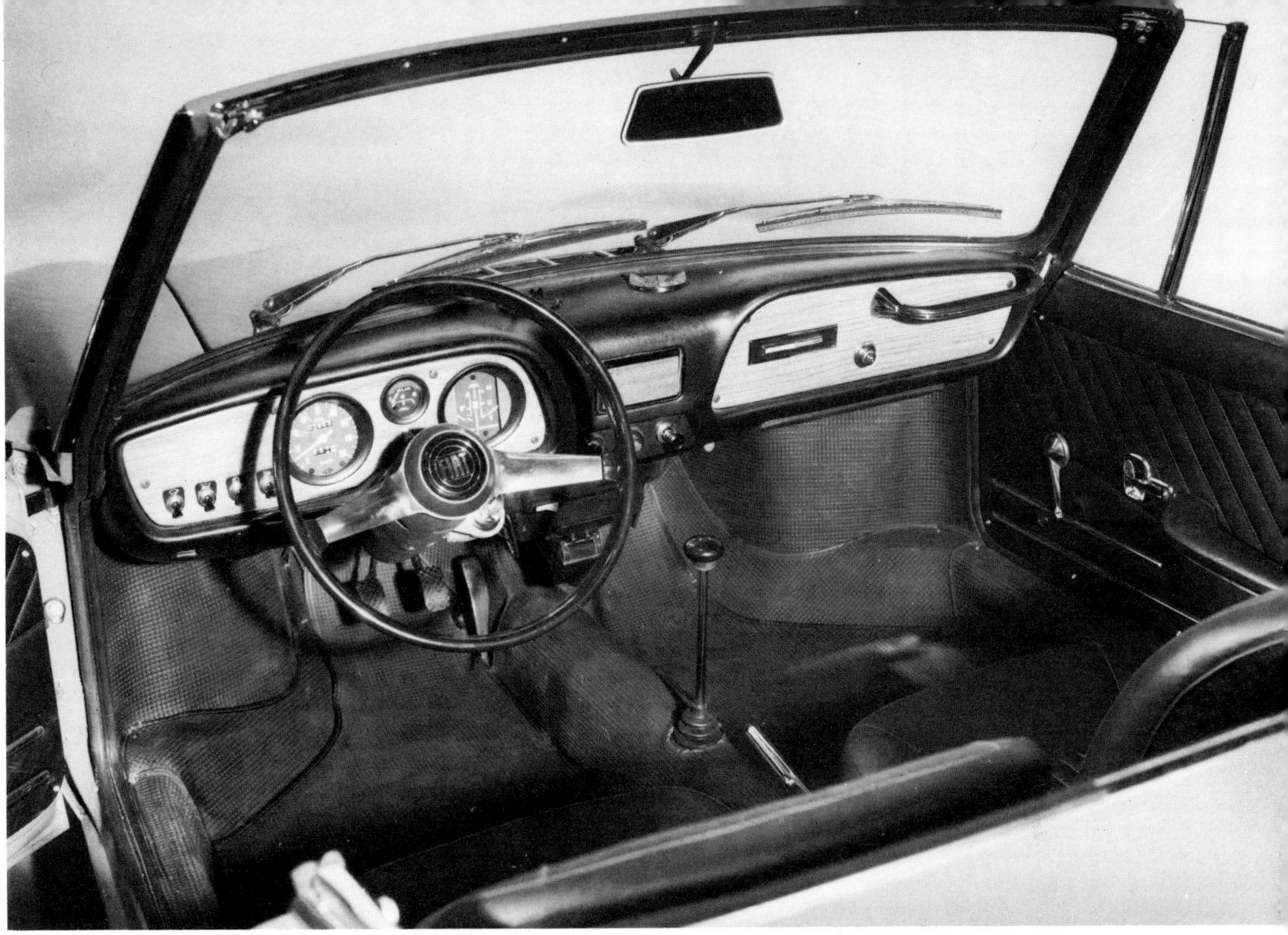

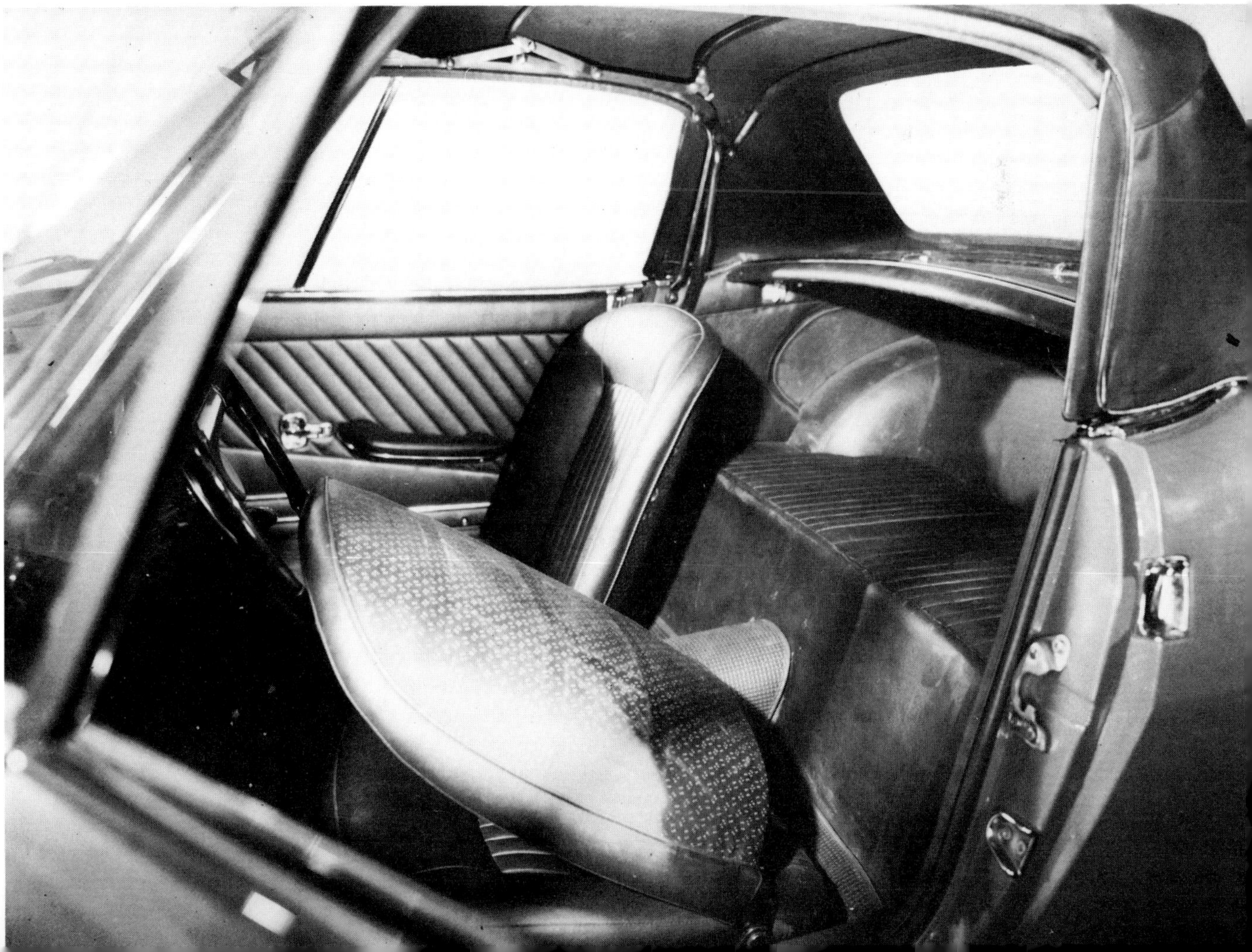

Fiat Sports Cars

ABOVE *Production in exalted company for the 850 Spider at Bertone's Grugliasco factory. On the right, 850 Spiders, on the left Fiat Dino Coupés*

RIGHT *At the Geneva Motor Show of March 1968, Fiat announced an improved 850 Spider. Now called the 850 Sport Spider, it had a 903 cc engine with more power and torque, vertical recessed headlamps instead of the original faired-in units, and bumper overriders*

mind. For the first time, they were preparing to make sporting versions of a cheap car, and if the style could be made right, the selling prices promised to be outstanding attractive. There was no doubt that such cars could be given high performance (considerably higher than the 75 mph top speed of the saloon), for Carlo Abarth and others had proved, not only that the engine could be enlarged considerably, but that it could be supertuned into the bargain.

It was at this point that Fiat took something of a momentous decision. Not only would they approve the development of a new coupé, but they would also commission the design of a spider as well. It was the first of a number of such moves that were to be made in the next few years, and it paid off handsomely.

There was never any doubt as to the source of the new fixed-head coupe style—it would be tackled 'in house' by the Fiat styling studio under the Boanos, father and son—but there was considerable discussion about the commission for the spider. Should it be styled by Fiat, or by a consultant? Should it be manufactured by Fiat, or partly by a consultant? There were a number of possibilities.

There were, of course, several stylists in the Turin area who could, no doubt, produce an acceptable style. But if Fiat decided that they wanted to see the bodies built by that styling house as well (thus repeating the Pininfarina exercise on the 1200/1500/1600S Cabriolets), their choice was severely limited, effectively to Bertone, Pininfarina, or perhaps (with a great deal of expansion and financial help) a company like Vignale.

We now have no way of knowing how the decision was made (except, perhaps, that Pininfarina were already fully committed to the existing 1200/1500 models, and were earmarked for the production contract on the forthcoming 124 Sport Spider), but Bertone's fine work in connection with the Alfa Romeo Giulietta and Giulia Sprint GTs must have been a factor. Whatever, in 1963, Bertone, who had a new factory (opened in 1960) at Grugliasco, a suburb of Turin only a few miles away from the major Fiat assembly plants, was invited to offer a style for an 850 Spider, and to quote for production of those shells in quantity. It was the first time Bertone had ever been associated with Fiat, and it would not be the last.

850 Coupé and spider

At the time, Bertone's chief stylist was a precocious young man called Giorgetto Giugiaro—yes, *that* Giugiaro—who had worked with Boano at Fiat for four years before joining Bertone in 1959. It was under his direction, though not necessarily from his own drawing board, that the new 850 Spider took shape. Fiat liked it at once, and decided to launch spider and coupé models together, at the Geneva motor show in March 1965.

As was to happen so many times in future years, both cars were based on the running gear, engine/transmission, and suspensions of the standard saloon, and in the case of the 850s they even picked up the same pressed-steel floorpan assembly, with the same wheelbase length of 6 ft 7.9 in. It meant that the Fiat-styled coupé could have really generous 2+2 seating without too much of a squeeze, while the new spider could be a spacious two-seater.

The coupé was shaped at Fiat's own studios at Via La Manta, in Turin, and apart from the hand-built 8V Coupé it is special because it was the first sporting Fiat of the postwar period to be styled 'in house', rather than by a consultant. Fiat, however, had bought their expertise rather than developed their own, for their styling chief, Mario Felice Boano, was a consultant who had originally had his own coachbuilding business in the city, and had been linked to Fiat since 1958.

The style which the Boanos produced was a neat and compact machine, with a fixed steel roof, intended for mass-production on press tools. The shape was so neat, integrated, and somehow understated that at a glance it was very difficult to see that the engine was in the rear at all. The fact that there was no front grille (for the cooling radiator was in the tail, alongside the engine), and that there were ventilation slots in the rear engine cover, almost went unnoticed. The coupé was not stripped out, or 'racer', which meant that Fiat knew exactly what their customers wanted. An 850 Coupé came complete with four plushly-trimmed seats, winding windows, and rear quarter windows which could also be cranked open to aid through-flow ventilation. The front wheel arches intruded considerably into the front foot wells, but this was because the car had such compact dimensions, and the seating was so far forward, and no-one complained too much.

The spider, styled and eventually to be manufactured by Bertone, was an altogether more dramatic-looking machine. Whereas Fiat merely side-lined their standard underpans to another part of the body shop at Lingotto, for the coupé bodyshell to be completed, they had to supply these floorpans in bulk to Grugliasco, just a few kilometres away, for Bertone to do their transformation act. The Bertone 850 Spider was a sleek little machine, but a puzzle for students of styling was that it really bore no relation to any previous Bertone shape. Most styling houses

63

Fiat Sports Cars

of the day seemed to develop some sort of family 'line', which made one shape superficially similar to the one before it. But not this time. The 850 Spider, with its smooth body side incorporating one feature line, its faired-in headlamps, and its cut-off tail, was not at all like the Iso Grifo, the Alfa 2600 Sprint or the Simca 1200S Coupé. It was, if anything, a Bertone 'one-off' (though, of all things, you can see traces of the same style in the Lamborghini Miura! Both were the work of Marcello Gandini), and it was said to have been influenced by the tiny front-engined Lotus Elan, which had first gone on sale in 1963.

Even though the spider was only a two-seater, Gandini's flowing lines meant that it was nearly seven inches longer than the coupé, most of the extra length being ahead of the front wheels. In spite of this, however, there was very little luggage space in the spider; whereas, in the coupé, the spare wheel was stowed vertically at the front of the forward luggage container, the lower lines of the Spider meant that this was not possible. The spare was mounted under the floor, and the resulting locker was very shallow indeed.

There was always likely to be a more restricted market for the spider than the coupé, if only because it was more expensive (1,050,000 lire compared with 950,000 lire when the two cars were launched in March 1965), and because it was never built in right-hand, drive form. Even so, the customers loved it, and within a year Fiat were already approaching the *total* production figures of the larger Pininfarina-built cars.

The great news for Fiat was that these cars were, after all, going to be a success in the USA, as well as in Europe. They were right for the times, and the Bertone-styled spider, in particular, was a very attractive alternative proposition to the old-fashioned front-engined MG Midgets and Triumph Spitfires. Not only that, but Fiat seemed to have tamed the handling characteristics completely. With a front/rear weight distribution of 38/62 per cent, it might have been reasonable to expect strongly oversteering machines, but there was little of this in the new Fiats. *Autocar*'s road test of 1966 summed up well: 'The days of unstable, oversteering, rear-engined cars are over, and the handling of the Fiat is a good example of the progress which has been made. Despite a rear weight bias of 62 per cent there is no noticeable oversteer on the road, quite the reverse in fact, with the car taking a naturally wide line that can easily be tightened by the steering as required.'

There was more to these new cars, of course, than good looks and gentle handling, for Fiat had boosted the engines considerably. No doubt with help from Abarth (who had done such an outstanding job with the 2300S Coupé's engine), the little 843 cc engines were given new camshafts, a higher (9.3:1-vs–8.8:1) compression ratio, and strikingly swept tubular exhaust manifolds. As a consequence, peak

Under the skin the 850 Sport Spider was much like the superseded 850 Spider, and the majority of the car's weight was still over the rear wheels

850 Coupé and spider

ABOVE LEFT *No major changes to the facia layout were made when the 850 Sport Spider of 1968 took over from the 850 Spider of 1965–68 vintage, though there was a neater and more comprehensive instrument display*

LEFT *A most handsome pair for the time (1965)—those that are left are well cared for today*

power rose to 47 bhp (DIN) on the coupé and to 49 bhp (DIN) on the spider. Top speed in each case was nearly 90 mph, so to keep this performance in check, front-wheel disc brakes were also standardized.

Before Fiat could achieve volume sales with these cars in North America, there was one minor hurdle to be cleared. They had to make sure that their engines complied with the latest wave of legislation concerned with exhaust gas emissions. Fortunately for Fiat, they were quick to spot a concession which confirmed that cars with engines of 817 cc or less did not have to comply. No sooner said than done. From the start of the 1968 model year, US market 850 Coupés and spiders had 817 cc—the reduction being achieved by a marginal reduction in cylinder bore, from 65 mm to 63.9 mm—and there was a negligible effect on the peak power output. This change, incidentally, was never inflicted on other markets, much to Fiat's credit.

The writer recalls these two small sporting Fiats with great joy, if only because they were the first Italian models he met when embarking on the life of a motoring journalist. It was such a pleasure to meet cars with such enormous character, and so very obviously Italian. There was no attempt to dress up unpromising mechanical components with glossy style and lush trim—quite the contrary, for these cars had serviceable, rather than plushy, rubber mats on the floor, exposed painted metal all around the cockpit, and a distinct air of 'function' rather than 'showroom appeal'. And yet, for all that, the coupé and Spider shapes had a great deal of visual appeal, especially the Spider, with its slippery-looking lines, the nicely special dashboard, and the optional metal hardtop to turn it into a snug little closed two-seater.

The Americans, clearly, liked the Spider and the Coupé very much indeed. As *Road & Track* testers commented, in April 1968: 'If, as we said, the Coupé was one of the handsomest designs ever seen on a small car, the Spider is certainly the most beautiful. Its carefully fashioned Bertone lines were admired

Fiat Sports Cars

RIGHT *From the three-quarter rear view, the style of the 850 Coupé was neat, compact, and understated. It was almost impossible to guess that the engine was in the tail*

ABOVE LEFT *Italian coachbuilders didn't ignore the 850 chassis—this is Moretti's effort of 1964 850 Coupé. Is there 124 Coupé influence there?*

LEFT *The shape of the 850 Coupé of 1965 was credited to Fiat's own studio, and it was a real credit to them. Generous 2+2 seating was provided*

by everyone who saw the car, and more than one owner of a small-displacement British roadster cast covetous eyes upon it.'

In the USA, after all, the Spider was a cheap little car in 1968 (it was priced at a mere $2215), and though it was significantly slower in acceleration and top speed, it handled a good deal better, particularly compared with the Spitfire. As *Road & Track* said of their car (which had, in fairness, optional cast alloy wheels):

'With suspension geometry that keeps its tail heaviness well in check, the Fiat can be flung about enthusiastically, giving an exceedingly high fun-dollar quotient.... If Fiat can import enough Spiders to meet the demand already created by the car's seductive appearance, the highways will be dotted with them.'

What was interesting, however, was that when the same magazine compared a Spider with the two British cars, and the Datsun 1600, calling in young non-journalist enthusiasts to drive all the cars in the same session, they summarized as follows:

'Almost all the negative remarks made by our drivers about the Fiat resulted from its small engine and its comparatively modest power. For around-town traffic where the indirect gears can compensate to some degree, the Fiat is lively, responsive, and good fun. Out on the highway, however, the engine whirs out a lot of revs, far more than any of our drivers felt comfortable with....'

As any pundit will tell you, some cars are 'too fast for chassis', while others are distinctly 'chassis too good for engine.' There was no doubt that the Fiat was one of the latter.

Help, however, was at hand. Fiat were in full flight in the late 1960s, when production was booming, when their domestic market share was almost ridiculously high, and when their seemed to be no possible end in sight to their expansion. At one time Giovanni Agnelli, Fiat's executive chief, was talking about a massive range of cars priced at £20 intervals, to provide something for everyone, and that eminent Fiat historian, the late Michael Sedgwick, went so far as to call the Torinese giant a 'General Provider'.

The 850 Spider and coupé models were, of course, somewhat dependent on the way that Fiat small *saloon* car development was heading, as the numbers of engines and components involved were so very much higher. Whereas average production of the sporting 850s was about 70,000 cars a year when they were at the peak of their reputation, annual Fiat production was about 1,300,000, of which at least a quarter of a million would be 850 saloons.

For the 1970s, however, Giacosa and his engineers had even more ambitious ideas, which would encompass (among other dramatic novelties) a whole series of new front-wheel-drive cars to be built with Fiat and Autobianchi badges. Working on the well-known 'building-block' principle, they were not only proposing to develop entirely new engines, but they also proposed to stretch the famous old 843 cc engine even further. Abarth, after all, had contrived to get the full 1000 cc from the same basic cylinder block, for racing purposes, so why should they not go partly along that route as well?

A new car, coded X1/2, and eventually to be known, in public, as the 127, was to replace the 850 saloon during 1971, and for this car the 843 cc engine was to be expanded to 903 cc. This change was only feasible by increasing the stroke, from 63.5 mm to 68 mm, for there was no more room in the cylinder block for the bores to be widened. This made the engine slightly undersquare, but it was not considered to be a serious drawback as the racing Abarth engines of 982 cc, which produced no less than 88 bhp (DIN) at 7600 rpm, had the even longer stroke of 75 mm. Well before Fiat were ready to launch the new 127 (or the Autobianchi A112, which was also to use the 903 cc engine), they used it, and other modifications, to improve the sporting 850s.

The new 850 Sport Coupé and 850 Sport Spider were launched at the Geneva Show in March 1968, where they instantly replaced the original 850s—and please note the addition of the 'Sport' word to their titles. Only for the USA, and then only until the end of 1969, was a smaller (817 cc) engine retained.

Compared with the original cars, the 'chassis' was virtually unchanged, except that wider-section radial ply tyres were specified. As before, the engines were matched to four-speed all-synchromesh gearboxes, whose ratios were not changed, nor was that of the final drive, so although the new cars might well be deeper breathing, they were no higher geared.

This is a simple comparison between the two engine types, as listed by Fiat for the coupé:

850 Coupé 843.cc 843 cc   47 bhp (DIN) at 6200 rpm   44 lb ft torque at 3600 rpm

850 Sport Coupé (903 cc) (1968)   52 bhp (DIN) at 6500 rpm   48 lb ft torque at 4000 rpm

It was slightly strange that the new engine, which

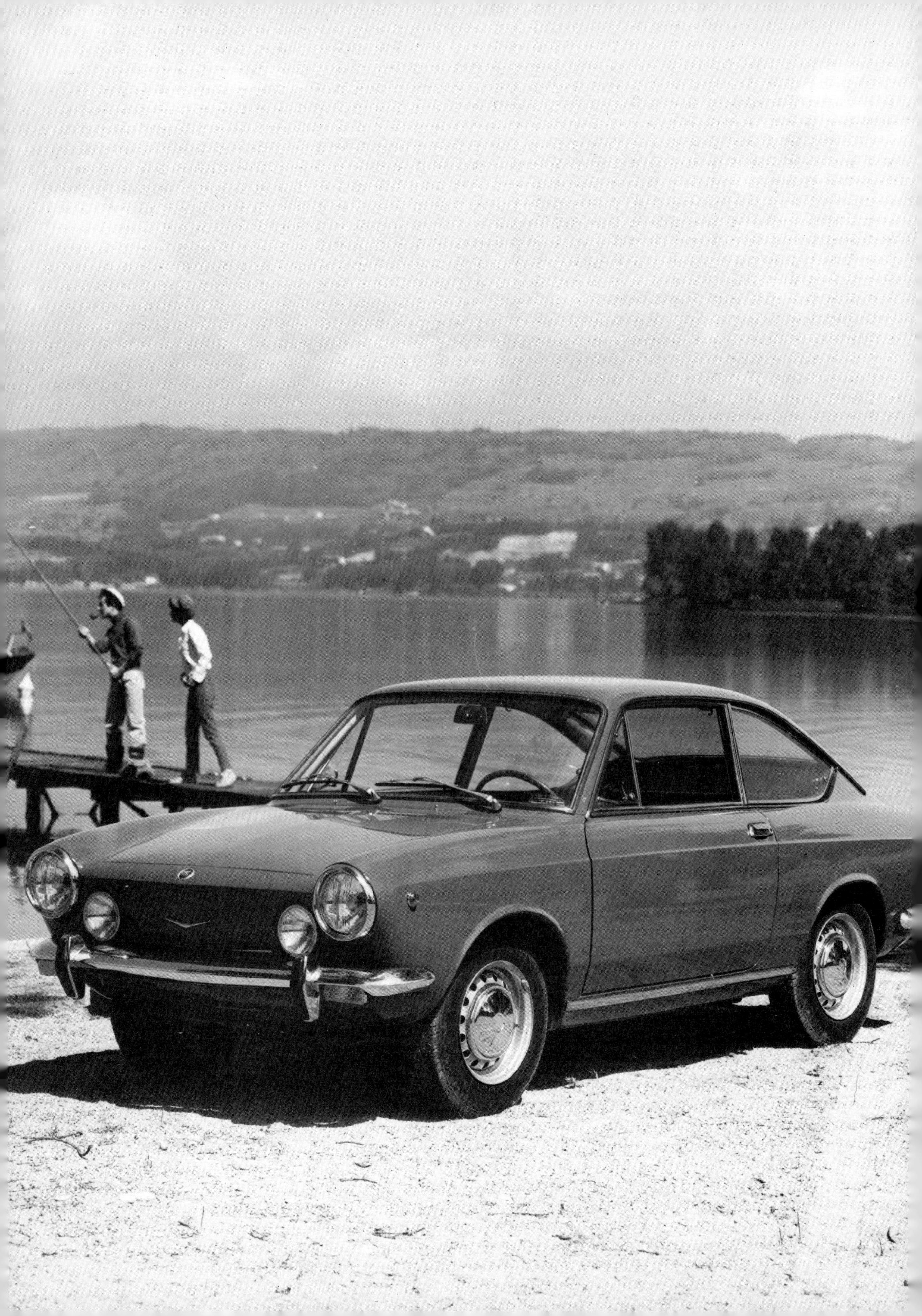

850 Coupé and spider

LEFT *When the 850 'Sport' categories were introduced in 1968, the coupé merely inherited extra long-range driving lamps recessed into the nose panel, but the main styling was unchanged until the car was dropped in the early 1970s. Considering its short (6 ft 7.9 in.) wheelbase, this is a remarkably well-balanced little car*

RIGHT *No doubt depicted in the most favourable way (for this is a Fiat publicity picture!) the 850 Coupé was nevertheless almost a full four-seater car, with neat and attractive seating*

had a longer stroke, should have developed its peak torque at a lower engine speed, if all the usual tenets of engine development had applied, but in the case of the 850 Sport engine the torque peak had actually increased, as had the speed at which maximum power was developed. This was, in fact, partly explained by the fact that a higher compression ratio of 9.5:1 had been adopted, along with minor improvements to the breathing.

Apart from the extra performance, which would have to wait to be proved by independent road tests, the most noticeable improvements—or, merely, changes, if one was feeling waspish—were to the styling. In neither case was the basic shape of the car changed, but the differences made the car immediately obvious.

On the coupé, a pair of additional driving lamps, which were automatically lit when the main beam setting was selected, were partly recessed into the front panel, inboard and rather below the level of the original headlamps, while at the rear there were four circular lenses in the vertical panel, sharing the functions previously compressed into just two lamps.

The most noticeable change, however, was at the rear, where a vestigial flip-up spoiler was incorporated on the engine lid and the corners of the rear wings, being accentuated by a chrome strip, horseshoe-shaped, all along the new sharp edge. I doubt if it had any noticeable aerodynamic effect, but it was visually distinctive. The styling changes, incidentally, were completed by the fitment of rubber-faced bumper over-riders (the original 850 Coupé had not had over-riders of any type).

Bertone's Sport Spider, too, was modified only in detail. Like the coupé, it had new rubber-faced over-riders, different from those of the coupé, while at the front the sloping headlamp cowls had been discarded, in favour of exposed, slightly higher, conventional headlamps. This change certainly did nothing for the smooth good looks of the Sport Spider, but had been necessary by the latest wave of legislation from North America. The Americans, for sure, had a lot to answer for, as this legislation also ruined the nose of the Jaguar E type, and did nothing for the style of the new Ferrari Daytona either.

The proof of the pudding was . . . in the performance recorded, and the favourable comments which appeared in the press. *Autocar*, for instance, opened their test of the 903 cc engined car by saying that: 'Even Fiat must have been surprised at the success of their little 850 Coupé. As soon as it was announced in 1965 demand ran at an extraordinary level, and today a high percentage of all 850s built are coupés. It is easy to see why the car has such an appeal; it fills a void in the market, and the price is right.' They found that the new Sport Coupé was not only significantly faster than before (with a top speed of 91 mph, compared with 87 mph for the 843 cc car), but that it was more accelerative, and quite remarkably economical, with 35 mpg (Imperial) easily within reach. The handling was still excellent, it was still a comfortable little machine, and a very appealing amalgam. In fact:

Fiat Sports Cars

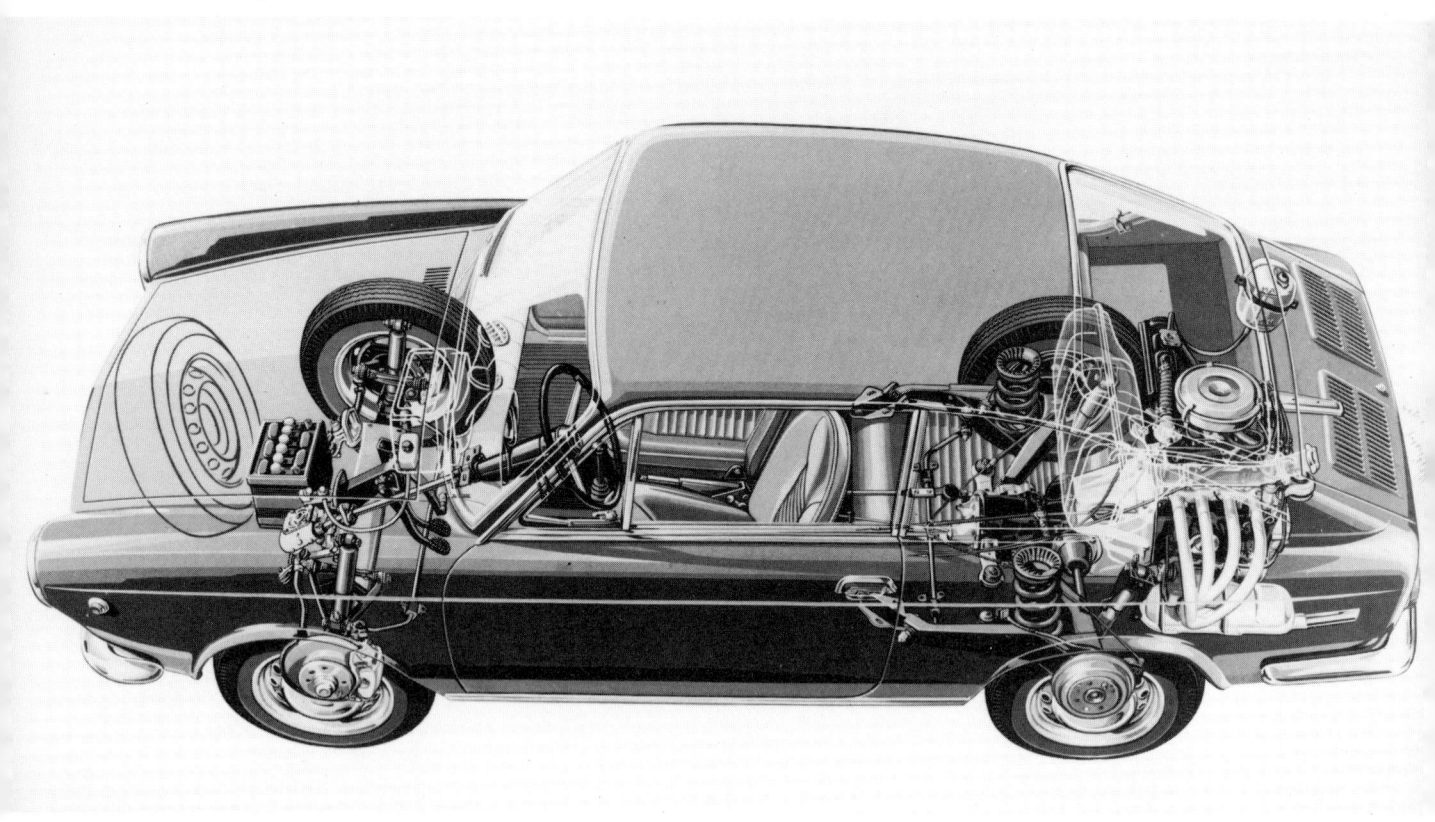

'Owners of Fiat 850 Coupés still ask us what else they might consider, and we have to say each time that there is little or nothing which offers the same blend of value, performance, economy, chic styling and reliability plus, above all, a sporting temperament.'

However, even though the 'Sport' models were great little cars—it wasn't only the press who thought so, but the tens of thousands of enthusiasts who ordered them—they were destined to have a relatively limited life. Their 'parent' car, the 850 Saloon, was rendered obsolescent by the new front-wheel-drive, overhead-cam engined, 128 saloon, and in the spring of 1971 it was finally forced out of production by the new and even more advanced, 127 hatchback.

Thereafter the 'Sport' range was on borrowed time, and even though it received enlarged inner headlamps at the Geneva Show of March 1971, that was really a final fling. The last of all was built in November 1971 at Lingotto, where it was immediately replaced by the new front-wheel-drive 128 Sport Coupé. In the long-term scheme of things, indeed, Fiat had always intended the 'Sport' 850s to be replaced by similar 128s, but fate had a hand in that, and there was no direct equivalent of the 128 Sport Spider in the offing. Instead, Bertone produced the miraculous X1/9, in a complex chain of events described in chapter 10, though the Sport Spider continued to be assembled at Grugliasco until 1973.

At the end of the day, the statistics supplied by Fiat for these two cars tell their own story. There is no detailed breakdown of sub-types, but Fiat say that 342,873 coupés and Sport Coupés were built, compared with 124,660 spiders—a grand total of 467,533 sporting 850s. Nearly half a million sports cars—it must have seemed incredible compared with the tiny number of 1100Ss, 8Vs and (relatively speaking) Pininfarina cabriolets which had gone before. But by the end of the 1960s, Fiat had become used to their own good fortune, and were basking in expertise, for their medium-sized models, all based on the 124, were doing equally as well.

ABOVE *The 850 Coupé shared exactly the same running gear as the 850 Spider, but 2+2 seating was provided on the same wheelbase*

LEFT *Oh yes! A very special 850 coupé from Ghia in 1967 with lines not dissimilar to those of the Porsche Abarth and the DeTomaso Vallelunga*

850 Sport Coupé and Spider

PRODUCED March 1968 to mid-1973
NUMBER BUILT Figures included in 843 cc version statistics
GENERAL LAYOUT As for original 843 cc versions, with following technical changes:
ENGINE Bore, stroke and capacity 65 × 68 mm, 903 cc (2.56 × 2.68 in., 55.1 cu. in.). CR 9.5:1. 52 bhp (DIN) at 6500 rpm. Peak torque 48 lb ft at 4000 rpm
CHASSIS AND SUSPENSION 155-13 in. radial ply tyres on 5.0 in. wide wheel rims
SPIDER Length 12 ft 6.5 in
COUPÉ Length 11 ft 11.8 in. Unladen weight 1642 lb
PERFORMANCE SUMMARY (*Autocar*, 16 January 1969) Maximum speed 91 mph, 0–60 mph 15.6 sec., standing start ¼-mile 20.4 sec., overall fuel consumption 34.1 mpg (Imperial)

850 Coupé and Spider

PRODUCED March 1965 to March 1968
NUMBER BUILT 342,873 coupés, and 124,660 spiders, all types including later 903 cc versions.
GENERAL LAYOUT Rear-engined sports coupé and spider models with unit-construction pressed-steel body/chassis units, with four seats (Coupé) and two seats (Spider). Four-cylinder engine driving rear wheels, with all-independent suspension.
ENGINE Overhead valve design, based on that used in all Fiat 600/850 saloon models. Four-cylinder, in-line, unit, with cast iron cylinder block and light-alloy cylinder head. Three crankshaft main bearings. Two valves per cylinder, operated by pushrods and rockers from single camshaft mounted in side of block, and driven by chain. Bore, stroke and capacity 64 × 63.5 mm, 843 cc (2.56 × 2.50 in., 51.4 cu. in.). CR 9.3:1. One downdraught dual-choke Weber carburettor. (Coupé) Maximum power 47 bhp (DI*N) at 6200 rpm. Peak torque 44 lb ft at 3600 rpm. (Spider) Maximum power 49 bhp (DIN) at 6200 rpm. Peak torque 43 lb ft at 4200 rpm.
NOTE For 1968 and 1969, in the USA only, the following engine size was used: 63.9 × 63.5 mm, 817 cc (2.51 × 2.50 in., 49.8 cu. in.). Maximum power quoted at 52 bhp (gross) at 6200 rpm, peak torque 46 lb ft at 4000 rpm
TRANSMISSION In unit with rear-mounted engine, and final drive, four-speed all-synchromesh manual gearbox. Final drive ratio 4.875:1. Overall gear ratios 4.69, 6.87, 10.02, 17.72, reverse 17.65:1. 13.8 mph/1000 rpm in top gear
CHASSIS AND SUSPENSION Rear engine, rear drive. Unit construction, pressed-steel body/chassis units. Independent front suspension by traverse leaf spring, wishbones, and anti-roll bar. Worm and roller steering. Independent rear suspension by coil springs, semi-trailing arms, and anti-roll bar. 8.9 in. front disc brakes, 7.3 × 1.2 in. rear drum brakes. 5.50-13 in. cross-ply tyres on 4.5 in. wheel rims. Bolt-on pressed-steel disc wheels
BODYWORK Pressed-steel shells, in unit with 'chassis', produced by Fiat (coupé), or by Bertone for Fiat (spider).
  Spider, in two-door, two-seat open sports style, with optional hardtop. Length 12 ft 4.9 in.; width 4 ft 11 in.; height 4 ft 0 in. Wheelbase 6 ft 7.9 in.; front track 3 ft 9.5 in.; rear track 3 ft 9.8 in. Unladen weight 1586 lb.
  Coupé, in two-door four-seat fastback coupé style. Length 11 ft 10 in.; width 4 ft 11 in.; height 4 ft 3.1 in. Wheelbase 6 ft 7.9 in.; front track 3 ft 9.5 in.; rear track 3 ft 9.8 in. Unladen weight 1586 lb
PERFORMANCE SUMMARY (*Autocar*, 3 June 1966) coupé: Maximum speed 87 mph, 0–60 mph 18.2 sec., standing start ¼-mile 21.0 sec., overall fuel consumption 32.5 mpg (Imperial)

6 124 Spider and coupé
An affair with the Americans

The chunky little 1100/103 saloon, which was more affectionately known as the *nuova Millecento* by the Italian public, went on sale in 1953, and was an instant success. For years, Fiat's only problem was to build enough of them, and the derivatives which came from it. It was the 1100/103, of course, which gave rise to the Pininfarina 1200 Cabriolet, Fiat's most successful sporting car of the 1959–66 period. It was not until 1963, a full ten years after the 1100/103 had been launched, that any serious thought was given to replacing it.

Apart from the need for a new body style, the most urgent engineering requirement was for a new engine—or, rather, a new family of engines. Accordingly, Fiat set Aurelio Lampredi to designing these, and gave him a fairly open brief, which included the need for a range of cubic capacities—at first envisaged as being between about 1.0-litres and 1.6-litres. it was this engine, which was given the title of Type 124 right from the start, which was to power so many of Fiat's new medium-sized cars—saloons, sporting and even outright competition models—in the next 20 years.

Lampredi, of course, was nothing if not versatile, for in addition to designing a series of vee-12s, twins, 'fours' and 'sixes' for Ferrari before 1955, he had also designed the new Fiat family of four-cylinder and six-cylinder engines for the 1300/1500, and 1800/2100/2300 saloons. This time the new engine was to be a relatively simple, but very sturdy, in-line four-cylinder unit. For the first time at Fiat it was to have a five-bearing crankshaft, and above all it had to be considerably lighter than the old 1100/103 engine which it was intended to replace.

As to a new car itself, there was considerable discussion at first. In 1963, with the imminent rebuilding of part of the Mirafiori factory in view, and with an eye to the potentially enormous cost of investment in a new body and a new engine, Fiat management favoured the idea of retaining the Type 116 (1300) underpan and suspension, gearbox and back axle, but fitting the new engine, and restyled superstructure. The new car, it was suggested, should be 70 kg/154 lb lighter than the 1300, and considerably cheaper to build.

However, after the styling department had been persuaded to produce a face-lifted 1100/103 complete with a longer wheelbase and wider tracks, it was decided that the new car, now also called a '124', would have a completely new bodyshell and suspensions. In the meantime, Dr Giacosa had become immersed in the merits of front-wheel-drive (see Chapter 8), and gave responsibility for 124 design and development to Oscar Montabone, back from a long sojourn at Simca, in Paris, where he had been the French firm's technical director. Perhaps it would be over-simplifying the issue to suggest that Montabone's 124, and Giacosa's 109 were direct rivals for the next hefty tranche of Fiat investment, for in the end both cars were produced. The 109, in fact, appeared first, in 1964 as the Autobianchi Primula, while the 124 was not revealed until April 1966.

Following the success, modest by future achieve-

TOP *After Fiat introduced the all-new 124 saloon in spring 1966, enthusiasts did not have long to wait for a Pininfarina-styled Sport Spider version to follow. Announced in November 1966, this car had the shortened 124 saloon underpan and running gear, except that the engine was enlarged to 1.4-litres, and had a twin overhead camshaft cylinder head. The lines were simple, almost understated*

RIGHT *The nose of the Pininfarina-styled 124 Sport Spider—everyone soon forgot the 'Sport' part of the title—with carefully styled details*

FAR RIGHT *The tail of the original 124 Sport Spider of 1966, modestly detailed, and hiding a surprisingly roomy boot*

124 Spider and coupé

Fiat Sports Cars

ABOVE *Neat and unpretentious facia and instrument panel layout of the 124 Spider*

RIGHT *Chunky, and purposeful, twin-overhead-camshaft engine—1438 cc/90 bhp—complete with four-speed gearbox, as fitted to the 124 Spider and coupé models from 1967. The front engine cover hides a cogged belt camshaft drive*

ments but praiseworthy enough at the time, of the 1200 Cabriolet, Fiat always had an ambition to repeat the exercise, and—if possible—to make more sporting cars, and even more money out of them. Accordingly, when the design of the new 124 was beginning to take shape, a coupé specification, and a very different open Cabriolet, or Spider version, were always pencilled into the plans. For that reason, the general layout of the 124, and especially that of the engine itself, are technically significant here, and must be described in some detail.

Until one looked closely, the 124 could initially be dismissed as 'just another car'. Indeed, I see that in my own technical analysis of the car, published in *Autocar* in 1966 after I had visited the factory to look at an early example, I said that: 'At first glance the 124 looks very ordinary indeed, having crisp if undistinguished styling, a conventional engine, gearbox and rear axle layout, and none of the interesting engineering features which one might have expected after studying its cousin, the Autobianchi Primula.' I then went on to say that it might represent the 'most up-to-date solution to the classic layout yet devised.'

The four-door bodyshell of the 124 saloon *was*, indeed, entirely conventional, and had a 7 ft 11.2 in. wheelbase, three inches longer than all the 1100/103 family, but exactly the same as that of the 1300/1500 saloons, with which there was no connection, and no common panels. The 124 was also just as wide as a 1300/1500, but two inches lower, and had simple styling, developed entirely in Fiat's own studios. There had only been a short time available for a styling study, and the only important point of evolution at the 'plaster mock-up' stage was that square-cornered glass shapes had become a little more rounded, and the grille detail rather more simple.

The front suspension was a conventional coil spring and double wishbone system, allied to an anti-roll bar, and with the telescopic dampers inside the springs themselves, not at all like that of the other medium-sized Fiats. Steering was by worm and roller, but at least the dreadfully tortuous arrangement of the 1100/103 (with pivots high up on the bulkhead behind the engine) had been abandoned for a more conventional installation behind, and under the engine sump.

At the rear there was a new lightweight hypoid bevel axle, generally similar to previous Fiat units of this type, but the suspension linkage was novel for Fiat. Actual suspension was by combined coil

124 Spider and coupé

spring/damper units mounted directly above the axle tubes, and there was a short anti-roll bar ahead of the axle itself. Location, however, was by parallel trailing arms running forward from the outer ends of the axle to points on the bodyshell under the rear seat pan, by a stout torque tube fixed to the nose of the axle, and by a long Panhard rod with almost ideal geometry, running across the car immediately behind the axle casing. It was neat, it was simple, and it looked as if it would be effective. Like many such Fiat designs, before or since, however, there were problems, and from the end of 1968 it would be modified considerably.

On the saloon car, befitting its intended price bracket, there were 13 in. pressed steel wheels, and Pirelli cross-ply tyres, but for the brakes there was a real surprise. Front wheel discs had, of course, been expected, but not the four-wheel discs, by Bendix of France, which were actually specified. These were of the latest sliding-caliper design, and at the rear they incorporated an integral hand-brake leverage, operating directly on the hydraulic cylinders.

The transmission was entirely as expected—a four-speed, all-synchromesh version of the new unit first seen on 1300/1500 models, and later (in five-speed form) on the 1500/1600S Cabriolets, allied to torque tube transmission and the new hypoid bevel axle already mentioned. For the 124, as for the 1500/1600S Cabriolets, there was a direct-action gear lever sprouting from the gearbox tunnel.

The only brand new 'building block' in the car was, of course, Lampredi's engine. Although at this stage is was only offered with a pushrod overhead valve cylinder head, 1198 cc and 60 bhp (DIN), it was already known that there was much more to come. I ought, therefore, to divert, to analyse the engine itself, and the changes to which it would eventually be subjected.

In any engine there will be certain 'untouchable' dimensions, due to the particular transfer line machinery to be installed, and in the case of the new 124 these were, respectively, the spacing of cylinder centres, and the height of the cylinder block face above the crankshaft bearings. In the next two years after the 124 was to be announced, pundits were to discover not only that the cylinder bore could be

Fiat Sports Cars

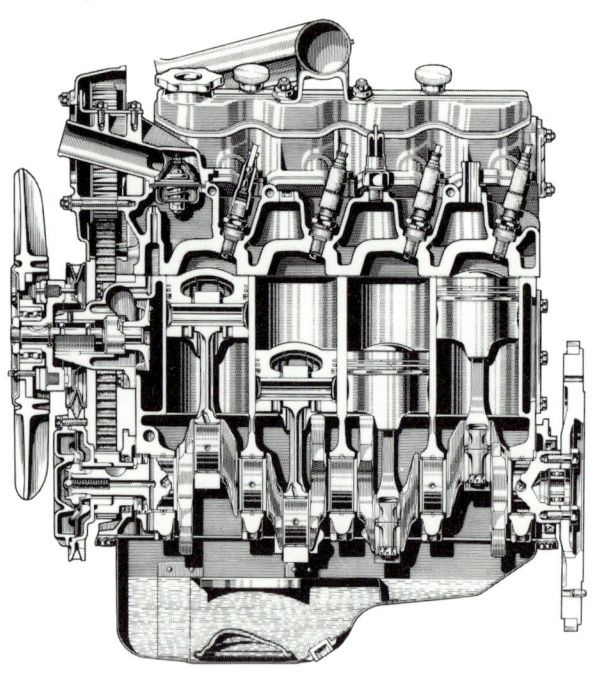

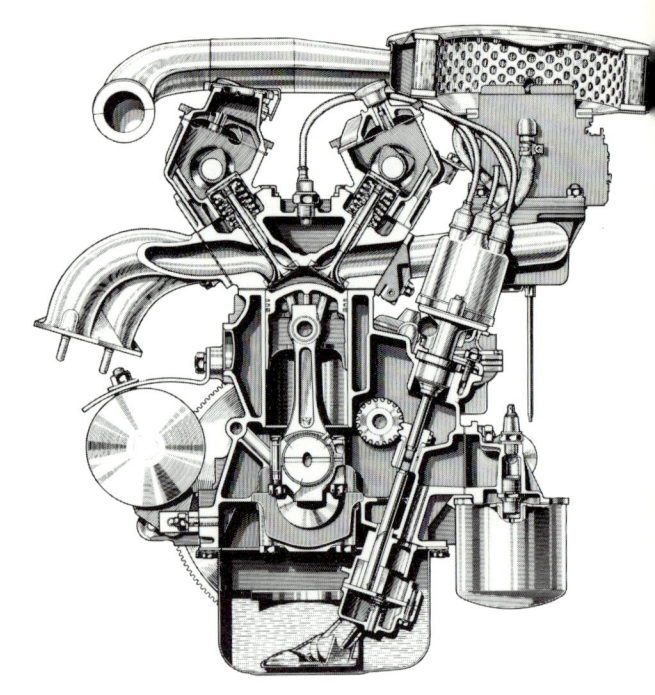

changed, but the stroke lengthened as well (sometimes together, sometimes in isolation), and not only that, but the entire cylinder head and mode of operation could be altered as well.

Lampredi, in short, had set out to design an engine with a cast iron cylinder block and light-alloy heads (which was conventional Fiat practice, of course) which even at first could be 1198 cc, 1438 cc, or 1608 cc, and could have pushrod overhead valve operation, or an advanced twin-overhead-camshaft cylinder head instead. The basic details of these units would be:

Model	Capacity	Bore × stroke mm	Valves	DIN power (bhp) rpm
124 saloon	1198	73 × 71.5	p/r	60 @ 5600
124 Special saloon	1438	80 × 71.5	p/r	70 @ 5400
124 Sport	1438	80 × 71.5	tc	90 @ 6000
125 saloon	1608	80 × 80	tc	90 @ 5600

(The 125 saloon, in fact, was not due to be launched until May 1967, and its significance to this story will be described later in the chapter.)

The pushrod engine which really formed the mass-production 'skeleton' for the more exciting derivatives (but would, nevertheless, be produced in huge numbers) was strictly conventional, for in 1198 cc form it had generous water passages around every cylinder bore, a sturdy overlap to its short-stroke crankshaft (made of cast iron, which *was* an innovation for Fiat), and a line of near vertical valves in wedge-shape cylinder heads, operated by a camshaft mounted in the side of the block, just above the line of the crank. There was quite a lot of space in the short but wide engine bay, so a side-draught dual-choke Solex PHH carburettor was fitted. Inlet and exhaust ports were all grouped together on the right side of the cylinder head.

The twin overhead camshaft version of this engine was altogether more advanced, and more exciting. The same basic cylinder block was retained, though the original camshaft was now only needed to act as a jackshaft to drive the skew shaft for the oil pump, and the ignition distributor.

The cylinder head, though housing twin overhead camshafts, and lines of valves opposed at 65 degrees, was designed with a careful eye to mass-production over a period of years, and by Jaguar, Alfa Romeo and Lotus-Ford standards was also conventional. The main advance was that it used one long, internally-toothed cogged belt to drive the camshafts from the nose of the crank—a feature pioneered in Europe by Glas, but only gingerly being adopted by large car-makers like Fiat. Like the pushrod engine, the 124S unit, as it was known, had a full-flow oil filter and a plastic cooling fan. The camshafts operated the valves in the classic racing engine way, via inverted 'bucket' tappets, and with adjustment by fat shims on top of, rather than underneath, those tappets. (It was typical of Lampredi, incidentally, that he arranged to use the same range of shims for this engine, the two different vee-6s for Dinos and the 130, and for the new 128 engine, which must have been an enormous help to standardization.)

124 Spider and coupé

FAR LEFT *Even in its original form, when it measured 1438 cc, there was no further space for later cylinder bore increases in the Type 124 AC twin-cam Fiat engine. It was sturdy and relatively simple, with cogged belt camshaft drive, and a five-bearing crankshaft.*

LEFT *The cross section of the 1438 cc 124 Spider/Coupé engine shows absolutely 'classic' Italian sporting car engine layout, with inverted bucket tappets, and concentric valve springs to operate the opposed valves*

BELOW *A question of ratios. This was the four-speed all-synchromesh manual gearbox fitted to some 124 Sports in the late 1960s*

BOTTOM *This was the five-speed gearbox which had been developed in parallel with the four-speed. The remote control linkage was added for a later (1.8-litre) derivative. This gearbox had originally been seen on the 1600S (Osca-engined) cars of 1965*

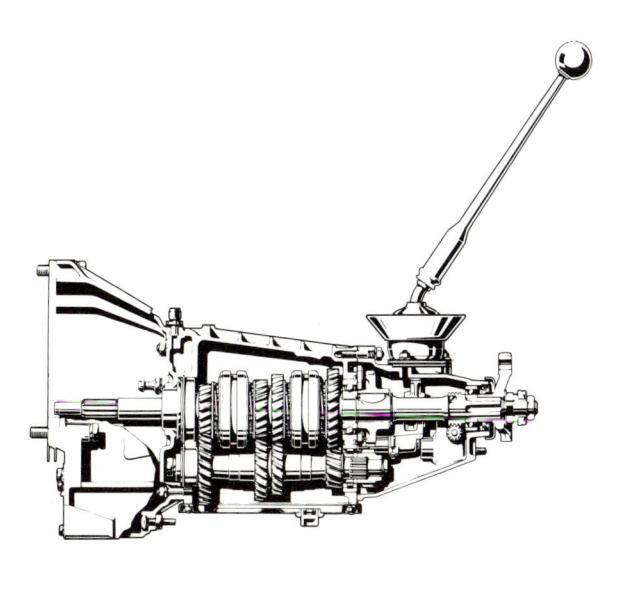

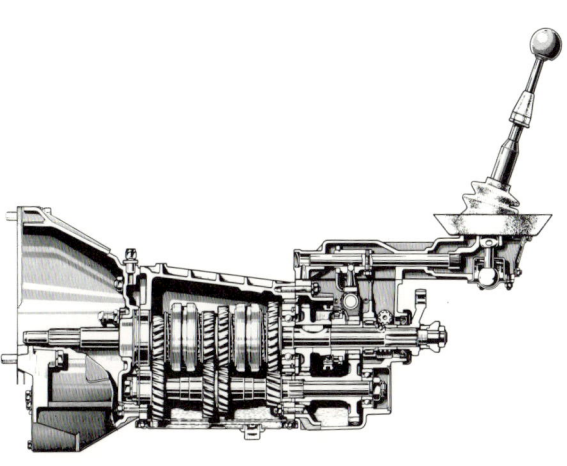

The fact that the two cambox faces were not machined in a single line made the engine look slightly strange—'knock-kneed' is how I have often heard it described—but it narrowed the unit and made it that important few centimetres more compact. The machined faces for inlet and outlet manifolds were in line with the valve angles, and of course this unit had classical cross-flow breathing. Whereas the pushrod unit had its horizontal carburettor on the right side, the twin-cam engine had a vertical, downdraught, dual choke Weber carburettor on the left, and the dual-outlet cast exhaust manifold was on the right side.

For the original 124 Sport installation, the engine was given a larger, 80 mm, cylinder bore, which meant that capacity was raised to 1438 cc, and it also meant that the block had to be recored, for there was no space for any water between adjacent cylinder bores. At a stroke, it seemed, the built in 'stretch' of the cylinder bore had been taken up.

This assumption was correct, for when Fiat announced the 1608 cc Fiat 125 saloon, it was seen that the extra capacity had been produced by increasing the stroke. In 1972, when the 132 appeared as a 125 replacement, the 84 mm cylinder bore of the engines used on that car were only produced by an expensive redesign of the entire engine, and the final 1995 cc capacity was only made possible by producing a longer stroke—of 90 mm—than the engine had ever been designed to accommodate.

Even so, it was a rugged little engine in 1.4-litre form, and was tuned to produce 90 bhp (DIN) at 6000 rpm. It is interesting to note that this mass-produced engine (and I use the phrase in its correct sense) was producing 63 bhp/litre at this very early stage of its development, whereas the very limited-production Osca-Fiat engine of the superseded cabriolets could only produce 57 bhp/litre—such is progress.

Another important mechanical change for the sporting 124s, compared with the saloon, was that the five-speed version of the gearbox became available. In fact there was no hard and fast rule as to which derivative was fitted with which box at first, for this varied with the market for which a car was intended. In Britain, for example, the coupé was to be sold with a four-speed box at first, and a five-speed box a year later. . . . In each case, the installation was like that of the 1965–66 1500 and 1600S Cabriolets, which is to say that there was no extra remote-control gearchange linkage.

The principle that Fiat had already established with the sporting 850s—that a closed car would be styled 'in house', and that an open version would be

Fiat Sports Cars

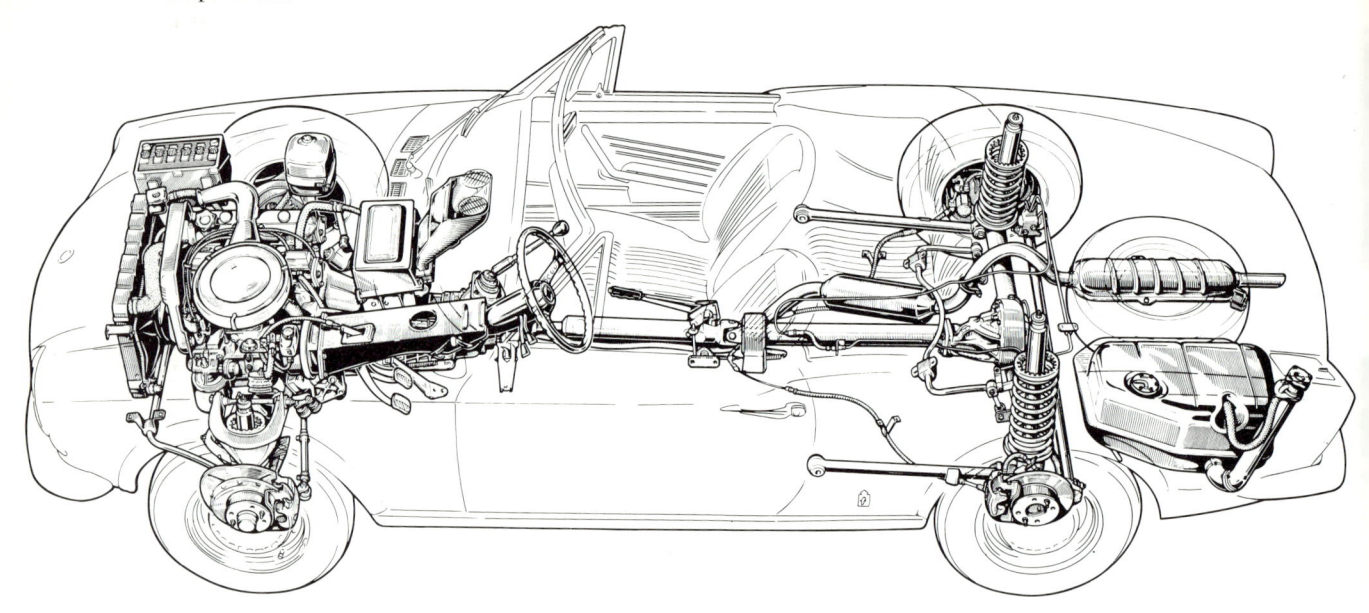

contracted out to a specialist coachbuilder, was upheld yet again with the two new 124 derivatives. Indeed, the same policy was also partly adopted for the Dinos, and for the 128s. For the 124s, unlike the 850s, Fiat chose Pininfarina as their outside contractor for the Spider.

Even Fiat could not tackle too many changes at once (especially in a year which was not only to see the launch of the 124 saloon, but a much revised and restyled 1100 called the 1100R, *and* the Ferrari-engined Dino as well), so they decided to phase their 124 Sport and Dino launches in the same way. At the Turin Show of November 1966, they would reveal the 124 Sport Spider and the Dino Spider, both with bodywork by Pininfarina, while the 124 Sport Coupé and the Bertone-styled Dino Coupé were both held back for launch at the Geneva Show of March 1967.

In 1966, therefore, Pininfarina had a very busy time, though his artistic standards did not seem to suffer because of this. In that year his stylists were responsible for the 124 Sport Spider, the Dino Spider and the Alfa Romeo Giulia Spider (Duetto), all of which were to be quantity-production machines built at the newly-expanded factory in Turin. Those production lines were in a state of upheaval, too, for the last of the old-type Fiat cabriolets and Alfa Romeo Giuliettas were built, after which tooling jigs and presses for the new models had to be installed. Who said that Italian workers were artists, but could not apply themselves to hard work? They were wrong.

For the 124 Sport Spider, Pininfarina were to be

ABOVE *The original 124 Sport Spider of 1966, with its twin-cam engine well hidden under engine bay accessories, and with the original type of rear axle location featuring trailing arms and a Panhard rod. The car really had two seats, and upholstering in the rear, but we can be charitable and call it a 2 + 2*

ABOVE RIGHT *In 1969, the 124 Spider was given a larger, 1608 cc, engine and minor styling changes including twin tiny bonnet 'power bulges', and a small-mesh radiator grille*

ABOVE FAR RIGHT *Very neat 124 Spider 1600 rear. Those who have heard that exhaust note know there's something special in that car*

RIGHT *By 1975, the 124 Spider was sold only in the United States, and looked like this, with yet another grille style, and massive energy-absorbing bumpers, but the basic sheet metal survived unchanged from the 1960s to the early 1980s*

supplied, from Fiat, with a structural underpan from the 124 saloon, modified only in that it was 14 cm/5.5 in. shorter in the wheelbase; this, in fact, meant that the 124 Spider had a slightly more squat stance than the 1500/1600S Cabriolet, for not only did have a slightly shorter wheelbase, but a considerably wider track.

Pininfarina did not, therefore, have enough space

124 Spider and coupé

Fiat Sports Cars

LEFT In 1975 the 100,000th bodyshell, painted and trimmed, was completed at Pininfarina. The car had twin small bonnet panel bulges and a 1.8-litre engine, the 150,000th car was not built until 1979, by which time a 2.0-litre engine was being fitted, and bigger but flatter bonnet bulges were in vogue. In 1982 the car continued to be built, but entirely assembled by Pininfarina

RIGHT Complete painted 124 Spider bodies beginning to accept much of their trim and electrical equipment, also at Pininfarina

BELOW 124 Spider bodyshell production at Pininfarina, with a great deal of handwork in evidence

124 Spider and coupé

on which to produce a full four-seater open car, but instead provided really generous and useful 2+2 accommodation; the '+2' seating, admittedly, was not very useful when the hood was erect. There was extra stiffening under the floor pan to restore beam stiffness, and extra bracing at the rear of it.

The styling of the 124 Sport Spider was understated and, from almost any other stylist, would have been considered ordinary. Somehow, even, it was not a shape which immediately screamed 'Pininfarina' to the observer, but on the other hand it was quite unmistakeable. Pininfarina's artists, in fact, had taken the theme of the 1500/1600S one stage further, barrelling the sides of the new car just a little more than the old, and left just a hint of a curved rear wing line by starting the swell of the pressing on the doors, above the door handle.

The inspiration behind the design, according to Pininfarina, was that of the one-off Chevrolet Corvette 'Rondine' of 1963. At first this was seen to have a permanent hardtop with a reverse-slope rear window. Later, as shown at Geneva in March 1964, the same car reappeared, slightly modified, with the same steel top, but with a new rear window swept back in a conventional style. The overall proportions certainly influenced the style of the new Fiat, especially the profile of the tail (described as having 'swallow tail' lines), and the hardtop, for the optional fitment on the new car.

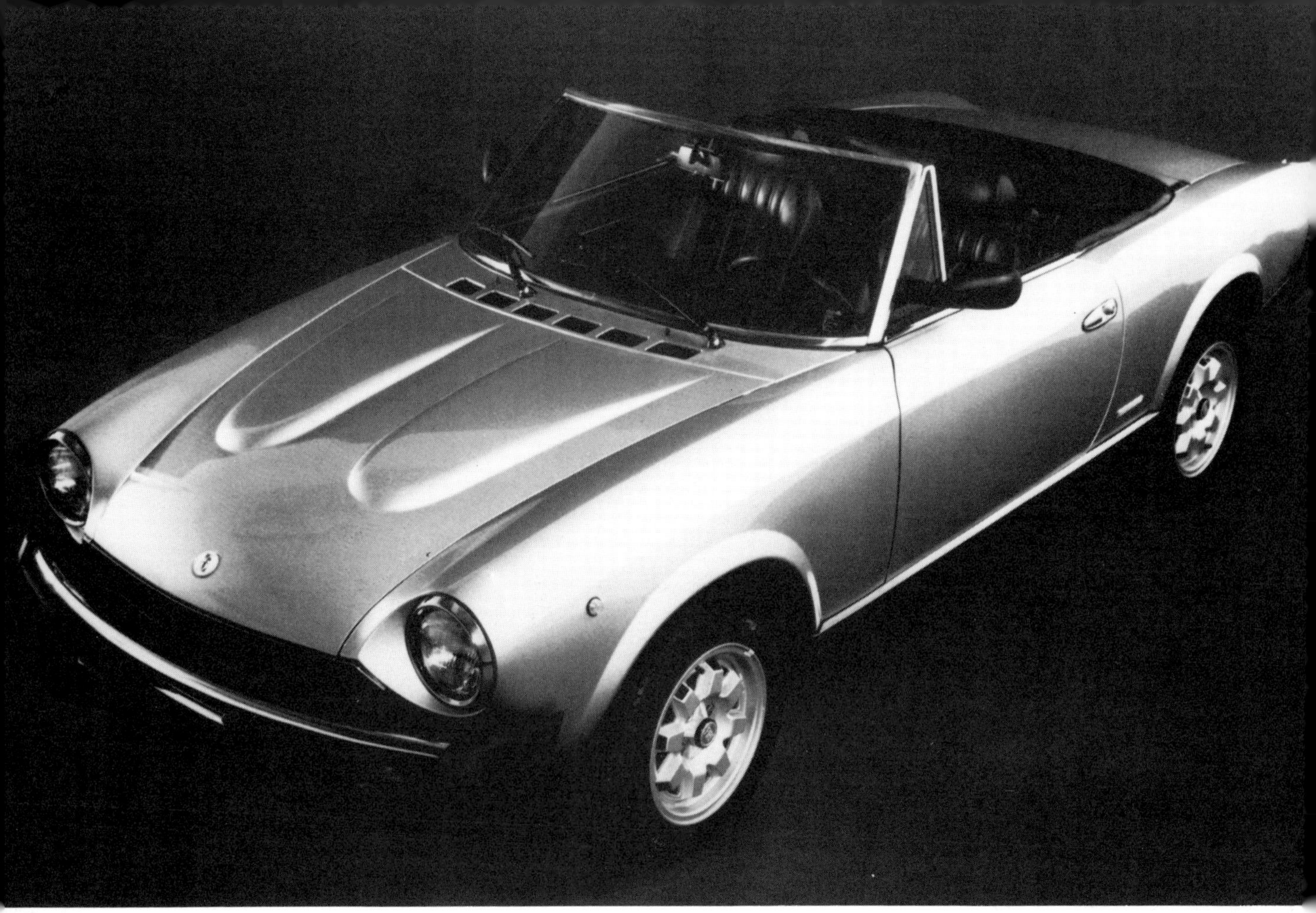

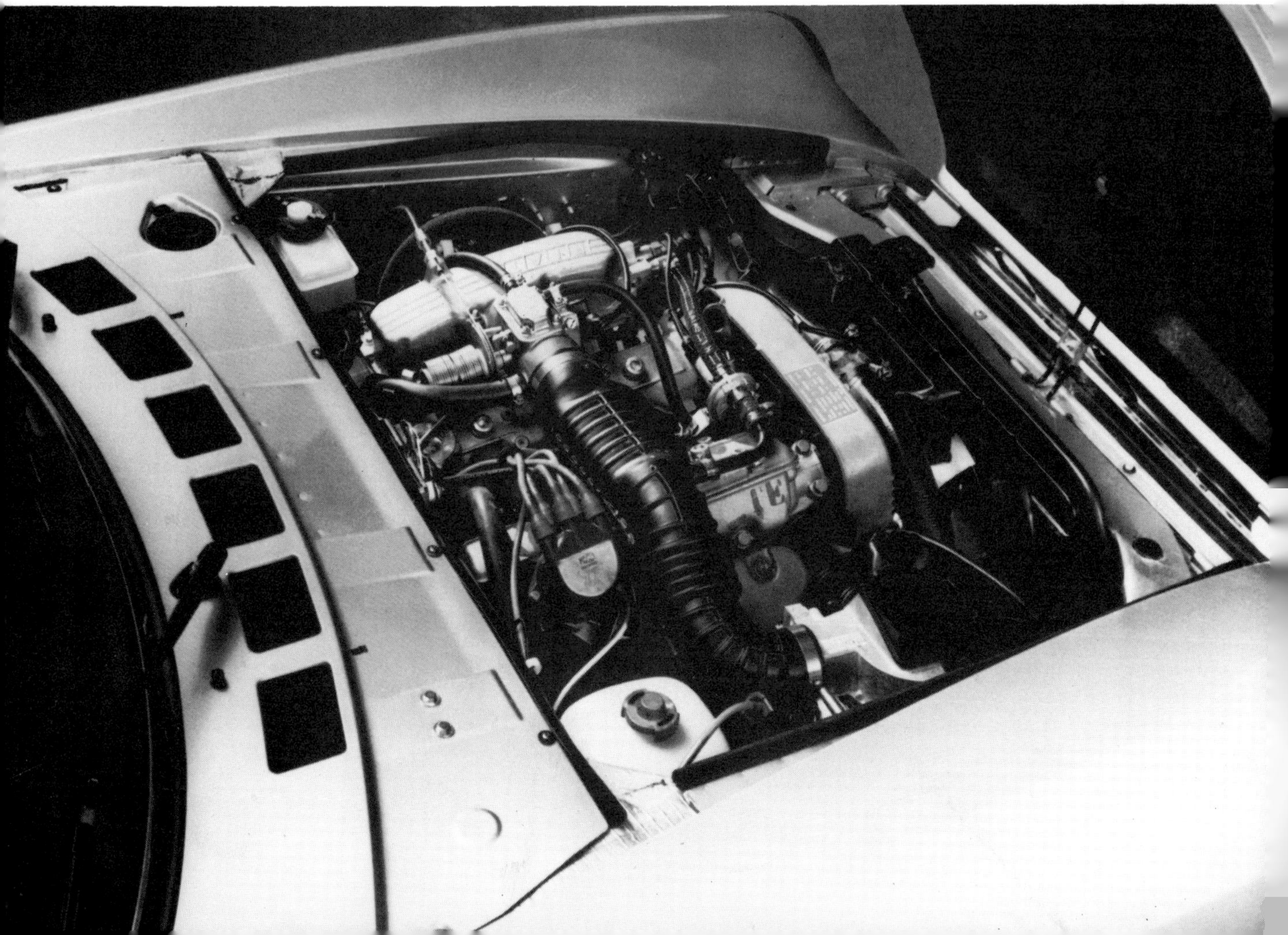

124 Spider and coupé

ABOVE *As with the 850 Coupé, the style of the 124 Sport Coupé of 1967 was by Fiat themselves, and almost everyone loved it. By utilizing the standard wheelbase from the 124 saloon, this was a full four-seater coupé, very stylish but very practical. The bonnet hid a 1.4-litre twin-overhead-cam engine*

LEFT (BOTH) *Probably the final development of the 124 Spider theme was the Pininfarina Spider Europa, badged as a 'Pininfarina' was not a 'Fiat'. It was announced in the spring of 1982, and featured fuel injection for its 1995 cc engine and very smart cast alloy wheels*

In its initial form, as revealed to the motoring press at the Turin Show of 1966 (where it was somewhat overshadowed by the exciting Dino Spider), there were no superfluous slots, bulges, or intakes, for there were still no USA regulations to get in the way of a good line. It was disappointing to be told that the 124 Sport Spider would only be built in left-hand-drive form (which meant that very few of these cars was ever sent to the UK, for instance), but on the other hand it was made very clear that the Spider was aimed fairly and squarely at the USA market, where it could be expected to face directly up to competition from the 1.8-litre MGB, whose size, performance and price were all similar. (In spite of some rumours at the time, by the way, there was no Pininfarina influence in the shaping of the MGB roadster, though the Italian firm was consulted over the MGB GT of 1965.)

There was widespread relief among Fiat enthusiasts when they saw the new 124 Sport Spider, that this was such a pleasing, if conventional, shape for a production car. In recent years, Pininfarina's efforts had fluctuated alarmingly, but the Fiat was clearly a more 'commercial' shape than that of the Alfa Romeo Giulia Spider, which was also released in 1966. This car was so controversial that it had to be reshaped after four years to make it more acceptable.

There was even more enthusiasm, from all quarters except those of Fiat's rivals, when the company 'completed the set' by announcing the 124 Sport Coupé at the Geneva show of March 1967. I have never forgotten that occasion, for I kept meeting colleagues with stunned expressions on their faces, and hearing comments like; 'Have you *seen* the new Fiat? It's beautiful—I don't understand it!'. And so it was—nothing quite so elegant, sleek, or

83

Fiat Sports Cars

ABOVE LEFT *In 1967, although Fiat ignored the Fiat 125 chassis as a sporting base, others didn't. Vignale produced a number of these coupés, some of which were exported. The five-speed 125S saloon was quite a flyer in its own right*

LEFT *The very simple but exquisitely detailed rear end of the 124 Sport Coupé. Neither Pininfarina nor Bertone, whom Fiat could have consulted, might have done any better*

practical, which had been shaped by Fiat, had been seen for years. It even put the chunky little 850 Coupé into eclipse, and those two cars, between them, overshadowed anything which Fiat had ever produced. It was no wonder that sales forecasts for the new car were enormous.

A few years later I was treated to a long diatribe from a rival stylist of a British (American-owned) firm about the deficiencies of the Fiat. At the time, and even today, I put this down to professional jealousy (the NIH—Not Invented Here—complex, possibly?), for it was clear that the customers loved the idea—and they were the ones who really mattered.

Fiat's coupé retained the 124 saloon's wheelbase of 7 ft 11.2 in., but the running gear was exactly the same as that of the Sport Spider except that only a four-speed gearbox was made available at first (for Fiat considered that the coupé was too heavy to pull a high 'overdrive' fifth gear). The unmodified 124 saloon floorpan and 'chassis' was used, and a remarkable sleek four-seater coupé bodyshell was completed entirely by Fiat. (The bodyshell of the Spider, of course, was constructed by Pininfarina and then transported to Lingotto for final assembly alongside the coupé.)

The coupé's lines were not startlingly different, but there was certainly not a curve, or a straight line, out of place. The nose was significantly lower than that of the saloon, there was a wide and simple grille between the headlamps, and the wing crown line ran smoothly through, almost in a straight line, to the tail, which was sharply cut off in what was to become a Triumph 'trade-mark' manner in the early

124 Spider and coupé

ABOVE RIGHT *Many industry analysts didn't like the 'middle period' 124 Coupé preferring the first and last instead. These were the common ones*

RIGHT *At the 1969 Turin Motor Show, the 124 Sport Coupé was given a 1.6-litre engine, and a revised nose style with four headlamps and a smoothed over bonnet shape. It was perhaps neater than before, but no more distinctive*

1970s. There were only two passenger doors, and the roof had slightly angular lines, but there was a great deal of glass area, splendid visibility from inside the cabin, and perfectly adequate room inside for four full-size occupants. Inside the car, dare I suggest this, the layout of the coupé's fully-instrumented dashboard was more pleasing than that of the Pininfarina Spider, and the seats looked both spacious and inviting.

There was no doubt that the 124 Sport Coupé was outstanding—perhaps even more promising than the spider. One reason was that it came as such a pleasant shock to so many people—they *expected* a Pininfarina Spider to be right, and to look right, but this Fiat-styled machine was such a pleasant surprise.

I cannot help but hark back to the first time I was involved in an *Autocar* road test of a 124 Sport Coupé, in 1968 when the five-speed transmission had been standardized for the British market. There had been a great deal of discussion in the office before the test was written and published, for none of us wanted to perpetuate an opinion which would not stand up to the passage of time. This, in the end, was the lead, and summary, of a rather historic test:

'Seldom have the *Autocar* test staff been so unanimous in their praise of a car. . . . Here is a bang up-to-date sports car, not from a specialist with a competition tradition, but from the world's fourth largest mass producer. By all that is sacred to the enthusiast this car has no right to be as good as it is. Yet judged absolutely and objectively, it is outstanding if not exceptional, not so much in what it does but in the way it does it.'

85

Fiat Sports Cars

ABOVE   *The graphics on the horn button remained much the same, however, with the 1600 Coupé*

LEFT   *Simple badging with the modernized company 'square' logo*

RIGHT   *The final version of the 124 Sport Coupé, introduced in the autumn of 1972, was the 1.8-litre example, with slightly modified front styling, which was generally not liked as much as the earlier, more pure, styles*

Cars like that do not often come along to captivate a hard-bitten motoring journalist. It was not that the coupé was enormously fast (it was faster in fourth than fifth gear, and 105 mph was just about the limit), nor very economical (24 mpg Imperial), but it did have outstanding roadholding, and in spite of being considerably heavier than the 124 saloon it had such amazing verve. In spite of the fact that the torque tube rear suspension was already being seen to have some inherent problems (which would be dealt with for 1969), the Coupé had that combination of roadholding, stability, and steering response that can never be designed into a car, but can only rarely be developed by accident.

The price of the cars—spider and coupé—were clearly very important to this overall impression, for if they had been marketed at Supercar prices no-one would have bothered to assess them on their merits. In Italy in 1967, when a 124 saloon was priced at 1,035,000 lire, the Sport Coupé cost 1,490,000, and the Spider 1,550,000. By comparison (and this is very important to the story) the newly-announced, and much faster, Dino Spider was priced at no less than 3,485,000 lire.

In the USA, in 1968, only one price *comparison* needs to be quoted to make my point. The 124 Sport Spider cost a mere $3226, and the coupé $2924, at a time when British Leyland's fashionable MGB GT was priced at $3160—clearly, the Fiats were in the very thick of the competition, in the biggest market for sports car in the whole world.

North American pundits loved the cars, in any case. *Road & Track*'s design analysis of 1968 (the first year in which these two sporting Fiats were put on sale in the USA) was headed: 'A pair that sets new standards of refinement for medium-price sports/GT cars', and later in the piece they wrote that: '. . . as for the Spider, it is the *only* car of its type being built today which is mechanically modern. . . .'

Fiat's only problem, at first, was to satisfy the demand for these splendid new machines, and although Fiat's own detailed coupé figures are not available, those supplied by Pininfarina for the Spider make interesting reading. In 1966, with series production just getting under way (the very first car was assembled in August), a mere 166 cars were built. In 1967, as production became established, this rose to 5478. Sales to North America began in 1968, once legislative matters had been satisified, and production leapt to 7789. A year later it had jumped again, this time to 10,643, and in 1970 (with the added attraction of a larger and more powerful engine) it rocketed to no fewer than 14,288 cars. In that year, incidentally, 76 per cent of all Sport Spiders were sent to the USA, a proportion which was set to rise steadily until the end of 1974, when *all* production was channelled in that direction.

Even though annual production figures for the entirely Fiat-built Sport Coupé are no longer available, the total sales figure is known, and this suggests that nearly three coupés were being built for every one spider. Accordingly, it looks as if Lingotto assembly had risen to about 50,000 coupés and spiders a year by the beginning of the 1970s—or about 1000 of these fine cars for every working week.

Interestingly enough, this is about 15,000 cars a year *more* than MG were building of their MGBs, at

When the 1.8-litre 1973 model coupé was announced, its side view was made more distinctive (or, at least, more recognizable) by the black triangle feature at the base of the rear quarter window

the same time, and it must have given Fiat management cause for some satisfaction. Alfa Romeo Giulia production, of course, was little more than half that of the Fiats, not only because the cars from Milan were more costly, but because their reliability reputation was often in difficulties.

Unlike MG, however, Fiat did not make the mistake of letting the same car soldier on, year after year, without making major improvements to it, though to some extent they were dependent on the changes being made to the (commercially) more important saloons from which various components were borrowed.

In May 1967, Fiat launched the 125 saloon, which was an ingenious amalgam of old Type 115 (1500) chassis engineering and underpan, modified 124 body structure and styling, and an enlarged version of the twin-cam engine from the new 124 Sport models. For the 125 saloon, the twin-cam became 1608 cc (with 80 × 80 mm bore and stroke), a downdraught twin-choke carburettor and 90 bhp (DIN) at 5600 rpm. Almost from the day it became available, the pundits began to suggest that it should also be fitted to the 124 Sport models—unfortunately they would have more than two years to wait.

In the meantime, an important change was being made to the rear suspension of the 124 saloon. As seems to have happened so often at Fiat, the engineers made a more satisfactory 'second-guess' at the installation, and made it available a mere 29 months after the car originally went on sale. As that eminent driver/engineer/journalist Paul Frère once commented, when writing in *Motor*:

'The 124 rear end has a torque tube that swivels in a big rubber ring of controlled radial stiffness, and there are twin radius rods, all of which require very careful alignment to prevent severe stresses from being fed into the rear axle casing on bad roads. This is not the case when a torque tube is not used.'

There could be no question of abandoning the rear axle location completely, but it was possible to make it very different. From September 1968 (but only publically acknowledged when the 124 Special saloon was announced in October), all 124s were equipped with a different layout.

The troublesome torque tube layout was abandoned, though the combined coil spring/damper units, and the long transverse Panhard rod were retained. The radius arms, too, were kept in place, but for the new cars they were also joined by an extra pair of short radius arms, above the line of the axle tube, and considerably inboard of the lower arms. Geometrically, the new suspension was by no means 'pure' when the car rolled significantly on corners, but a degree of rubber bushing at the end of all the links made it all practical. In effect, all 1969-model year 124s had this system.

Important changes were made to the 124 Sports *and* to the Dinos at the Turin Show of November 1969. Not only was the nose of the coupé restyled (with four headlamps, a full width grille) and an even more smoothly profiled bonnet line), and the Pininfarina spider given a mesh grille and twin 'power bulges' in the bonnet panel (which it did not really need), but the latest Type 125BC 1608 cc engine was fitted, and with two Weber carburettors was tuned to produce no less than 110 bhp (DIN) at 6400 rpm. By this time, too, the five-speed gearbox had been standardized for both body types, though for North America the 1438 cc engine was retained for another year.

According to all the figures, the 1.6-litre 124 Sports were faster cars, no less economical cars, and all-round better cars. Unfortunately, by the time the 124 Spider was imported to the USA (for 1971), *Road & Track* recorded a maximum (gross) power figure of only 104 bhp, 0–60 mph in 12.2 sec., and a top speed in fifth gear of 112 mph.

For them, at least, it was not better *enough*. As they headlined their test report of March 1971: 'Added flexibility is the only measurable advantage of the new 1608 cc version.' In 1970 they had compared the car with its rivals and concluded that its only serious flaw was a small, low-torque, engine. Now, for 1971, in theory, there was more power and torque, but according to their figures it had not been translated into better performance.

Perhaps the Americans were unlucky, for there was no doubt that the un-strangled European version was a much more rapid car. That was all to the good, but there were disturbing signs that as a car the 124 Sport was gradually being 'de-specialized', if I might invent such a phrase. *Autocar*'s testers tried a 1.6-litre 124 Sport Coupé in 1970, and thought it 'No longer quite an outstanding car'. This was due to a combination of factors—the higher price, the wider-ratio gearbox, the lower overall gearing, the extra weight, the softer (less precise) handling, and less fade-free braking among others—and on hindsight this looks disturbingly like the start of the 1970s trend which was to take so much character out of Fiat cars. Once Dr Giacosa retired, or began to withdraw from day-to-day influence on the specification of the new models, Fiats began to be less exciting to know.

The company, incidentally, was hedging its bets with the new 'Sports', for the 1438 cc engine was retained as an option to the 1608 cc unit. To make the choice more easily understood, the 1.4-litre car was not only made cheaper, but fitted with less desirable equipment; a four-speed gearbox was still available on the 1.4-litre car, for instance, but five speeds were standard on the 1.6-litre version.

For 1973, however, yet more important changes were in prospect. In the summer of 1972, Fiat introduced their new 132 saloon which, frankly, was a very disappointing replacement for the 125. Even though it has survived to the early 1980s (as the Argenta), it has never been a best seller, nor ever admired for its looks. However, one important 'building block' feature of the car was its new range of engines, the Type 132 twin-cam units.

These looked like the familiar 124 Sport/125 twin-cams, but were actually quite different. Although they retained the usual iron block/alloy head/twin-cam/cogged belt camshaft drive details, they had been considerably redeveloped. The main requirement had been to produce more space for a larger cylinder bore (and, eventually, if only we had known it at the time, a longer stroke), and even though this increase was small—from 80 mm to 84 mm—it meant that the cylinder bore spacings had all been changed, and that the cylinder block and head castings were quite new. Even so, neither size of engine for the 132 (a 1.6-litre and a 1.8-litre) had any water between adjacent cylinder bores, so it was clear that no further stretch remained for the future.

The 125's bore and stroke dimensions had been abandoned, and there were two new sizes for the 132:

125-type 1.6-litre 80 × 80 mm 1608 cc
132-type 1.6-litre 80 × 79.2 mm 1592 cc (98 bhp)
132-type 1.8-litre 84 × 79.2 mm 1756 cc (104 bhp)

In the autumn of 1972, therefore, no-one was surprised to see that the new engines were applied to the 124 Sports. To rationalize the building of twin-cams at Fiat, the original 1438 cc engine was abandoned, and for 1973 the Sport Coupé and Spider models were sold with the 1592 cc and 1756 cc engines, respectively in 108 bhp and 118 bhp (DIN) tune.

To match this change, there were new sets of gear ratios—a four-speed cluster actually being the *old* five-speeder without fifth, and the *new* five-speeder being exactly the same as that fitted to the 132 saloon. In both cases, the ratio sets were closer together than before, though for the first time there was to be a neat remote-control linkage (and shorter gear-lever), grafted onto the familiar casing.

All this change was good, and looked like something of an advance over the older 1.4-litre/1.6-litre cars, but unfortunately the stylists had been allowed to meddle. There was a new grille design for the Coupés along with new vast vertical tail lamp clusters, which quite spoilt the sleek good looks, along with the use of ventilation extractors in the rear quarters, and revised interior trim. Pininfarina, however, had been wise to leave the Spider alone.

In any case, Pininfarina had been very busy on Abarth's behalf, for one of the 1972 Turin Show's star exhibits was the new 124 Abarth Rallye, which was an extensively-modified version of the Pininfarina spider. I describe the design, development and competition history of these cars in Appendix A, at the back of this book.

Fiat Sports Cars

The new 1.8-litre engine was not as powerful as might have been expected, for Fiat had reverted to the use of a single twin-choke Weber carburettor (the 1.6-litre of 1969–72 had used two such instruments), and somehow the latest cars were not as outstanding as might have been hoped. There was a year's delay before the 1756 cc engine was made available in the USA, after which it was standardized for the next four years. It was a measure of the way in which USA exhaust emission rules were strangling engines that the 1974 model 1756 cc Fiat engine could only produce 92 bhp (net), which was not better than the original 1438 cc engine had produced in 1966. Unhappily, too, regulations made heavy new bumpers mandatory, so the 1974 model was also 250 lb heavier than the original.

By this time, of course, the inflationary effects of the Middle East 'Yom Kippur' war were beginning to affect Fiat's commercial fortunes, as was the fact that they had not only acquired Lancia, but were actively developing new medium-sized, Fiat-engined models to carry the Lancia badge.

In the early 1970s, Fiat's intention was not only to see the new transverse-engined twin-cam Lancia Beta into production, but to evolve coupé, Spider, HPE (estate car) and mid-engined X1/20 derivatives from it. Until 1974, at least, the new mid-engined X1/20 machine, which was effectively the same layout as the X1/9, was going to be badged as a Fiat, and carries the type number of '137' to this day. My understanding is that it was to have replaced the 124 Sport Coupé, just as the X1/9 effectively replaced the 850 Coupé in the end. All these events are described more comprehensively in Appendix C—where it is made clear that X1/20 finally became the Lancia Monte Carlo.

Even though the car's name changed at the last minute, the strategy for sales in the USA did not. The 124 Sport Coupé was withdrawn at the end of the 1975 selling season, and for 1976 the Lancia Monte Carlo (named Scorpion for the United States because of trade mark difficulties) took over. The 124 Sport Spider, however, was carried on, alone, in almost the same way as the MG MGB was being built in Britain.

Perhaps Fiat thought that the 124 Sport Spider would fade away quite soon (and, if they were honest, they probably wished that it would, for with the 131 replacing the 124 in 1974, many of the chassis components would become unique to the open sports car—not a very economic proposition, as BL were to discover with the MGB of the late 1970s as well), but they kept it in production *purely for sale in the United States*. In 1973, 10,213 spiders were sold in the USA, and 2085 in Europe, but in 1974 no fewer than 15,117 of the 1.8-litre cars crossed the Atlantic and a mere 417 stayed in Europe. The actual date of the start-up of 1975-model body assembly at Pininfarina was 25 September 1974, after which no further 124 Sport Spiders were built for sale in Europe. Not that this worried Pininfarina, or Fiat, one tiny bit, for it meant that they could both concentrate on building cars to one legislative specification.

There was a temporary drop in demand in 1976 (almost certainly caused by the initial reaction of enthusiasts to the potential charms of the sensational-looking mid-engined Lancia Scorpion, which was on show at the same dealerships), but otherwise the Spider maintained, and indeed slightly increased, its sales. In 1980, just before demand finally slumped, nearly 19,000 cars were sold in the USA.

From July 1978 (in other words, at the start of 1979 model year build at Pininfarina), the Spider was given the long-stroke 1995 cc engine (84 × 90 mm, bore and stroke) which is the final stretch of the long-running twin-cam engine design, and was also offered for the first time with the option of a three-speed (GM Strasbourg) automatic transmission, which seemed to help demand more than it had ever done for MG with the MGB.

This, in fact, was vitally necessary to the very viability of the Spider in the USA, for ever-tightening exhaust emission regulations had clawed the peak output of the 1978-model 1756 cc engine to a mere 83 bhp. The 1995 cc Spider 2000 (as it was now called) only had three more horsepower, but considerably more torque than before (104 lb ft compared with 89 lb ft). It was that sort of strangulation which had helped to kill off the Lancia Scorpion (see Appendix C), but Fiat were determined that it should not happen to the well-loved Spider.

In 1978, after all, Fiat in North America was still a large organization, with 100,000 sales a year of all types, the most important of which were the Spiders and the X1/9s, which was a considerably higher total than BL's achievement at the time. They were, on the other hand, stoking up considerable customer resistance, not only because there had been nothing new from Fiat in sports cars (visually, that is) since the arrival of the X1/9 in 1974, and because the quality control standards of existing models were not high enough. The 600-odd USA-based Fiat dealers were getting restive about their future, particularly after the failure of the Lancia Scorpion.

To improve the Spider 2000, and to extend its life even further, Fiat USA, made two significant

The 124 Sport Coupés kept the same basic type of facia panel throughout their lives. This, in fact, was the 1973 1.8-litre version, complete with cold air vents above the radio mounting position, and with a remote control gear change

improvements for 1981. One was to boost the performance of the 1995 cc engine by conventional methods, which in conventional terms was to give it fuel injection, and the other was introduce an extra model, the Spider Turbo, with an engine conversion developed by Legend Industries of Detroit and Hauppage, New York State.

Fuel injection, built into Spider 2000s from May 1980 Pininfarina production, was by courtesy of Bosch (the familiar L-Jetronic system used on so many successful European cars), and it allowed peak power to be raised to 103 bhp (DIN) at 5200 rpm, and peak torque to 112 lb ft at 3500 rpm. This made the automatic transmission option much more viable than before, and it restored the car's top speed to something like 110 mph.

The turbo, however, was originally designed by Fred Dellis of Legend Industries, who also just happened to be a Fiat dealer as well, and it was Karl Ludvigsen who did so much to champion its development in the two years in which he was Fiat USA's vice-president of Corporate Relations.

It was by no means a 'wild' turbocharging installation, as the peak figures of 120 bhp and 130 lb ft torque confirm, but it made the car even more flexible to drive, more broad-shouldered, while still remaining inside the fuel-emission regulations. When the car was new, Fiat suggested that they would build 1000 in 1981, but later events overtook them, and this figure was not achieved.

However, although this produced a really noticeable improvement in performance (0–60 mph sprints were possible in about 9.2 seconds, compared with 10.3 seconds for the normally aspirated Spider 2000), it could not rescue the fading image of Fiat. Throughout the 1970s, complaints about poor corrosion resistance had been growing, which culminated in Fiat having to confront the US government in courts of law. In the end, a massive recall campaign was necessitated, and some cars (mostly earlier, older, Fiat models) were actually bought back from complaining customers, then scrapped, rather in the same way that Lancia Betas

A favourite type of Fiat picture—with the new 1.8-litre 124 Sport Coupé and Spider of 1973 formating along an autostrada *close to Turin*

were bought in, and broken up, in the UK in the late 1970s.

In 1981, sales of Spider 2000s (and X1/9s, incidentally) slumped badly, so hard and so fast that Pininfarina, and Fiat, both produced far too many cars. For 1981 model year, 10,472 cars were built, but only 5911 were sold. Unsold stocks built up, and the future for the cars looked bleak. The Spider's age, and its past, had finally caught up with it. Like the MGB, for which demand had slumped in 1979 and 1980, time had run out, and repeat orders were simply not appearing.

One radical, and final solution, would have been for Fiat to abandon the Spider 2000 (and the X1/9, which was in exactly the same type of trouble), sell off existing stocks, and withdraw from North America. Instead, they chose an alternative method which now, on hindsight, appears to have been a failure.

Fiat proposed the same deal with Bertone (for the X1/9) and Pininfarina (for the Spider 2000). Instead of the coachbuilders merely pressing, assembling, painting and trimming the body/chassis units, they should take over complete assembly, market the cars direct, without involving Fiat in Italy, and even be granted the privilege of rebadging their products, so that—for example—the Spider would officially become a Pininfarina Spider Europa.

Pininfarina must always have known that this was a smart move on Fiat's behalf, and a rather desperately inconvenient move for them, but they concurred. From March 1982, therefore (at the Geneva Show) the car officially became known as a 'Pininfarina' rather than a 'Fiat', and the 'Europa' part of the title meant that there was to be a European specification of the fuel-injected 1995 cc engine. This, in fact, was almost identical to that being fitted to similar sporting Lancias, and it boosted the power to a best-ever figure of 122 bhp (DIN) at 5300 rpm.

The truth of what actually happened in 1982 is, however, not at all easy to establish. (See Chapter 10 for a similar comment about the Fiat/Bertone/X1/9 deal!) Although I visited Pininfarina in the autumn of 1982 when gathering material for this book, I was not allowed to tour the production lines due to some form of industrial relations problem. The figures supplied to me later, however, indicated that sales had continued to slump (to a mere 2079 cars for the whole of 1982), and that in spite of all the brave words being produced about building a 'European' version of the car, that no such machine had been built before the summer holiday close down at the factory. So, Italian reticence triumphs again!

It now seems that the long-running career of the 124 Sports—Coupé and Spider—is over, and that the saga spanned 18 years. Even though full and final figures could not (would not?) be supplied by Fiat or Pininfarina for the Spider, those which were provided make impressive reading. No fewer than 279,672 124 Sport Coupés were built from 1967 to

1975, and 190,546 124 Sport Spiders from 1966 to the end of 1982—making 470,218 in all. This makes these models by far the most numerous of all medium-sized sporting Fiats, and it almost (but not quite) matches the MG MGB's record.

Now, at the end of 1983, it really is all over for the sporting cars from Fiat. When European journalists visited Florida to try out the new Fiat Uno hatchback saloon, car chief Vittorio Ghidella announced the imminent closing down of Fiat Motors of North America. Although a new sales organisation was to be set up, it was not expected to have any major effect. Like BL, Fiat had found the latter-day United States market to be unrewarding—and, also like BL, they were now out of the sports car market completely.

124 Sport Spider—1.4-litre

PRODUCED November 1966 to July 1970
NUMBER BUILT 60,233 1.4-litre and 1.6-litre versions.
GENERAL LAYOUT Front-engined open sports car, with unit-construction pressed-steel body/chassis unit, and 2 + 2 seating. Four-cylinder engine driving rear wheels, with independent front suspension. Closely related to 124 Sport Coupé design
ENGINE New corporate Fiat design of 1966, twin-overhead-camshaft version of 124 ohv unit, intended for many cars in next decade. Four-cylinder in-line layout, with cast iron cylinder block, and light-alloy cylinder head. Five crankshaft main bearings. Two valves per cylinder, opposed in part spherical combustion chamber, operated by twin overhead camshafts, driven by cogged belt from nose of crankshaft. Bore, stroke and capacity 80 × 71.5 mm, 1438 cc (3.15 × 2.82 in., 87.5 cu. in.). CR 8.9:1. One downdraught dual-choke Weber carburettor. Maximum power 90 bhp (DIN) at 6000 rpm. Peak torque 80 lb ft at 3600 rpm
TRANSMISSION In unit with engine, five-speed all-synchromesh manual gearbox. Final drive ratio 4.1:1. Overall gear ratios 3.74, 4.1, 5.78, 8.93, 15.58, reverse 14.96:1. 17.8 mph/1000 rpm in fifth gear
CHASSIS AND SUSPENSION Front engine, rear drive. Unit construction, pressed-steel body/chassis unit. Independent front suspension by coil springs, wishbones, and anti-roll bar. Worm and roller steering. Live rear axle, suspended by coil springs, twin radius arms, torque tube, Panhard rod, and anti-roll bar. (From late 1968, rear suspension modified to be: coil springs, upper and lower radius arms, Panhard rod) 9.0 in. front disc brakes, 9.0 in. rear disc brakes, with vacuum servo assistance. 165-13 in. radial ply tyres, on 5.0 in. wheel rims. Bolt-on pressed-steel road wheels
BODYWORK Pressed-steel shell, in unit with 'chassis', produced for Fiat by Pininfarina, on basic of standard Fiat 124 underframe (shortened wheelbase) and some inner panels. Two-door, two-seater spider body style, with optional hardtop. Length 13 ft 0.4 in.; width 5 ft 3.5 in.; height 4 ft 1.25 in. Wheelbase 7 ft 5.8 in.; front track 4 ft 5 in.; rear track 4 ft 4 in. Unladen weight 2083 lb
PERFORMANCE SUMMARY (*Road & Track*, July 1968) Maximum speed 106 mph, 0–60 mph 11.9 sec., standing start ¼-mile 18.3 sec., overall fuel consumption 30 mpg (Imperial)

A fitting on some, but not all, 1.8-litre late-model 124 Sport Coupés were these smart sculptured road wheels

Fiat Sports Cars

124 Sport Spider—1.6-litre

PRODUCED October 1969 to July 1973
NUMBER BUILT Total included with 1.4-litre cars
GENERAL LAYOUT As for original 1.4-litre Sport Spider, except for:
ENGINE Bore, stroke and capacity, 80 × 80 mm, 1608 cc (3.15 × 3.15 in., 97.5 cu. in.). CR 9.8:1. Maximum power 110 bhp (DIN) at 6400 rpm. Peak torque 101 lb ft at 3800 rpm.
(From autumn 1972), bore, stroke and capacity 80 × 79.2 mm, 1592 cc (3.15 × 3.12 in., 97.3 cu. in.). 108 bhp (DIN) at 6000 rpm, 101 lb ft at 4200 rpm)
TRANSMISSION Final drive ratio 4.3:1. Overall gear ratios 3.79, 4.3, 5.85, 9.03, 15.77, reverse 15.17:1. 17.5 mph/1000 rpm in top gear
BODYWORK Slightly revised Pininfarina shell, no dimensional changes. Unladen weight 2201 lb
PERFORMANCE SUMMARY No details available—approximately same performance as 1.6-litre Sport Coupé.
NOTE USA version with 104 bhp (*Road & Track*, March 1971) Maximum speed 112 mph, 0–60 mph 12.2 sec., standing start ¼-mile 18.6 sec., overall fuel consumption 27.8 mpg (Imperial)

124 Sport Spider—1.8-litre

PRODUCED August 1972 to July 1978
NUMBER BUILT 69,208
GENERAL LAYOUT As for 1.6-litre Sport Spider, except for:
ENGINE Bore, stroke and capacity 84 × 79.2 mm, 1756 cc (3.31 × 3.12 in., 107.1 cu. in.). CR 9.8:1. Maximum power 118 bhp (DIN) at 6000 rpm. Peak torque 113 lb ft at 4000 rpm. (If four-speed gearbox fitted, maximum power 114 bhp at 6000 rpm)
TRANSMISSION Four-speed or five-speed gearboxes available. Final drive 3.9:1 with four-speeds, 4.3:1 with five-speeds. Overall gear ratios: (four-speed) 3.90, 5.50, 8.48, 14.81, reverse 14.24:1. (five-speed) 3.79, 4.3, 5.85, 9.03, 15.77, reverse 15.17:1. 17.00 mph/1000 rpm in top gear (four-speed box), 17.5 mph/1000 rpm in top gear (five-speed box)
PERFORMANCE SUMMARY As for 1.8-litre coupé
NOTE For North America, engine details as follows: 1974, CR 8.0:1. Maximum power 93 bhp (DIN) at 6200 rpm. Peak torque 92 lb ft at 3000 rpm. 1976, CR 8.01:1. Maximum power 86 bhp (DIN) at 6200 rpm. Peak torque 90 lb ft at 2800 rpm. Weight 2440 lb
PERFORMANCE SUMMARY (*Road & Track*, 1976) Maximum speed 95 mph, 0–60 mph 14.8 sec., standing start ¼-mile 20.0 sec., overall fuel consumption 27.6 mpg (Imperial)

124 Sport Spider—2.0-litre

PRODUCED July 1978 to 1983*
NUMBER BUILT 48,998 to August 1982, plus 1021 Pininfarina Spider Europa* built to the end of 1982 to same cut-off date
GENERAL LAYOUT As for 1.8-litre Sport Spider, now for USA only, except for:
1979 AND 1980 Bore, stroke and capacity 84 × 90 mm, 1995 cc (3.31 × 3.54 in., 122 cu. in.). CR 8.0:1. Maximum power 87 bhp (DIN) at 5000 rpm. Peak torque 104 lb ft at 3000 rpm
TRANSMISSION Five-speed gearbox with 3.90:1 final drive. Overall gear ratios 3.43, 3.90, 5.30, 8.19, 14.27, reverse 13.73:1. 19.4 mph/1000 rpm in top gear. Optional three-speed GM automatic transmission. Final drive ratio 3.58:1. Overall automatic ratios 3.58, 5.30, 8.59, reverse 6.87:1. 18.6 mph/1000 rpm in top gear. Unladen weight 2475 lb
PERFORMANCE SUMMARY (*Road & Track*, July 1979) Maximum speed 102 mph, 0–60 mph 10.6 sec., standing start ¼-mile 18.1 sec., overall fuel consumption 25.2 mpg (Imperial).
1981 and 1982: Engine size as before, but Bosch fuel injection fitted. Maximum power 103 bhp (DIN) at 5200 rpm. Peak torque 112 lb ft at 3500 rpm.
1982 Spider Europa. Engine size as before, and with Bosch injection, but CR 9.0:1. Maximum power 122 bhp (DIN) at 5300 rpm. Peak torque 127 lb ft at 3500 rpm
PERFORMANCE DETAILS (Factory claim) Maximum speed 106 mph. No other details
*NOTE Fiat 124 Sport Spider renamed Pininfarina 124 Spider Europa from March 1982

124 Spider Turbo

PRODUCED 1981 and 1982, as conversion, in USA
NUMBER BUILT Not known
GENERAL LAYOUT As for 2.0-litre Spider, only sold in USA, except for:
Maximum power 120 bhp (DIN) at 6000 rpm. Peak torque 130 lb ft at 3600 rpm. Bosch fuel injection plus turbocharging. 185/60HR 14 in. tyres, on 5.5 in. alloy rims
PERFORMANCE DETAILS (*Road & Track*, April 1981) Maximum speed (approx) 110 mph. 0–60 mph 9.2 sec. No other details

124 Sport Coupé—1.4-litre

PRODUCED March 1967 to 1972
NUMBER BUILT 279,672 of all types, 1.4-litre to 1.8-litre. No breakdown possible (see text)
GENERAL LAYOUT Front-engined coupé with unit-construction pressed-steel body/chassis unit, and four seats. Four-cylinder engine driving rear wheels, with independent front suspension. Closely related to 124 Sport Spider design, having similar layout and underpan but 124 saloon wheelbase.
ENGINE As 124 Sport Spider
TRANSMISSION As Sport Spider from mid-1967 (five-speed manual gearbox option), but four-speed all-synchromesh manual gearbox also available. Final drive ratio (four-speed box) 4.1:1. Overall gear ratios 4.1, 6.11, 9.41, 13.35, reverse 15.86:1. 16.2 mph/1000 rpm in top gear
CHASSIS AND SUSPENSION As 124 Sport Spider, with same rear suspension change from autumn 1968
BODYWORK Pressed-steel shell, in unit with 'chassis', produced by Fiat, on basis of standard-wheelbase Fiat 124 underframe, and some inner panels. Length 13 ft 6 in.; width 5 ft 5.4 in.; height 4 ft 3.8 in. Wheelbase 7 ft 11.2 in.; front track 4 ft 5 in.; rear track 4 ft 4 in. Unladen weight 2116 lb
PERFORMANCE SUMMARY (*Autocar*, 12 September 1968) Maximum speed 102 mph, 0–60 mph 12.6 sec., standing start ¼-mile 18.8 sec., overall fuel consumption 22.2 mpg (Imperial)

124 Sport Coupé—1.6-litre

PRODUCED October 1969 to September 1975
NUMBER BUILT Total included in all 124 Coupé figs (see 1.4-litre)
GENERAL LAYOUT As for 1.4-litre model, except for mechanical changes introduced with 1.6-litre Sport Spider
TRANSMISSION As 124 Sport Coupé 1.4-litre, with four-speed or five-speed gearboxes available, same final drive and overall ratios as before
BODYWORK Unladen weight 2194 lb
PERFORMANCE SUMMARY (*Autocar*, 31 December 1970) Maximum speed 109 mph, 0–60 mph 10.7 sec., standing start ¼-mile 17.8 sec., overall fuel consumption 23.6 mpg (Imperial)

124 Sport Coupé—1.8-litre

PRODUCED August 1972 to September 1975
NUMBER BUILT Total included in all 124 coupé figures (see 1.4-litre)
GENERAL LAYOUT As for 1.6-litre model, except for mechanical changes introduced with 1.8-litre Sport Spider
PERFORMANCE SUMMARY (*Autocar*, 14 June 1973) Maximum speed 107 mph, 0–60 mph 10.5 sec., standing start ¼-mile 17.4 sec., overall fueld consumption 24.6 mpg (Imperial)

7 Dino – the Maranello connection
Ferrari + Fiat = homologation special

In February 1965, the CSI (*Commission Sportive Internationale*) confirmed the rules for a new Formula 2 racing series, to take effect on 1 January 1967. At the beginning of March, Fiat and Ferrari announced that they were to produce a high-performance engine to suit. It was a classic case of cause and effect—and it made sensational headlines all over Italy. The result, in the fullness of time, was not only that Fiat built a new vee-6 engine called a Dino, but that there were Fiat and Ferrari Dino cars powered by such units.

Fiat and Ferrari had been friends, if not collaborators, for some years, but the Dino project came about as a matter of necessity. The new Formula 2, in which Ferrari were determined to take part, required the use of an engine derived from an homologated production car, one of which at least 500 examples had been built in the previous 12 months, and it could only have a maximum of six cylinders; the maximum capacity could be 1600 cc, and such engines could have up to two overhead camshafts per cylinder head.

Ferrari were in trouble as soon as they heard about this proposal, for although they could always find a suitable engine (that was never a problem at Ferrari!), they would find it very difficult to build so many cars in a year. (They might *say* they had built so many cars, even if it was not strictly true, but the CSI were well versed in such Ferrari tricks, as they had locked horns with the Italian firm over the number of mid-engined 250LMs built in 1964. . . .)

Enzo Ferrari's first-ever contact with Fiat was in 1918–19, when he had been discharged from the Italian army, and was looking for a job. He was out of luck on that occasion, but once he gained a position of importance at Alfa Romeo he soon attracted Fiat engineers to help him design racing cars. By this time, reputedly, he had become a distant admirer of Fiat's Vittorio Valletta, so perhaps it was no surprise that the very first 'Ferrari' (though it was never badged as such) was based largely on Fiat components.

Immediately after World War 2, Ferrari started building his own cars, and for some years these became progressively more prominent, and increasingly more successful, not least due to the genius of two engine designers—Gioacchino Colombo and Aurelio Lampredi, both of whom developed separate vee-12 units.

By the mid-1950s, however, Ferrari's fortunes were in decline, mainly because their engines were becoming less and less competitive. Short-term assistance came from Lancia, who handed over their entire Grand Prix team—D50 cars, vee-8 engines, *and* the designer, Vittorio Jano—but this was not going to help Ferrari when a new Formula 2 came into force, from January 1957. That Formula specified engines of no more than 1.5-litres, without supercharging, and Ferrari was determined to compete.

Ferrari's only son, Alfredino ('Dino' for short) had joined his father as an engineer, and it was clear that

Three masters: Pininfarina, Fiat and Ferrari

Fiat Sports Cars

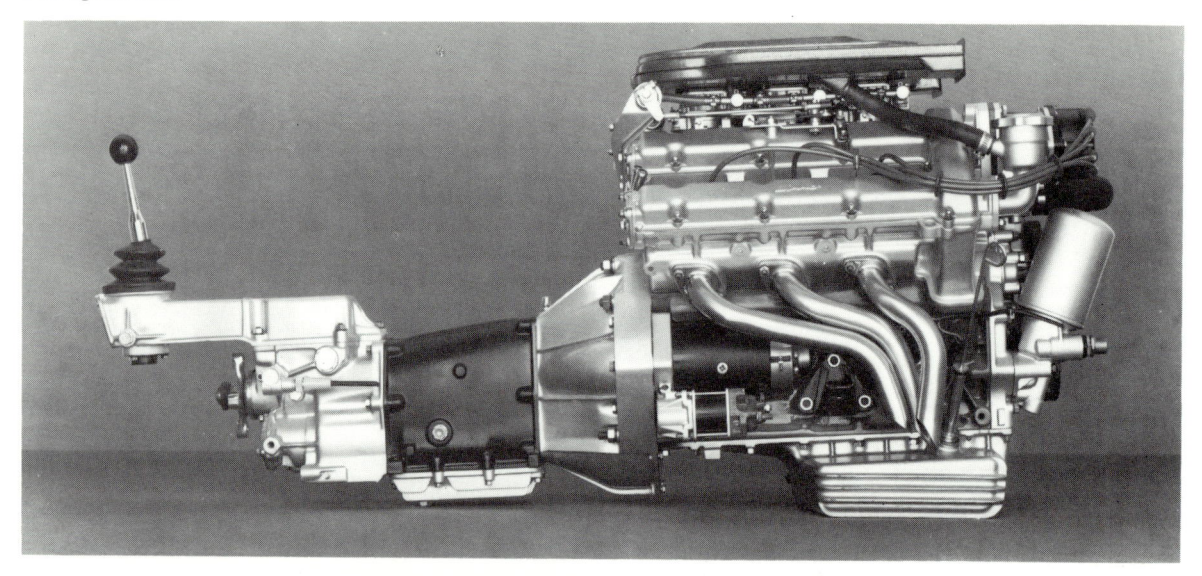

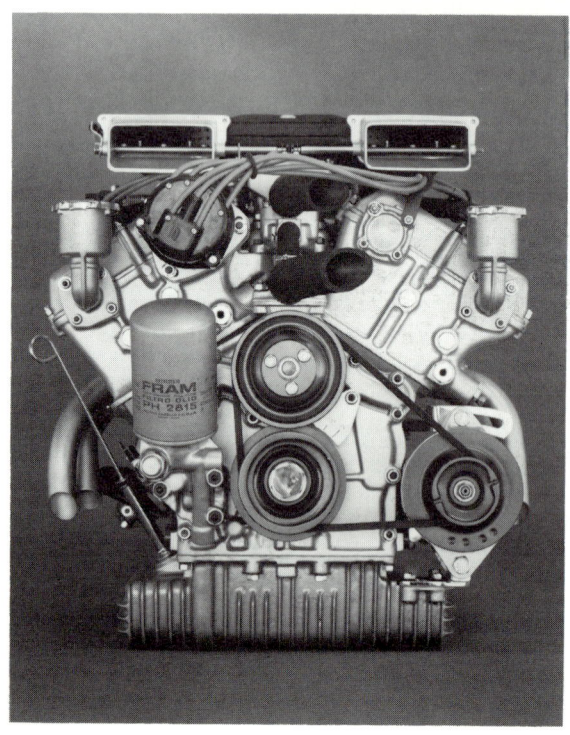

ABOVE Head-on view of the 65 degree 2.0-litre Fiat Dino vee-6 engine. The extra five degrees of engine 'vee' angle was supposed to give extra space for carburettors and manifolds in the centre of the unit

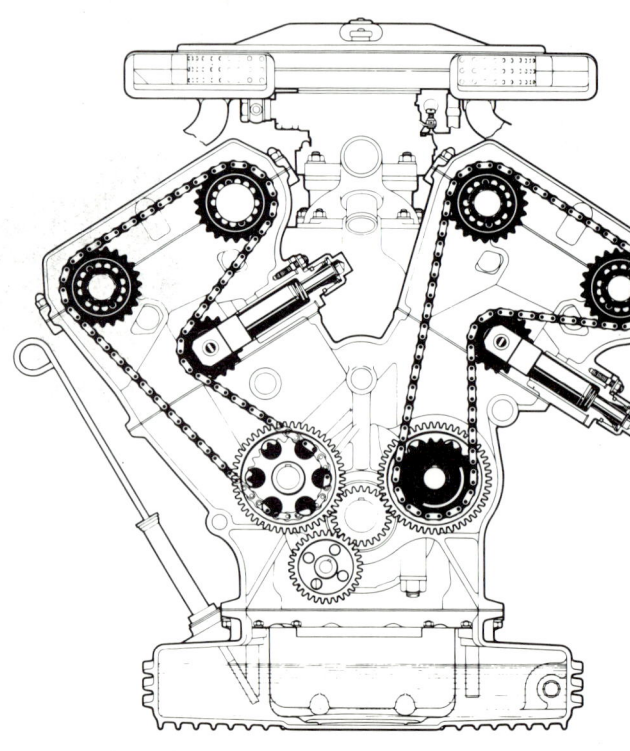

ABOVE The Rocchi/Lampredi Dino engine, whose parentage stretched back to 1955, and Vittorio Jano, had distinctive camshaft chain drives, not direct from the nose of the crankshaft, but from sprockets geared to the crank itself.

TOP The most exciting engine produced by Fiat in modern times—the Ferrari-inspired vee-6 Dino unit. This was fitted to Fiat and Ferrari Dinos, plus the charismatic Lancia Stratos of the mid-1970s. Here it is in original light-alloy block 2.0-litre Fiat guise, complete with Fiat-built gearbox, with its separate fifth gear casing

96

Dino—the Maranello connection

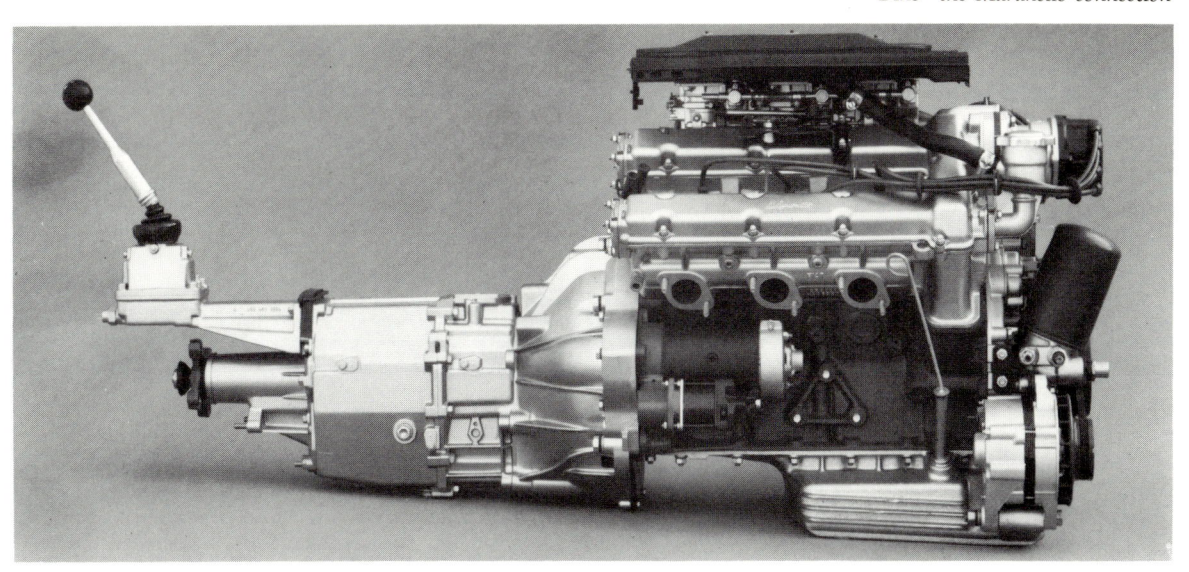

ABOVE Compare this 1970 Fiat Dino engine/gearbox installation with the earlier 1967 variety. The cylinder block is now cast iron rather than light-alloy, the alternator is on the right instead of the left of the engine, and the massive five-speed ZF gearbox (later to become famous on racing and rally cars) had been fitted, to deal with the increased torque of the 2.4-litre engine

BELOW The 1967–69 2.0-litre Fiat Dinos had very simple rear suspensions, by leaf springs, with forward facing (from the tail) radius arms, and twin dampers each side. This was not really adequate for the performance of the car

Fiat Sports Cars

father doted on him. Unhappily, Dino was never very robust, and by 1955 was suffering from a progressive kidney disease.

Legend has it that Dino Ferrari, in consultation with his father, and Jano, who spent long hours at his bedside in the winter of 1955/56, conceived a new engine, which would be a vee-6 and that, according to Ferrari himself: 'Dino came to the conclusion that the engine should be a vee-6, and we accepted this decision.'

Doug Nye, who has cronicled the complete Dino story in great detail, is more analytical about the process, and says: 'In view of Vittorio Jano's impeccable engineering credentials and vast experience, this is a little hard to believe.'

Chronologically, the facts are that Aurelio Lampredi had left Ferrari in 1955, when Jano arrived, that poor Dino Ferrari died in June 1956, and that the first of a new family of vee-6 engines called Dinos (not yet with the 'Dino' name cast into its camshaft covers) ran on a test bed at Maranello before the end of 1956.

A Dino vee-6 first raced in 1.5-litre form in 1957, but for the next seven years a bewildering variety of engines in the family were to be raced in F1 and F2 racing cars, hillclimb specials and racing sports cars. Their engine capacities ranged from 1477 cc to 2962 cc, their cylinder block vee-angles from 60, to 65, even to 120 degrees, while some had twin overhead camshafts and some one, while they might have downdraught Weber carburettors, or even fuel injection, and two valves, or four valves, per cylinder. They were, in other words, typical of the way in which Ferrari would modify, improve, and remodify a family of engines to suit his many needs. In this case, their greatest single achievement was to power the Ferrari Grand Prix cars which won the Constructors' *and* the Drivers' World Championships in 1961.

The original Dino engine, which was completely designed by Vittorio Jano, was not merely a Ferrari vee-12, cut in half, but was a brand new design in its

ABOVE *Pininfarina did their best with the Dino Spider, but it always looked a rather stubby car, with such a short (7 ft 5.8 in.) wheelbase, and the two seats well forward. But there was no mistaking it, as the discreet badging made clear*

RIGHT *The anatomy of the original Dino Spider of 1966, with the Ferrari-inspired vee-6 engine sitting atop the front suspension crossmember, and the two seats almost in mid-wheelbase positions*

BELOW RIGHT *It was always a delight to study the detail styling of the Dino Spider—such as, for instance, the light-alloy road wheels, the wrap-around indicators, and the door handle layout*

own right. It was a compact unit, and 'conventional' according to Ferrari's standards—which is to say that it had a wet-liner light alloy cylinder block, light alloy cylinder heads, chain drive to the twin overhead camshafts per bank, and one carburettor throat per cylinder.

Conventional wisdom suggested that it should be a 60 degree unit, but because Jano wanted to use twin-cam cylinder heads, and could visualize a lack of space inside the vee to arrange adequate inlet port ducting, he very boldly decided to use a 65 degree angle instead! Although this meant that balancing the six throw, four main bearing, crankshaft was made more difficult, Jano achieved this, and there have never been any complaints about the unit on the score of vibrations.

By the mid-1960s, however, the Dino engines which Ferrari were using were not at all like those which Jano had originally laid down. For a time there had been a 60-degree single-cam unit, which had vee-12 cylinder dimensions, and almost was a vee-12 chopped in half, while for 1961 Jano's successor, Carlo Chiti, produced a 120-degree four-cam 1.5-litre unit for the new generation of Grand Prix cars.

After Chiti defected, to help found the unsuccessful ATS concern, Ing. Franco Rocchi was briefed to

98

develop a new, more robust 'endurance' version of the original Dino vee-6, and although the 1964 and 1956 engines were visually similar it might be instructive to compare their vital statistics:

	1956 'Jano Dino vee-6	1964 'Rocchi Dino vee-6
vee angle	65 degrees	65 degrees
capacity	1489 cc	1592 cc
bore × stroke	70 × 64.5 mm	77 × 57 mm
peak power, @ rpm	175 @ 8500	175 @ 9000

The engine was not ready for display, or even for mention, at Ferrari's annual press conference in December 1964 (at the time, indeed, he talked about producing a new Dino 168, which would have used a 1.6-litre version of the quite different 90-degree vee-8 Grand Prix engine), and details of the Fiat-Ferrari accord were released before the very first vee-6 Rocchi-powered Dino 166P made its first appearance, on test, at Monza in April 1965.

There had been talk of a new Formula 2 category for some time at the beginning of the 1960s. When F1 was for 1.5-litre cars with no limit as to the

Fiat Sports Cars

number of cylinders they could use, F2 was for 1.0-litre cars, but with F1 being upgraded to 3.0-litres from 1 January 1966, F2 was also in line for an upgrade as well.

Fiat had already been supporting Ferrari financially since the 1950s (nowadays we would call it sponsorship), but serious talks between Enzo Ferrari and Vittorio Valletta began in 1964, talks which were to remain secret even from important engineers like Dr Giacosa and Aurelio Lampredi. Ferrari saw that his only hope of competing in the new F2 was to use the latest vee-6 Dino-type engines, and that he should persuade Fiat to collaborate with him. Already, by the time he first contacted Fiat, the engine was available in 1592 cc, 1987 cc and 2417 cc with a choice of different bores and strokes. Clearly the structure of the engine was very strong, for the most powerful (the F1 unit intended as an interim engine for 1966, could produce up to 280 bhp at 8500 rpm.

The time was certainly ripe for two of the most famous Italian car-makers to get together, and it now seems certain that Pininfarina (who had strong links with both Fiat and Ferrari) helped to act as marriage brokers, as did Signor Bellicardi, the manager of Weber carburettors (a subsidiary of Fiat).

The deal they cooked up was extraordinary. Not only would Ferrari hand over the Dino vee-6 engine design to Fiat, for reworking as necessary, and for manufacture in series, but Fiat would undertake the design of a new model to be sold as a Fiat Dino, so that the production numbers could be achieved as soon as possible, for Ferrari to use the engine in F2 in 1967.

In the meantime, Ferrari also decided to make his own production car, the first to use the Dino vee-6 engine, and to make matters very confusing he not only proposed to call it a Dino, but officially it was not a Ferrari at all—just a Dino, in its own right.

I might as well make the confusion complete, right away, by pointing out that Fiat Dinos always had conventional front engines and rear-wheel-drive, whereas 'Dino Dinos' (i.e. Ferrari Dinos) had mid-mounted engines and rear-wheel-drive. But there is more complication to come. The original 'show-car' extravaganzas on this theme, by Pininfarina, showed a Ferrari-type Dino with the vee-6 engine mounted in line (1965), but the production car of 1967 had a transversely mounted engine and a completely new transaxle. Complicated.

All this was commercially complex. As Ian Webb has said, in his *AutoHistory* about the Ferrari Dinos: 'It can hardly have been a complete act of altruism

ABOVE *Four headlamps and a full-width bumper on the Pininfarina-styled Dino Spider of 1966—not a line out of place*

RIGHT *The 1966 Dino Spider instrument display. Look carefully, for the speedometer reads up to 250 km/h, and the warning sector on the rev-counter does not start until 7200 rpm. What more could a sports car lover want?*

BELOW RIGHT *Even at its first motor show—Turin 1966—Pininfarina found time to produce a special version of their Fiat Dino, this one having a permanent hardtop...*

on the part of Fiat, but it did allow the two companies to decide whether they liked the look of each other. Despite enormous misgivings on each side—by Ferrari at the prospect of once more having to rely on an outside source for such a vital component, and by Fiat at the thought of having to make an engine for which they had not been responsible and which was probably not even designed for mass-production methods—the vee-6 was to be produced in Turin. That it came out of a Fiat factory was plain whenever one of the engines was taken apart; all components were embossed with the Fiat logo, which must have been galling for Ferrari diehards to accept.'

Time was short if the necessary 500 cars had to be built before the end of 1966 (or, at least, the part for those cars be made available, even if all had not been completed), so that Ferrari could go racing in 1967. In the event, the prototype F2 1.5-litre Dino-engined Ferrari was shown in February 1967, and made its

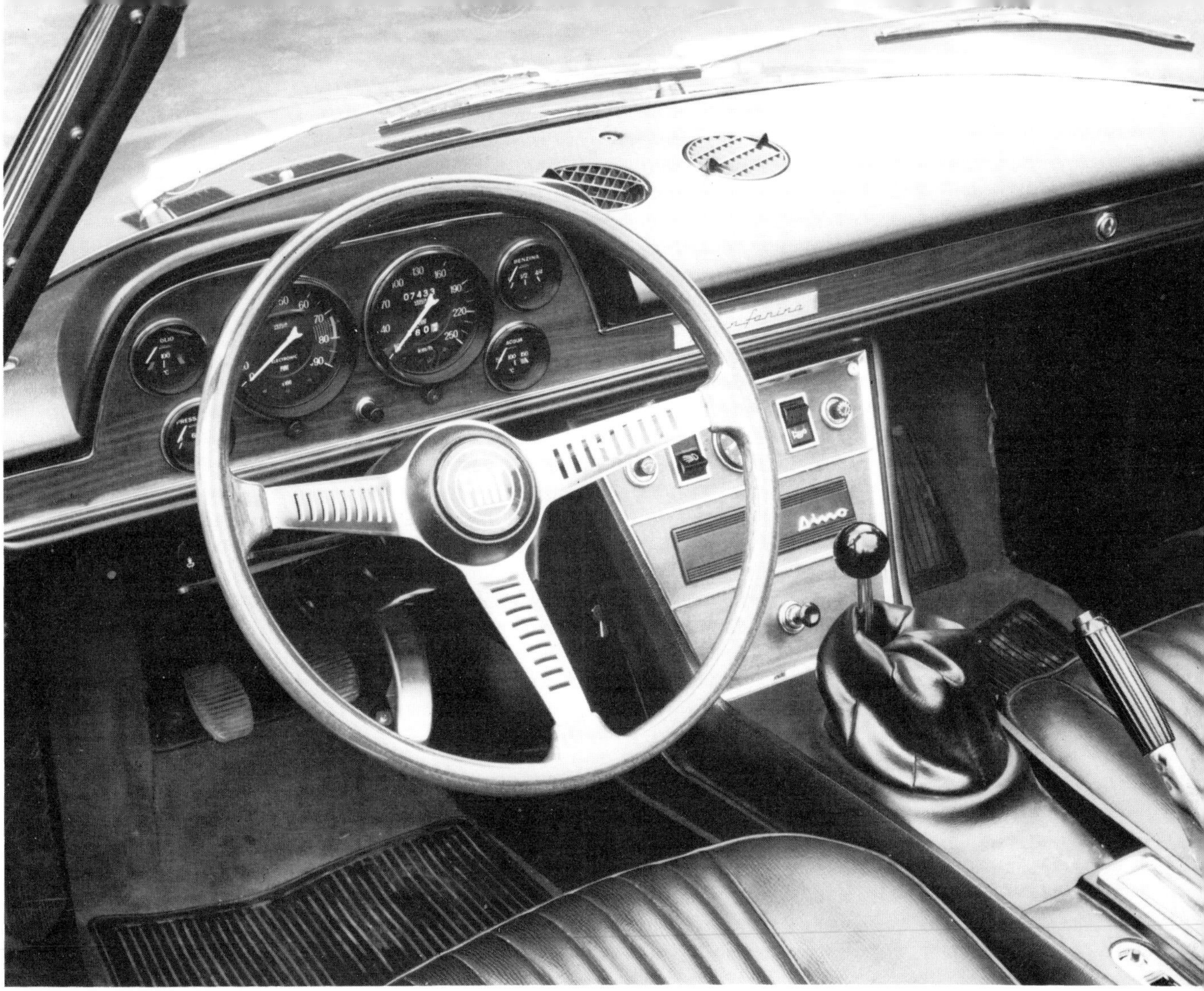
OLIO
BENZINA
ACQUA
Dino

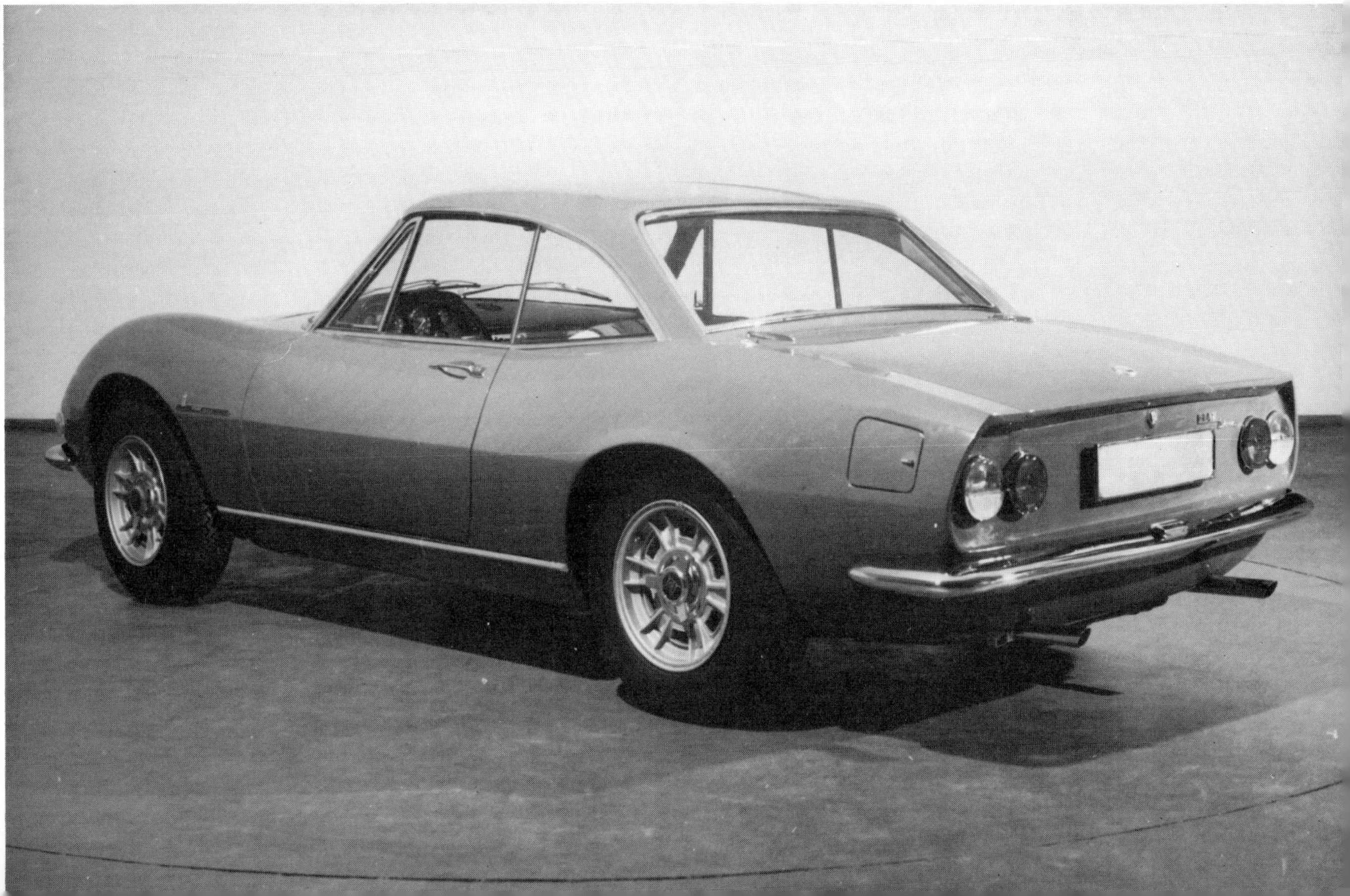

Fiat Sports Cars

race debut in July, but it did not race again until 1968, so perhaps all the rush was not needed.

Nevertheless, Fiat's amazingly versatile designers set up a new project for the Type 135, began to evolve a new chassis, and set Aurelio Lampredi to 'productionize' the engine. Such a task must have been bitter-sweet for the talented Lampredi—bitter because it no doubt reminded him that the original layout was by Jano, whose arrival at Ferrari in 1955 had forced him to leave, and sweet because he was now in charge of the refinement of that very same unit.

Because of the tearing hurry—there were only 20 months between the public acknowledgement of the Fiat-Ferrari accord, and the opening of the Turin Show of November 1966, when the Fiat Dino production car would have to be put on sale—a great deal of compromise was necessary to produce cars at all. As I have pointed out elsewhere in this book, the definitive Fiat Dinos were really those launched in 1969, by which time they had transmissions and suspensions worthy of the magnificent engine; the original cars, in almost every way, were 'homologation specials', and like most other cars of that type, they were only really valuable as high-status machines for those wishing to identify with the racing programme.

In planning for the new cars, Fiat decided on precisely the same approach as that already being prepared for the sporting derivatives of the 124—they would offer a two-seater spider, and a close-coupled four-seater coupé. Like the 124, the spider would have a shorter wheelbase than the coupé, and like the 124, the Dino Spider would be styled by Pininfarina, and would be announced alongside it, at the 1966 Turin Show. The difference came with the coupé—Fiat were styling and building their own 124 Coupé, but for the Dino they entrusted the job to Bertone instead.

Although the wheelbase of the Dino Spider and the 124 Spider were the same (at 2280 mm/7 ft 5.8 in.) this was probably no more than a coincidence. Perhaps there were a few common panels in the floor pan of the two cars, but essentially the designs were quite different, and of course they supported entirely different front and rear suspensions, engines and transmissions. As in other cases, in fact, Fiat designed the structural underbody, building and supplying the short wheelbase version to Pininfarina, and the longer wheelbase type (2550 mm/8 ft 4.4 in.) to Bertone, for these two concerns to manufacture, weld-up, and complete their own bodyshells, before returning them to Rivalta for final assembly.

RIGHT *This 1968 effort was a more way-out Pininfarina 'show car' style on the basis of the 2.0-litre Fiat Dino. It was called 'Ginevra' (Geneva) for that was the motor show at which it appeared . . .*

BELOW *. . . and a year later they converted it into a flowing and rather nice fastback hardtop car. Neither car went into series production*

The independent front suspension had much in common with the forthcoming 125 saloon, which is to say that it was also like that of the 1300/1500 saloons first seen in 1961 (for the 125 retained the same underpan and suspension layout), having a sturdy double wishbone layout with a combined coil spring/damper unit fixed to the top of the top wishbone, rather than being installed inside the wishbones. There was a sturdy anti-roll bar, and steering was by the usual Fiat worm and roller, with a three-piece universally-jointed steering column being needed to thread its way down the side of the bulky engine; right-hand-drive Fiat Dinos were never made.

Fiat had very little to say about the rear suspension, partly because, I believe, they were not very proud of it. Dr Giacosa dismisses it in just two lines in his autobiography, for it was really no more sophisticated than a conventional live axle with half-elliptic leaf springs, except that single-leaf springs were used, and there were two forward-facing radius arms (from the tail of the car to the axle line itself) to control axle tramp. In fairness, it was a little more clever than it sounds, for there was no inter-leaf friction, and the alignment of the radius arms and the forward section of the leaf springs made an effective Watts linkage; in addition, the rear mounting of the radius arms ensured minimum protrusion into the restricted passenger space. There were two telescopic dampers at each end of the 2300-based axle beam—one ahead and one behind the line of the tube—to complete the installation.

There was no Panhard rod, and no other precise sideways location of the suspension.

Braking, of course, was by big four-wheel Girling discs—10.6 in. diameter at the front, 10.0 in. at the rear—with a vacuum servo. The handbrake lever was placed between the seats. Fat, 185-14 in. Michelin or Pirelli tyres with a high-seed rating were standard, mounted on cast-alloy centre-lock road wheels with 6.5 in. wide rims. It all added up to a simple, squat, and purposeful chassis, which promised tenacious roadholding, if not a boulevard ride.

Lampredi's work on the Ferrari-designed engine was not to increase its output, but to improve its durability. Naturally, compared with Ferrari's original specification, it also had to be de-tuned considerably to make it docile in heavy traffic conditions. Of all the available permutations of bore and stroke, Lampredi chose to make the production engine a 2.0-litre unit, 1987 cc to be precise, picking up the 86 × 57 mm bore and stroke dimensions from the racing sports car derivative.

Distinctive features of the engine were not only its 65 degree vee-angle, its wet-liner construction, and its twin-overhead camshaft cylinder head layout, but the three downdraught twin-choke Weber carburettors, and the fact that the camshafts were driven by two separate chains, one serving each cylinder head, and being driven by sprockets geared to the crankshaft, rather than directly from the crank nose. As prepared for road car use, the engine produced 160 bhp (DIN) at 7200 rpm, with a

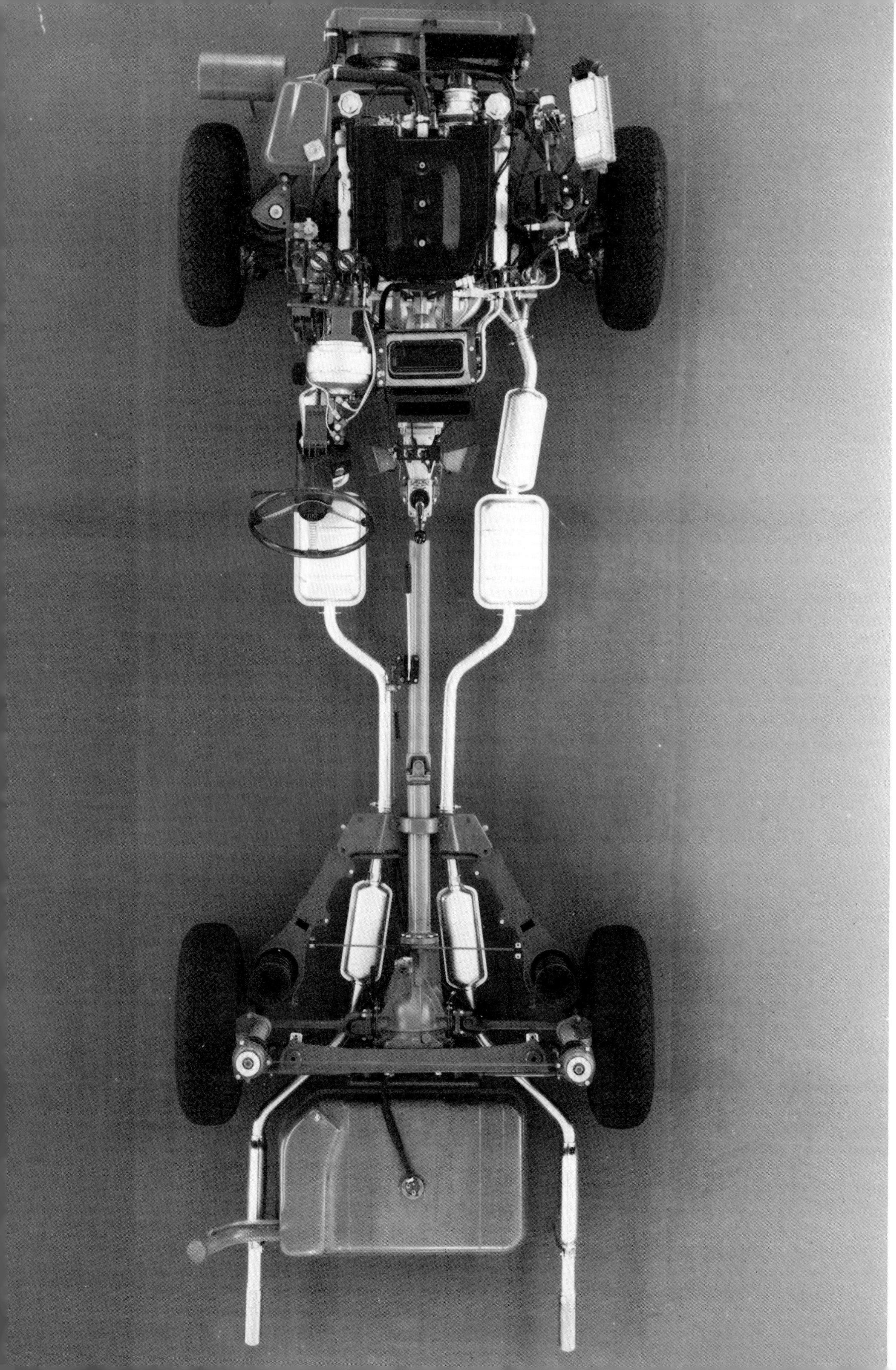

Dino—the Maranello connection

LEFT *At the Turin Motor Show in November 1969, the Fiat Dino design was comprehensively updated, with the new 2.4-litre iron-block engine and ZF gearbox being fitted, along with coil spring independent rear suspension (of 130 saloon type) instead of a live axle. It made a good car into something sensational*

RIGHT *The semi-trailing link independent rear suspension chosen for the Dino 2400 was like that developed for the executive-class 130 saloons and coupés. The final drive casing and its torque tube were mounted up to the bodyshell at four widely-spaced points*

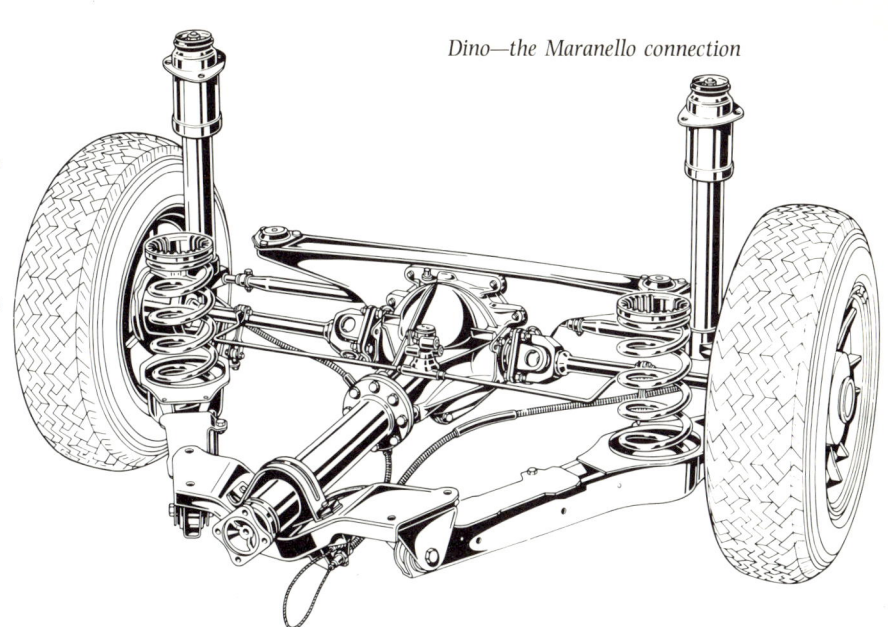

maximum torque figure of 127 lb ft at 6000 rpm.

(Two sidelines: The same 1978 cc engine was sent by Fiat to Ferrari for the mid-engined Dino, and in that guise it was supposed to be more highly tuned, at 180 bhp, and 138 lb ft. A study of comparative part numbers, however, shows differences only in carburettor jets, and the exhaust system, so perhaps the Ferrari Dino's extra power was only for 'image' purposes!

In addition, the Ferrari Formula 2 engine, for which this production unit was really evolved, had a capacity of 1596 cc, produced by reducing the stroke to a mere 45.8 mm—the shortest stroke ever found in this family, by the way—and its peak power output was 210 bhp at 10,500 rpm).

The clutch was a Borg & Beck diaphragm spring unit, and behind it there was a specially-developed Fiat five-speed all-synchromesh gearbox. This used the casing from the 2300 model, but in what was now a typical Fiat system, there was also a secondary casing bolted behind it and underneath the remote control change housing; the top four gears were in the main housing, with fifth and reverse finding a home in the secondary casing. The back axle, too, was a 2300-based casing, but with a new final drive ratio of no less than 4.875:1 to match the high-revving qualities of the engine, and the fact that fifth gear in the box was a 0.87:1 'overdrive'.

As I have already explained, the Pininfarina-styled Dino Spider was announced at the Turin Show of November 1966, at the same time as the rather more ordinary (also Pininfarina-styled) 124 Spider also made its bow. It was a short, rather stubby, style with quite unmistakeable lines, which included low-mounted quadruple headlamps, and a sharply cut-off tail to which the tail lamps (similar to those on the mid-engined Ferrari Dino of 1967) were fixed. The cast-alloy wheels were by Cromadora, and these wheels were also to be used on the Ferrari Dino—quite a lot of commonization went into these joint projects.

Pininfarina, however, was not merely content to take the credit for the basic style of the car, striking though it was. At Turin in 1966, he also showed one car complete with a conventional extra hardtop, rather like that later used on the 124 Abarth Rallye, and yet another machine with a fixed hardtop, more glass area, and more flowing roof lines.

The Bertone-styled Fiat Dino Coupé appeared four months later, at the Geneva Show of March 1967, by which time production of the 'chassis' and underbodies had actually begun. This was a distinguished occasion, not only for the styling of the coupé, but because it was the first time that Bertone had been associated with such a high-powered Fiat model (their links, of course, had already been established with the cheeky and appealing little 850 Spider).

Mechanically, the Bertone coupé was like the Pininfarina Spider, except that it had the longer wheelbase version of the same underbody. However, the superstructure, and layout, was entirely different, and the Bertone car was more practical because it had a four-seater arrangement. There were no common skin panels between coupé and spider, of course, and somehow the coupé was an altogether more appealing car, trimmed and furnished like any up-market (dare one say 'Ferrari-type'?) Supercar, and looking smooth and refined into the bargain.

The prices asked were interesting—for these were much the most expensive Fiats ever put on the

Fiat Sports Cars

market. In 1967, a Dino Spider cost 3,485,000 lire and a Coupé 3,650,000 lire, and I ought to put these prices in perspective by quoting the 124 Spider price of 1,550,000 lire. You could, in fact, buy a 124 Spider, a 124 Coupé *and* a 500 F saloon for the price of one Dino ... but who would want to?

Almost as soon as the Dinos went on sale, there was a rush to buy, and the necessary 500 to allow Ferrari to race were soon on their way to customers. There was no doubt that although they were complex and expensive cars to run (no Ferrari-engined car has ever been simple), they also had enormous charm which could almost overcome the heart-failure brought on by perusing service and repair bills.

Perhaps Geoffrey Howard, writing in *Autocar* in February 1968, about the coupé, came closest to capturing this appeal, and I'm grateful to the magazine for letting me quote a few extracts: 'Above all she was a lady. Like a lady she arrived late, breathless, full of apologies, and looking like a billion lire.... Just as I was about to make a third phone call there was a yelp of tyres, a thrash of camshaft chains and the zoom-zoom of six Weber throats.... She sounded like an orchestra. At the top were the treble chords of her four cams, whining and whirring up to 5000 and screaming like a circular saw on to 7500 or 8000. From 2000 she would pull like a lion with a deep throaty growl which hovered and burbled, then picked up to rise in a crescendo with all the other sounds—gearbox, wind and exhaust—joining in with a double *forte*.'

There was also high praise for the handling (though there was no doubt that the rear axle location was simple, if not primitive, and would twitch the tail if provoked), and above all for the car's character.

John Bolster, writing in *Autosport* about the Dino Spider, was equally ecstatic, and he also quoted performance figures which (considering the car's pre-launch build-up) were creditable rather than extraordinary. The Spider, he said, could reach 127 mph (Geoffrey Howard had quoted 131 mph for his Coupé), sprint to 60 mph in 8.1 sec., and reach the quarter mile from rest in 16 sec. There was, however, a rather pointed comment about the rear suspension which must have given Fiat cause to think, if they were not already doing so: 'The car handles well on fast corners, even when the road is bumpy. On sharper corners the rear end can be made to break away, and when the surface is wet it is necessary to apply opposite lock fairly smartly, for which purpose the steering is suitably quick. On open bends the Dino is tremendous fun, and the occasional rear-end breakaway adds to the pleasure of handling this high-spirited animal.'

In fact, by the time that 1163 Pininfarina-styled Spiders and 3670 Bertone-styled Coupés had been

TOP RIGHT *The Bertone style of Fiat Dino, the Coupé, was not only beautiful, but very spacious as well*

BELOW RIGHT (BOTH) *Bertone and Pininfarina were supplied with Dino underpans like this, and started fabricating their own bodies on top of those; the Bertone Coupé style going on the longer (actually 124 Coupé) length wheelbase*

BELOW *For the 2.4-litre Dino Spider, tiny styling changes were made, notably a new twin-chrome strip grille, slightly different wheels, and different facia layout. Why modify a great shape?*

Dino—the Maranello connection

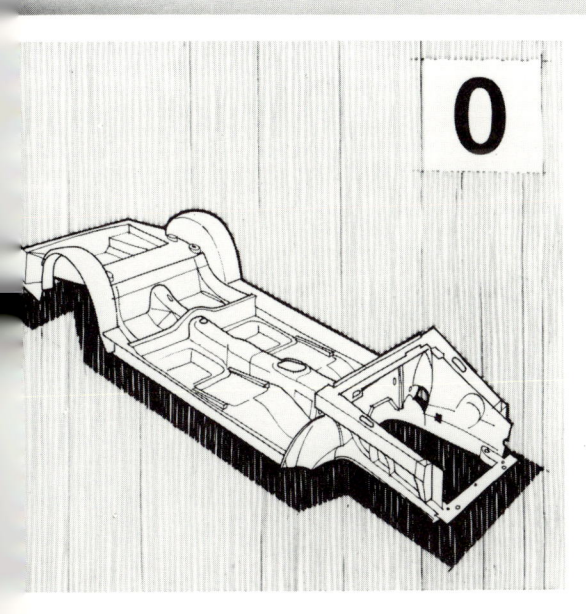

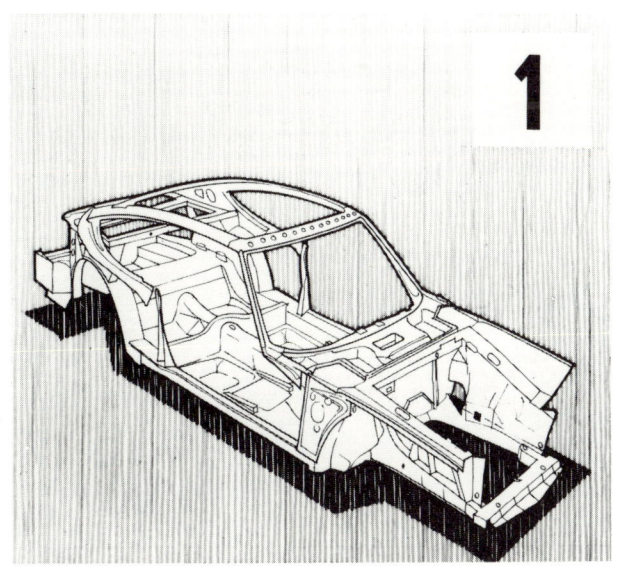

Fiat Sports Cars

built, Fiat were ready to put a much more highly developed Dino on sale, and this was duly announced at the Turin Motor Show in the autumn of 1969. This derivative, the Dino 2400, would not have been possible without the new 'Executive-class' 130 saloon, which had been launched rather prematurely at the Geneva Show earlier in the year. For a technical analysis of that car, in particular its suspension, I invite the reader to consult Chapter 9.

The fact is that the Dino 2400 was a much better car than the original Dino, if not exactly as specialized, or full of racing-car-like character. It was the 'Mk II' Dino which should really have been announced in the first place, if only Dr Giacosa's engineers had been given time to develop it. There were major changes to the engine, the transmission, and the rear suspension, but none at all to the basic style of either car.

Fiat, who were building all the engines, for themselves and for Ferrari, decided not only to enlarge the unit, but to make it cheaper to build, and a little more silent. Many engine designers would agree that although an alloy cylinder block is great for saving weight, it is also very good for transmitting noise, so it was no surprise that Lampredi chose a cast iron cylinder block for the enlarged engine. Its bore and stroke were both increased (from 86 × 57 mm to 92.5 × 60 mm) and the capacity therefore became 2418 cc. Compared with the original 2.0-litre engine, the 2400 was both more powerful, and had more torque. Here are the comparisons:

1987 cc	Fiat Dino	160 bhp at 7200 rpm	127 lb ft at 6000 rpm
	Ferrari Dino	180 bhp at 8000 rpm	138 lb ft at 6500 rpm
2418 cc	Fiat Dino	180 bhp at 6600 rpm	159 lb ft at 4600 rpm
	Ferrari Dino	195 bhp at 7600 rpm	165 lb ft at 5500 rpm

—statistically, for the Fiat Dino, this meant that for a 22 per cent increase in capacity, that engine power had risen by 12.5 per cent, and peak torque by 25 per cent. All these figures indicate not only that the new, enlarged, engine was more powerful, but that it was more flexible, and certainly easier to drive. In the mid-engined Ferrari application perhaps this was not a vital improvement, but in the relatively heavy front-engined Fiat Dino it most certainly was.

I should make it clear, in passing, that although the 2.4-litre Dino engine, and the vee-6 engine of the Fiat 130 were introduced in the same year, they had no common parts, nor were they of the same basic design. It is merely enough to point out that the 130 was a larger engine, with a different (60 degree) vee-angle, single overhead camshaft cylinder heads, and belt-driven overhead camshaft drive. It is true that Aurelio Lampredi designed both of them, but that was the only connection.

The manual gearboxes of the Dino 2400 and the 130, however, *were* the same. Fiat had found that the original Dino (neé 2300) box was only marginally up to its job, so for the new cars they called in the German specialists, ZF, and bought a new five-speed design from them. Brand-new at the time, this was a versatile transmission later found on several other high-performance cars in Europe, most noticeably in rally cars like the Ford Escorts and Opel Kadetts, where one of its principal advantages was the number of alternative gear ratios available, long and short gear lever extensions, and its great strength.

For the Dino 2400 an 'overdrive' set of gears were chosen, and it is interesting to compare these with the superseded Dino '2300' ratios:

Dino 2000   3.01, 1.82, 1.35, 1.00, 0.87, reverse 2.88:1
Final drive 4.875:1

Dino 2400   2.99, 1.76, 1.30, 1.00, 0.87, reverse 3.67:1
Final drive 4.778:1

The new gearbox, however, while strong, also had a heavy action, and was neither as silent or refined as Fiat would have liked. But it did the job, and did it

ABOVE LEFT *Quite, quite special was Bertone's Dino Coupé. Their next try was the Ferrari 308GT4 which has become highly respected since it went out of production*

LEFT *Splendidly trimmed sports seats for the 1967 Dino Coupé and adequate, if not lounging, space in the rear seats as well*

RIGHT *Trim detail of the Bertone Dino Coupé's rear quarter. That window clamp would eventually reappear on the doors of the Lancia Stratos*

Fiat Sports Cars

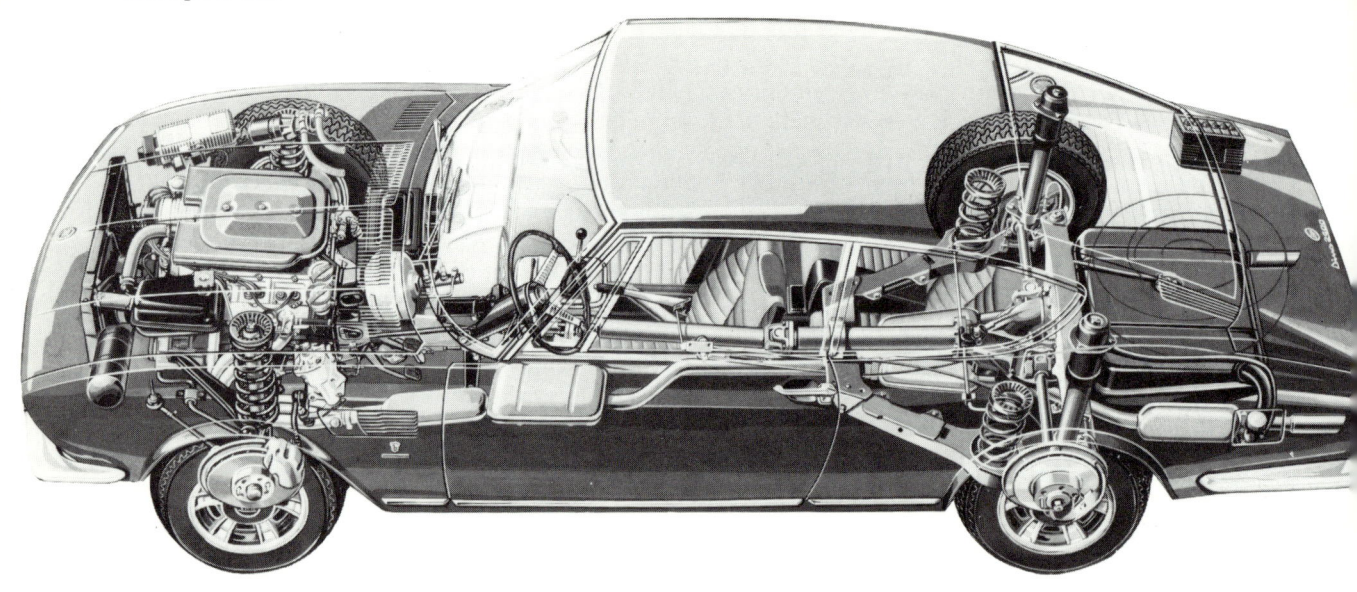

ABOVE *The Dino Coupé's facia can be compared with that of the Dino Spider. The actual instruments are the same, but their layout entirely different*

TOP *Like the Dino Spider, the Dino Coupé was thoroughly revised for 1970, and was given the 2.4-litre engine and independent rear suspension*

well, as did the new limited-slip differential standard in the 2400's final drive.

The major chassis change, however, was the use of independent rear suspension, and naturally this necessitated a wholesale carve-up of the underside of the car. Instead of simple leaf springs and radius arm location of a beam axle, there was a bodyshell mounted final drive unit, springing by coil springs ahead of the line of the rear wheels, separate dampers acting on the hub carriers, all allied to

110

semi-trailing arms (pivoting, at their forward end, near the body mounting for the torque tube) and adjustable track-control arms.

There were few other changes, and almost none at all to the body styling and appointments, though the wheels were altered to have conventional five-bolt fixings, this change being shared with the Ferrari Dino 246GT which also came into existence in 1969. One important change was to the prices, which were even higher than before—3,930,000 lire

ABOVE *A 2.4-litre Dino Coupé 2400 slipping through the traffic in the centre of Turin. Only the very smallest exterior styling changes were obvious, including a chrome strip picking out the outline of the front grille*

TOP *The very smart new facia/instrument layout for the 2.4-litre Dino Coupé introduced in November 1969*

Fiat Sports Cars

for the spider and 4,100,000 lire for the coupé, which compared with 5,500,000 lire for the Ferrari Dino 246GT, and a mere 1,680,000 lire for the 1.6-litre 124 Sport Coupé. (Incidentally, even the large and exotic 130 Coupé, described later, was priced at 4,750,000, which gives a very good indication to the high Dino prices of the day.)

Even though Fiat, and Ferrari, were both beginning to lose interest in the Dino by the beginning of the 1970s (Fiat because of the low sales volume they were achieving, and Ferrari because their vee-6 engine was nearing the end of its life, and there was an all-new 90 degree vee-8 on the way) the cars were kept in production until 1973. The motoring press carrying out road tests did not have to relate too closely to the price of the Dinos, so their comments continued to be favourable. Sales, however, gradually fell away, such that only 420 2400 Spiders and 2398 2400 Coupés were to be built in rather more than three years.

In the meantime (as detailed in Appendix B) Fiat and Ferrari had moved even closer together. From mid-1969, Fiat had taken a 50 per cent share in Ferrari SpA. Two early consequences were that there was an injection of Fiat management into Maranello, and that final assembly of the 2.4 litre Fiat Dinos was moved to a new factory extension at Maranello.

In total, therefore, there were 1583 open Dinos, and 6068 of the four-seat closed coupés, an extremely creditable achievement for what had turned out to be anything but an 'homologation special'. Incidentally, in the same period, a total of 150 Ferrari Dino 206GT models, 2732 246GTs and 1180 GTS (Spiders) were also built—which means that Fiat Dinos considerably outsold Ferrari Dinos.

The death of the Dino in 1973 really represented the last of Fiat's indulgencies, for the Energy Crisis was just about to erupt, and Fiat's commercial fortunes were about to take a turn for the worse. No other Fiat was ever fitted with this engine, but it did not die immediately, or completely. Perhaps the most famous use for this fine engine was in the Lancia Stratos homologation special, a car so bound up in Ferrari politics, Fiat money, and the development of Fiat-Lancia competitions strategy that I have given it a section all of its own.

Since Fiat are now out of the sports car business, the four-cam Dino engine may go down in history as the finest Fiat-built engine ever to be put on sale. The cars themselves, particularly the 2.4-litre Spiders (which are almost viewed as Ferraris as they were Maranello built), are now highly-valued—and, surprisingly, the Dino Register is based in the UK.

Dino Spider and coupé—2.0-litre

PRODUCED November 1966 to October 1969
NUMBER BUILT 1163 spiders, 3670 coupés
GENERAL LAYOUT Front-engined model in two types—two-seater open spider and four-seater closed coupé, with unit-construction pressed steel body/chassis unit. V6-cylinder engine driving rear wheels, with independent front suspension.
ENGINE Developed from original Ferrari Dino design, produced by Fiat, fitted to Fiat and Ferrari Dino models. V6-cylinder, 65 degrees between cylinder banks, light-alloy cylinder block (and steel liners) and light-alloy cylinder, with double overhead camshaft operation, by chain from nose of crankshaft. Bore, stroke and capacity 86 × 57 mm., 1987 cc (3.39 × 2.44 in., 121.2 cu. in.). CR 9.0:1. Three downdraught dual-choke Weber carburettors. Maximum power 160 bhp (DIN) at 7200 rpm. Peak torque 126 lb ft at 6000 rpm
TRANSMISSION
In unit with engine, five-speed all-synchromesh manual gearbox. Final drive ratio 4.875:1. Overall gear ratios 4.24, 4.875, 6.58, 8.87, 14.67, reverse 14.04:1. 17.5 mph/1000 rpm in top gear
CHASSIS AND SUSPENSION Front engine, rear drive. Unit construction, pressed steel, body chassis unit. Independent front suspension by coil springs, wishbones, and anti-roll bar. Worm and roller steering. Live axle rear suspension, by half-elliptic leaf springs, and twin leading radiu arms. 10.62 in. front disc brakes, 10.0 in. rear disc brakes, with vacuum servo assistance. 185-14 in. radial ply tyres on 6.5 in. wheel rims. Bolt-on cast-alloy road wheels
BODYWORK Pressed-steel shells, in unit with 'chassis', produced for Fiat by Pininfarina (spider) and Bertone (coupé).
  Spider, in two-door, two-seat open sports style, with optional hardtop. Length 13 ft. 5.8 in.; width 5 ft 7.4 in.; height 4 ft 2 in. Wheelbase 7 ft 5.8 in.; front track 4 ft 6.5 in.; rear track 4 ft 5 in. Unladen weight 2535 lb.
  Coupé, in two-door, four-seat fastback coupé style. Length 14 ft 9.5 in.; width 5 ft 6.8 in.; height 4 ft 3.8 in. Wheelbase 8 ft 4.4 in.; front track 4 ft 6.8 in.; rear track 4 ft 6.4 in. Unladen weight 3042 lb
PERFORMANCE SUMMARY (*Autosport*, 3 March 1967) Maximum speed 127 mph, 0–60 mph 8.1 sec., standing start ¼-mile 16.0 sec., overall fuel consumption 20 mpg (Imperial)

Dino Spider and coupé—2.4-litre

PRODUCED October 1969 to January 1973
NUMBERS BUILT 420 spiders, 2398 coupés
GENERAL LAYOUT Specification as for 2.0-litre Dino models, except for modified engine, different gearbox, and new independent rear suspension. Details differ from 2.0-litre as follows:
ENGINE Cast iron cylinder block, no separate cylinder liners. Bore, stroke and capacity 92.5 × 60 mm, 2418 cc (3.64 × 2.36 in., 147.6 cu. in.). Maximum power 180 bhp (DIN) at 6600 rpm. Peak torque 159 lb ft at 4600 rpm
TRANSMISSION Final drive ratio 4.778:1. Overall gear ratios 4.18, 4.778, 6.22, 8.42, 14.29, reverse 17.54:1. 17.1 mph/1000 rpm in top gear
CHASSIS AND SUSPENSION Independent rear suspension, coil springs, MacPherson struts, semi-trailing arms, track control arms, anti-roll bar. 10.6 in. rear disc brakes. 205/70VR14 in. tyres.
BODYWORK (Spider) Length 13 ft 6.7 in. Unladen weight 2800 lb
(Coupé) Unladen weight 3042 lb
PERFORMANCE SUMMARY Maximum speed 130 mph, 0–60 mph 8.7 sec., standing start ¼-mile 16.1 sec., overall fuel consumption 20 mpg (Imperial)

8 128—front drive

Style and performance in two varieties, 128 Coupé and 128 3P

It is quite amazing that Fiat began studying front-wheel-drive layouts at such an early date, but took so long to put such a car on sale. A big decision had to be made, no doubt, not only on technical grounds, but in terms of financial investment and the re-equipment of factories. Even so, it was ten years after BMC had put the revolutionary Mini-Minor on the market that Fiat launched the 128, even though their first diversion had already been put on sale as an Autobianchi.

The front-wheel-drive story begins in 1943, when Fiat became interested in the prototypes being developed in France by J.A. Grégoire. From time to time in the next two decades Giacosa encouraged his engineers to consider front-wheel-drive for new cars, but it was not until the Type 123 project took shape that these studies took root.

The 123 projects, four in number, began to take shape in 1958/1959, involved front-wheel-drive and rear-engines, three-cylinder and four-cylinder engines mounted vertically and horizontally, in-line or transverse, but a gradually evolving style. Eventually 123E4 became the preferred project, and after Oscar Montabone returned to Fiat after a sojourn as technical director of Simca, Fiat's French associate company, a new project, Type 109, was started in 1962. It was this car, which combined the final development of 123E4's style with the latest design-office thinking of a transversely-mounted four-cylinder engine and an end-on gearbox, which was eventually put on sale as the Autobianchi Primula in 1964. Autobianchi, of course, was another Fiat subsidiary so none of the pundits were fooled—but it was indeed significant that the 850 saloon had been launched in May 1964 with a rear engine, while the front-drive Primula appeared only months later, in October. In terms of what was to follow, the Primula was both simple and relatively old-fashioned, for its

The very upright Fiat 128 was an unpromising basis for a new Fiat sporting car. This one's a 1971 128 Rallye, with uprated engine

113

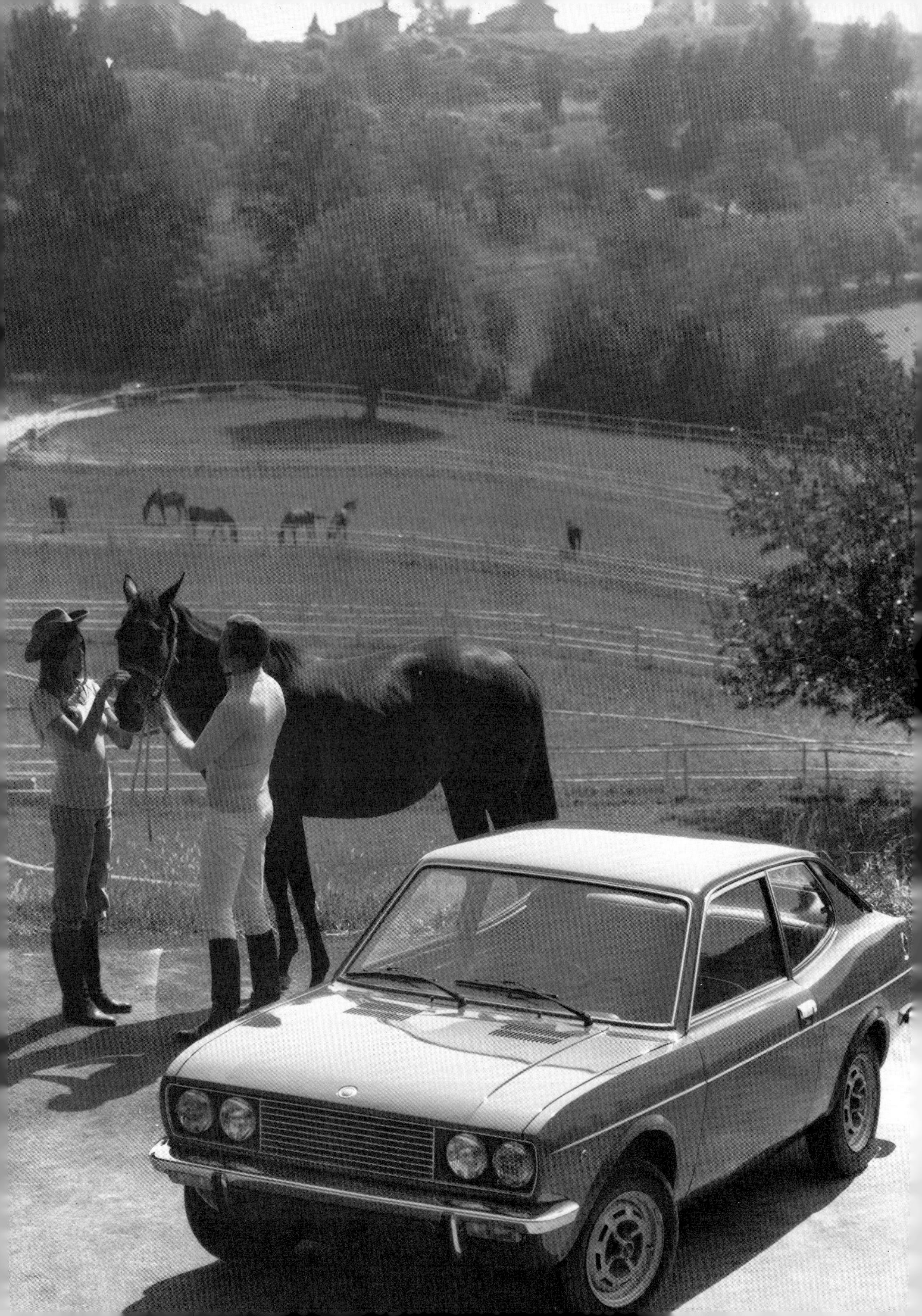

128—front drive

engine was the old 1221 cc pushrod engine from the 1100/1200 family, and its rear suspension was nothing more complicated than a 'dead' axle beam suspended on half-elliptic springs.

By this time, however, Giacosa, Montabone and Lampredi had begun thinking about the definitive all-new front-drive car, which they gave the code name of X1/1. This was the first of a new series of project codes, sometimes used in conjunction with the old 100 Series projects, and sometimes alone. So that I do not cause any more confusion in this chapter, I should say at once that X1/1 eventually became the Type 128, and it was the 128 name which was applied to the car when it was launched.

The styling of X1/1 really began before the main mechanical layout was settled, but by 1967 the project had become firm. Giacosa saw X1/1 as a replacement for two existing Fiats—the conventional (and very old, in design terms, 1100R saloon, and the rear-engined, but relatively new rear-engined 850s—and proposed that it should have at least the same amount of accommodation as the 1100R but that it should be a more compact, and technologically advanced, machine.

Giacosa was convinced that the new car needed an engine of at least 1000 cc, and although he had a prototype built with a modified version of the conventional overhead valve 124 model's engine mounted transversely, he knew that a new family of engines would be needed, and commissioned Aurelio Lampredi to tackle this. Fiat was large enough and profitable enough to consider this, for in 1967 they would build 1,365,000 cars, and in 1969 (when the 128 was announced) this achievement would rise to a magnificent 1,633,088 including Lancia and Autobianchi.

It was in 1967 that Vittorio Valletta, Fiat's long-serving president, died suddenly, and his place was taken by Giovanni Angelli, but this had no effect on the progress of X1/1. The launch was timed for 1969, a year in which all manner of new or modified Fiats were to appear.

X1/1's styling came in for a good deal of modification between 1964 and 1968. Originally it had rather more distinctive lines including rectangular headlamps, and a semi-sloping tail which would have allowed the fitment of a hatchback, but the final design was a very characteristic 'Fiat' shape, rather square, and with noticeable family resemblance to the 124 and 125 saloons. Right from the start it was meant to have a two-door, four-door, and three-door (estate) layout, and it was always tacitly understood that a sporting version would follow.

The bodyshell, therefore, was a conventional pressed steel unit construction assembly, and all the technical interest lay in the chassis and running gear. In effect, X1/1 took the philosophy of the Autobianchi Primula one very full step further, and was a car by which several other manufacturers all began to set their own standards.

At one time, Giacosa was happy to see X1/1 (the 128), X1/2 (which became the Autobianchi A112) and X1/4 (which became the 127) all having the same transmission, but in the event the Autobianchi was given its own special transmission, as the car itself was to be built in a different factory with, of course, a different engine.

LEFT *But the stylists at the factory produced a very attractive little coupé shape on the same floor pan and front-wheel-drive power pack. This was the 128 Sport Coupé of 1971*

RIGHT *Even though the 128 Sport Coupé had a shortened wheelbase compared with the saloon, space was still found for four seats. This one's a prototype*

115

Fiat Sports Cars

Lampredi's all-new engine for X1/1 was a masterpiece, and one which is still in use in Fiats such as the Ritmo/Strada models of the 1980s. Not one dimension, or component, was the same as an existing engine. However, apart from its intended use for transverse mounting, it was a relatively conventional five-main-bearing unit, with a cast iron cylinder block and a light alloy cylinder head. The major advances were that it was quite obviously designed with a future 'stretch' in mind, for its 1116 cc capacity was achieved by a bore of 80 mm and a stroke of a mere 55 mm; yet there was still water around all the cylinder bores, and the stroke/bore ratio of 0.68:1 was extreme by all except current Ford standards.

There was a line of valves angled at 18 degrees towards the manifolding side of the cylinder head, operated directly by a single overhead camshaft mounted in the cylinder head, via inverted bucket-type tappets. The camshaft itself was driven from the nose of the crankshaft by an internally-toothed cogged belt. In general layout, and in detail design, though with no common components, the 128's cylinder head was remarkably similar to those of the new Fiat 130's vee-6 unit. This was not remarked upon at the time, but it was really not all surprising, for the same man (Aurelio Lampredi) had been responsible for both engines, and had moved on to tackle the design of the 128 as soon as that of the 130 had been schemed out.

So that it should take up the minimum possible space in the engine bay of the new car, the engine was mounted over towards the right (off) side, with the transmission 'in-line' towards the left, and it was angled forward at 16 degrees towards the nose. In this way the fore-and-aft dimension was minimized,

ABOVE *No hatchback on the 128 Sport Coupé, just a smart fastback style, a conventional boot lid, and a choice of 1100 or 1300 engines. Above the floor pan/wheelarch package, every panel of the coupé was different from the saloon*

RIGHT *This 128 Sport Coupé drawing shows why Fiat had so much difficulty in making the car any lower, as the transverse front-wheel-drive engine-transmission power pack was very lofty. For the later 128 3P, the structure was revised behind the doors*

and the inlet and exhaust manifolds were both at the rear of the engine as installed. The only drawback (which did not seem to cause trouble in service) was that the sparking plugs and distributor were facing the front grille, and a bit vulnerable to water splashing.

The transmission was that first used in the Fiat-designed Autobianchi Primula, being a two-shaft all-indirect, all-synchromesh four-speed unit, with spur gear drive to the final drive, which was mounted below and behind the main gearbox, almost in line with the flywheel end of the engine itself. The only snag with this layout was that there were unequal-length drive shafts to the front wheels—that to the right (off) side wheel being much longer than that to the left side. In no Fiat application, however, does it seem to have caused any problems of 'balance', or disturbed the suspension geometry, and in the original 128, where peak output was only 55 bhp, there was no noticeable effect.

The suspension of the 128, too, was a great advance on any previous small Fiat. At the front, to

128—front drive

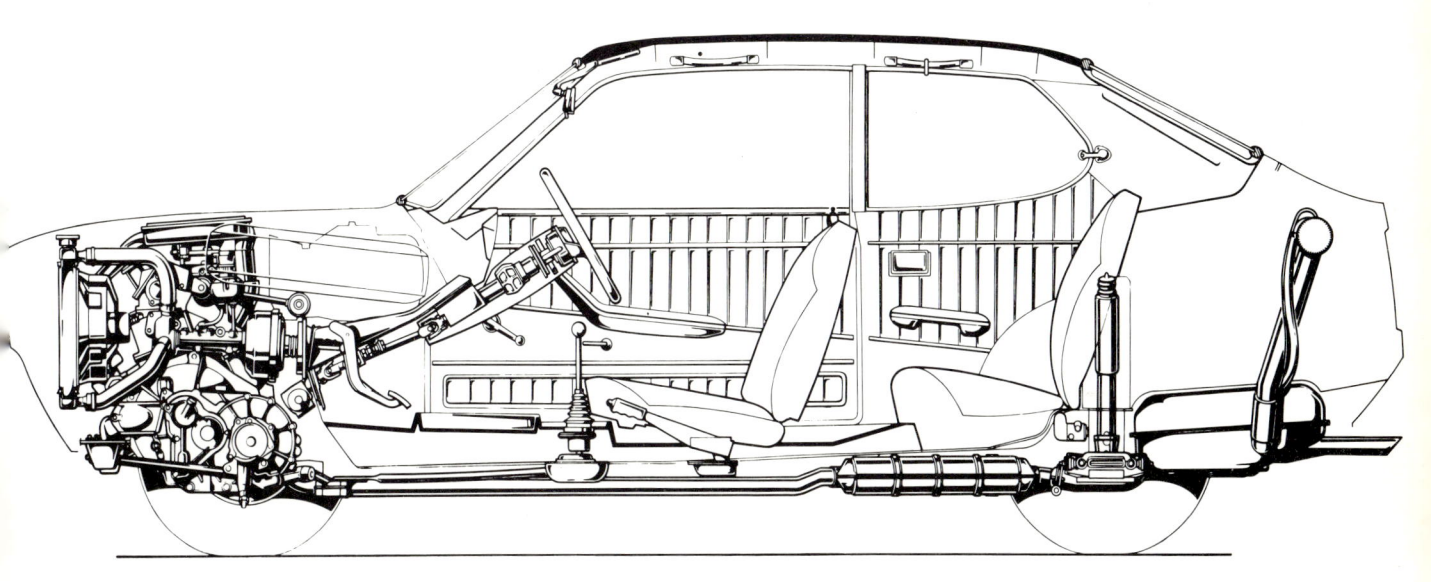

suit the front-wheel drive installation, Giacosa chose a simple MacPherson strut installation, in which the anti-roll bar also formed part of the lower 'wishbone', while at the rear he combined the merits of MacPherson with the well-proven transverse leaf spring of the old 600s and 850s. The spring itself was clamped at two points, near the inner pivots of the lower wishbone, which meant that it could act as a pure spring and as an anti-roll spring as well, while the 'MacPherson' part of the linkage was a telescopic damper fixed rigidly to the hub, and rubber-mounted to the body shell high up under the corner of the rear windows. The whole of this neat and advanced all-independent layout was complemented by rack and pinion steering (for the first time on any Fiat), by radial ply tyres, and by front-wheel disc brakes.

Observers drew comparisons between the new 128 and the relatively new Simca 1100, which was not surprising, since Oscar Montabone had been closely concerned with the layout of both cars at the project stage.

As it stood, on announcement, with a wheelbase of 8 ft 0.4 in., an unladen weight of about 1800 lb, uncompromisingly square styling, and a top speed of no more than 84 mph, the 128 was not very appealing to the enthusiast, but most people realised at once that this was just the start of a dynasty, rather than a definite statement of what Fiat were going to build throughout the 1970s. In the next few years, it was reasoned, there would be more powerful, and faster, 128s, and it was highly likely that there would be different bodies to complement these. The 128, after all, would eventually take over from the old 850, which meant the end of the smart coupé and spider. So, then. . . .

They were not to be disappointed, but I should admit that the sporting 128s never had the character and dash of the sporting 850s. On the other hand, the mid-engined X1/9s, which evolved from the 128 (see Chapter 10) were prettier, and more sporting, than anything seen on the old basis.

Well before the 128 saloon was put on sale, Boano's styling studio at Fiat was already looking at derivatives of the basic car. Fiat management wanted to capitalize on the success of their new engine, and the front-wheel-drive layout which went with it, and asked for new coupé and spider styles to be developed. As with the existing 850s, they thought that Fiat could be entrusted with the styling of the new 128 coupé, while Bertone should be asked to tackle a new 128 spider. As I shall make clear in Chapter 10, Bertone were never convinced that a front-wheel-drive spider could be made to look right, produced their own mid-engined scheme instead—and the X1/9 was the result.

Boano's brief for a new 128 fixed-head coupé was that the same basic mechanical layout as the 128 saloon should be used, along with a shortened version of the pressed-steel underpan, but that an entirely new superstructure could be prepared. As with the 850 Sport Coupé, 2+2 seating accommodation was considered necessary for this market sector. In the meantime, Fiat engineers were finishing off the first 'stretch' of the new engine design. With a larger bore of 86 mm, but the same stroke of 55 mm, the capacity was pushed up to 1290 cc, and the peak power increased to 67 bhp for the 128 Rally saloon, and to 75 bhp at 6600 rpm for the new sporting Fiats, so there was a promise of considerably more performance if the shape of the new coupé was right.

Fiat Sports Cars

Compared with the 128 saloon, the floorpan of the 128 Coupé Sport was shortened by 22.5 cm/8.9 in., though the general machanical layout of the 'chassis' and the running gear was not altered. In spite of this cut-and-shut operation, and the fact that the new car's roofline was more than four inches lower, there was still adequate, if not ample, room for four adult passengers to be carried.

The Fiat style was a two-door coupé with a conventional separate boot. The coupé was altogether lower, sleeker, and obviously more purposeful than the very austere saloon from which it had been developed, and the bonnet line had been lowered as much as possible bearing in mind the considerable height and bulk of the transverse engine, which was ahead of the line of the front wheels. In some details, such as the way that the waist (belt) line was kicked up under the rear quarter windows, the new coupé was influenced by the styling of the smaller 127 saloon which had been prepared for launch in 1971, but in general it was an entirely predictable, even staidly conventional, shape.

The 128 Coupé Sport was revealed in time for showing at Turin in November 1971, when it was seen not merely to be one, but four new versions of a

TOP *To produce a successor to the 128 Sport Coupé, and to make the new car more distinctive and practical, Fiat produced the 128 3P. The front style was as before, the more sweeping changes being made at the rear*

ABOVE *A feature of the 128 3P of the mid-1970s was its hatchback body style, so very much more practical than that of the 128 Sport Coupé*

new model. Not only was there to be a 64 bhp 1116 cc and a 75 bhp 1290 cc choice of engines, but there were to be standard or deluxe trim specifications. 1100 models and 1300 models, if produced as 'S' (standard) versions, were built with rectangular headlamps, unmodified 128 wheels, and one type of grille, while 'SL' types (de luxe trim) had four circular headlamps, a different grille, and special wheels with exposed wheel nuts. Internally, however, the SL was much more desirable, for it had reclining front seats, floor carpets, and an engine rev-counter to make it more suitable for a 'sporting' job.

The 128 Coupés were direct replacements for the similar 850s, which were withdrawn at once, and the new front-drive cars began to sell very well indeed, not only because they looked new, but because they were considerably faster than the 128 saloons which had preceded them. The fact was, however, that the style was controversial, not only because it was still relatively high, narrow and conventional (there was really no answer to this because of the position of the engine), but because it did not have a hatchback feature, something which was already becoming fashionable in Europe. It was not nearly as distinctive as the old 850 Sport Coupé had been, and it was not destined to be a success in North America.

What made the 128 Sport Coupé so attractive when fitted with the larger engine was that it was a 100 mph car. When *Autocar* tested an early example in the summer of 1972, their At-a-Glance summary was: 'Nimble and quick coupé version of well-established front drive saloon. Remarkably refined despite low overall gearing, though noisy at very high speeds. Excellent handling and good fuel consumption, well finished but apparently rather expensive.'

It was, in other words, cheap and cheerful in the nicest possible way, and clearly it appealed to people all over Europe. Predictably, perhaps, many more of the larger-engined, and more powerful, versions were to be sold. One factor which contributed to the new car's splendid handling and stability was that it was equipped with modified MacPherson strut front suspension. In place of the dual-purpose anti-roll bar, which was discarded altogether, there was a new drag link, to locate the wheel more precisely. Incidentally, the 1290 cc engined car could not only reach 100 mph in ideal conditions, but it might also average 32 mpg (Imp.) in day-to-day motoring.

But by 1974, this was no longer enough, for the car was already beginning to look rather conventional. By this time Ford had launched their Capri II which, though well above the price range of the sporting 128s, featured a very practical hatchback, and fold-down rear seats, and this was seen as an important pointer to the layout of future

It was able to swallow a great deal of luggage, for the rear seats could be stowed in a folded down position

Fiat Sports Cars

LEFT *A masterful car with lots of space, the 128 3P combined speed with space like no other 128 except perhaps a non-standard 128 Estate*

BELOW *This was Fiat's own drawing of the dimensions of the 128 3P, with rear seat erect (left) and folded down (right). All dimensions are in millimetres*

sporting cars. Closer to home, too, the 128 Coupés had been hard-hit by the impact of the Bertone-styled X1/9, whose mid-engined elegance had caused a real sensation when it was launched at the end of 1972.

Fiat's response was not to order up a new car to replace the existing coupé (for the model was far too new, and the investment in body tooling too high, for that to be practical), but to prepare a major restyling and re-engineering exercise on the same underpan and front end. Accordingly, from June 1975, the coupé was joined by a new car, the 128 3P, and by the end of the year it had been superseded by it.

The 3P (3P means *tre porte* in Italian, or three doors) was a smart and ingenious derivation of the Coupé. Up to and including the front doors, from the nose, and of course including the rear suspension layout, the 3P was pure coupé, but aft of that a clever rearrangement had taken place. In place of the kicked up side window style of the coupé, the sloping tail, and the separate boot compartment, there was straight through side-window styling, a neater tail, a hatchback, and versatile fold-down rear seating.

When they launched the car, Fiat had this to say about it: 'The Coupé had personality; the new 3P is *universale*', and the statistics which accompanied the launch material proved that. In the revised bodyshell there was a little bit more rear passenger space, a completely flat load floor when rear seats were folded forward, and a total capacity in the tail of 32.4 cu. ft.

By this time, incidentally, EEC anti-pollution laws were beginning to take effect and, compared with the coupé's engine, there had been several minor changes. On the one hand the compression ratio had been increased (8.8:1 to 9.2:1) but on the other the shape of the cylinder head had had to be modified, and the result was that peak power of the 1290 cc engine was slightly down, from 75 bhp to 73 bhp, though its effect on vehicle performance was only marginal. Fiat claimed economy improvements of between four and eight per cent which, in view of the way in which petrol prices were soaring after the Yom Kippur war of 1973, was just as well. As before, there was a choice of engines, 1116 cc or 1290 cc, and as before the attraction of the smaller-engined derivative was mainly confined to Italy, where the vehicle tax laws were graded according to the size of a car's engine.

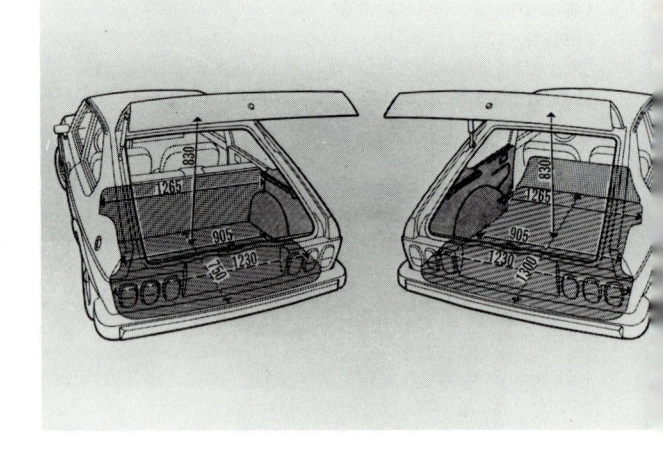

The 3P was an extremely likeable little car, more

versatile and—some say—more stylish than the original coupé, it's only real failing being the height of the rear sill for loading heavy baggage. The reduction in peak power caused by the new engine settings had more than been offset by an increase in torque, and the result was that the 3P was no faster in maximum speed, but quite a bit more spritely in acceleration, and potential fuel economy was considerably improved. *Autocar*'s lead-footed testers achieved 32.7 mpg overall with their 1300, and thought that up to 36 mpg was quite feasible in normal day-to-day motoring. It was, however, a very high-revving little car, for the near-100 mph top speed was equal to engine speeds of 6600 rpm, so it was by no means a quiet little car to drive fast. On the Italian *autostrada*, where everyone seemed to drive flat out in those days, it must have been a very noisy little car.

In this short chapter you may have noticed that I have made no mention of the word 'exciting', for somehow the 128 Coupé and the 128 3P were not cars of that sort. Pleasant, yes, and effective, certainly, but not exciting. But this does not mean that they were boring, or unsuccessful.

Fiat, in fact, had placed these cars very carefully in their range of models. If they had been less sporting, they would merely have been extra derivatives of the 128 family car scene. If they had been more extremly tuned or styled, they would not have been as attractive to so many people. The sales figures prove their point, perfectly. Although Fiat have not been able to give me a detail breakdown of the figures, they confirm that nearly 331,000 128 Coupés and 3Ps of all types were built and sold in seven years (1971 to 1978), which works out at nearly 50,000 cars a year. Small beer to Fiat, perhaps, but undoubtedly profitable. I need to ask only one rhetorical question—wouldn't BL have been delighted if their Midgets or Spitfires were selling at anything like the same rate?

By the late 1970s, Fiat were progressively beginning to reduce their model scope, and were gradually turning themselves into a large-production manufacturer of bread-and-butter cars. The Strada of spring 1978 was acknowledged to be an eventual successor to the 128, and this meant that the 'chassis' of the old car would soon be discontinued. No-one was surprised, therefore, that the 3P disappeared from the production lines at Lingotto before the end of the year, or that there has never been an equivalent replacement on the basis of the Strada.

128 Coupé Sport—1100 and 1300 models

PRODUCED November 1971 to December 1975
NUMBER BUILT 330,897 including all 128 3P models, 1975–8
GENERAL LAYOUT Transverse front-engined four-seater sports coupé, with pressed-steel unit construction body/chassis unit. Four-cylinder engine driving front wheels, with all-independent suspension
ENGINE Tuned versions of new overhead camshaft design produced for 128 saloon range. Four-cylinder in-line unit, mounted across the car, with cast iron cylinder block, and light-alloy cylinder head. Five crankshaft main bearings. Two valves per cylinder, overhead mounted, operated by single overhead camshaft driven by cogged belt from nose of crankshaft. Two engine sizes: 1100: Bore, stroke and capacity 80 × 55.5 mm, 1116 cc (3.15 × 2.18 in., 68.1 cu. in.). CR 8.8:1. Maximum power 64 bhp (DIN) at 6000 rpm. Peak torque 61 lb ft at 4400 rpm.
1300: Bore, stroke and capacity 86 × 55.5 mm, 1290 cc (3.38 × 2.18 in., 78.8 cu. in.). CR 8.9:1. Maximum power 75 bhp (DIN) at 6600 rpm. Peak torque 68 lb ft at 3600 rpm)
TRANSMISSION In unit with engine, and with final drive, four-speed all-synchromesh manual gearbox. Final drive ratio 4.077:1. Overall gear ratios 4.24, 5.91, 9.13, 14.60, reverse 15.13:1. 15.0 mph/1000 rpm in top gear
CHASSIS AND SUSPENSION Front engine, front drive. Unit construction pressed-steel body/chassis unit, using underframe of Fiat 128 saloon. Independent front suspension by coil springs, MacPherson struts and anti-roll bar. Rack and pinion steering. Independent rear suspension by transverse leaf spring, MacPherson struts, and lower wishbones. 8.9 in. front disc brakes, 7.3 × 1.2 in. rear drum brakes, with vacuum servo assistance. 145-13 in. radial ply tyres, on 4.5 in. wide wheel rims. Bolt-on, pressed steel disc wheels
BODYWORK Pressed-steel shell, in unit with 'chassis', produced by Fiat, on basis of standard Fiat 128 underframe and some inner panels. Two-door four-seater coupé body style. Length 12 ft 6 in.; width 5 ft 1.5 in.; height 4 ft 3.5 in. Wheelbase 7 ft 3.5 in.; front track 4 ft 4.4 in.; rear track 4 ft 4.5 in. Unladen weight 1787 lb (1100) or 1797 lb (1300)
PERFORMANCE SUMMARY (*Autocar*, 17 August 1972), 1300 version, Maximum speed 99 mph, 0–60 mph 13.1 sec., standing-start ¼-mile 18.8 sec., overall fuel consumption 28.5 mpg (Imperial)

128 3P—1100 and 1300 models

PRODUCED June 1975 to October 1978
NUMBER BUILT 330,897 including all Sport Coupés of 1971–5
GENERAL LAYOUT Basic layout, and engineering as for 128 Coupé model, but with restyled rear and new 'third door' hatchback. Technical difference, as follows:
ENGINE Slightly retuned:
1100: Maximum power 65 bhp (DIN) at 6000 rpm. Peak torque 64 lb ft at 4100 rpm.
1300: Maximum power 73 bhp (DIN) at 6000 rpm. Peak torque 74 lb ft at 3900 rpm
BODYWORK Unladen weight 1875 lb
PERFORMANCE SUMMARY (*Autocar*, 21 February 1976) 1300 version, Maximum speed 98 mph, 0–60 mph 11.7 sec., standing start ¼-mile 18.4 sec., overall fuel consumption 32.7 mpg (Imperial)
NOTE This model lightly modified, and renamed 128 Sport from Spring 1979.
For the US market, the 1290 cc 128 Sport had: CR 8.5:1. 62 bhp (DIN) at 5600 rpm. Peak torque 67 lb ft at 3800 rpm. Final drive ratio 3.76:1 or 4.42:1. Overall gear ratios 3.91, 5.47, 8.40, 13.47, reverse 13.96:1, or 4.60, 6.43, 9.88, 15.84, reverse 16.42:1. 16.3 or 13.8 mph/1000 rpm in top gear.
Unladen weight 1995 lb

9 130 Coupé—speed with dignity
Pininfarina's genius on an unpromising chassis

It took a long time to develop a larger, more up-market, replacement for the 2300S Coupé which, considering the work-load in Fiat's design departments in the 1960s, is hardly surprising. But the delay was justified. The graceful 130 Coupé of the 1970s, which was sporting rather than a sports car, was one of the most unexpectedly successful Fiats, and a classic Grand Tourer in every way. Compared with the Plain Jane saloon car from which it evolved, the 130 Coupé was so elegant, and had so much style, that it still seems something of a miracle that it ever appeared at all.

It is a fact that, in spite of their great resources, Fiat have never had much success with their large cars. It didn't seem to matter how hard they tried, or even who they consulted for advice, but their big-engined cars rarely seemed to inspire much enthusiasm. It's been like this for many years, with small cars like the Topolinos, 600s and Pandas making all the headlines—and taking most of the sales. Perhaps the state of the Italian market had something to do with this—somehow, the Italians never took to buying their cars in bulky packages, and they seemed to prefer their motoring in smaller machines, preferably urged on by tuned-up engines.

The Fiat 130 was produced as a replacement for the 2300 saloon, though by the time it appeared in 1969 it had become considerably larger and more

122

130 Coupé—speed with dignity

complex than that car had ever been. One reason was that it had suffered a very protracted design and development period and, like Topsy, it 'just growed'. The 130 of 1969 was not at all like that which had originally been conceived in 1963.

I should start, however, by briefly mentioning the Fiat 140 project, which began to take shape in a special design office in Milan, many miles away from Turin, and Dr Giacosa. However, as Giacosa has admitted in his autobiography: 'The reader will have already noticed that large automobiles intended for the privileged few have never much appealed to me . . .', which might explain why Valletta was persuaded to initiate Project 140, under Cesare Tonegutti. The 140, of which only one prototype was built in the late 1950s, was very 'American', in that it was large, had a 4.2-litre vee-8 engine, American automatic transmission, hydropneumatic suspension, and power steering and braking. It seems to have been a failure, too large and heavy, and not at all 'Fiat-like', so it was scrapped in 1958.

By the early 1960s, however, Fiat was so prosperous, and expanding so fast, that management began to look for ways of extending the range. It could not be extended downwards (the *nuova 500* was already the smallest practical car which Giacoas's team could devise), but the attraction was to produce a large car, something with which to confront Mercedes-Benz and others.

The original 130 of December 1963, existing only as a plaster mock-up in the styling studios, was little more than a longer and wider version of the 2300, using the car's running gear. This, on hindsight, seems to have been no more than a 'sighting shot', for it rapidly outgrew this original concept. By 1965, when more serious work began, it had also been given an alternative project code, X1/3, which helped to confuse not only prying journalists but Fiat management who were not yet closely involved!

Once the 124 saloons, and the 125 models which developed from those cars, were finalized, Giacosa's team could begin to concentrate on the 130 project.

LEFT *The extremely elegant 130 Coupé (left) was developed by Pininfarina on the unlikely basis of the square-rigged (Fiat-styled) 130 saloon, using the same underpan and all mechanical components. The saloon had appeared prematurely in 1969, and the coupé made its bow in March 1971*

BELOW *With the Tower of London as background, this was a 1974 British-market 130 Coupé—large, but by no means ungainly*

Fiat Sports Cars

If only Pininfarina had got their way, their concept of 130 styling could have been turned into a complete family. The 130 Coupé itself (above), the two-door car which was built in thousands. However, only one estate car (centre) and one four-door saloon (bottom) were ever made, both as show cars. Surely the Pininfarina four-door saloon would have been more distinguished than Fiat's own uninspired saloon?

130 Coupé—speed with dignity

As Giacosa himself has said: 'By now I had given up my initial idea of an automobile that would be the logical development of the 2300. The 130 had come to resemble a Mercedes 300 in weight and size; it needed a much bigger 6 or 8V engine.'

Which meant that he, and his engine specialist Aurelio Lampredi, once again had a major new project to consider, and new toys to be built, and the styling process was left to the studio, under the direction, as usual, of Mario Boano. However, it was by no means the most important new model on the go at this time—that must surely have been the all-new front-wheel-drive 128 saloon, which was to be launched within weeks of the 130 itself.

The choice of engine was central to the whole project, and it soon became apparent that no existing Fiat engine was suitable. The largest existing engine was the 2.3-litre straight-six cylinder unit used in the 2300 and 2300S models, but this was already at the limit of its development, and was too long to be fitted to the compact type of engine bay dictated by modern styling trends.

At the time (1965) the new Ferrari-based Dino vee-6 unit had not been finalized, but as this was a 2.0-litre design, with light-alloy cylinder block, four overhead camshafts, and was highly tuned, it was not really suitable. Even in its definitive form, as used from 1969, it was still a complex 2.4-litre engine, though it had, at least, been given a cast-iron cylinder block by this stage.

Lampredi, therefore, was faced with designing a new engine for the 130, and chose a vee-6 for the purpose. But it was not even a stretched derivative of the Dino vee-6. Along with many other writers, I was originally confused by the rather vague information released about the 130 engine, but close study of the two engines clears this up straight away—the Dino engine, and the 130 engine, were entirely different.

Here are the basic reasons. The 2.4-litre Dino had a bore and stroke of 92.5 × 60 mm (2418 cc), a 65 degree angle between cylinder banks, and chain drive to four overhead camshafts (two per cylinder head), and with opposed valves. The original 130 engine had a bore and stroke of 96 × 66 mm (2866 cc), a 60 degree angle between the cylinder banks, and cogged-belt drive to two overhead camshafts (one per cylinder head), with in-line valves.

It may seem illogical, even for a company like Fiat which loved to have engines to play with, not to produce one common new vee-6 design to cover the Dino and the 130 models, but the fact was that the company had become locked in to the Dino design, which was at the limit of its capacity at 2.4-litres, whereas the need for the 130 was for a more simple and refined engine, with more torque and a larger displacement.

The hard-working Lampredi, indeed, was concerned with the design and development of both 'iron-block' Fiat vee-6 engines at the same time, for work on the iron-block Ferrari-type Dino vee-6 began in 1966, at which point work on the 130-type vee-6 was also under way.

The first prototype 130 saloon was not completed until the summer of 1967, and was still not at all like the production car in many respects. At the time it had a 2.6-litre vee-6 engine, and was fitted with live axle rear suspension, but it was planned to evaluate the De Dion system in due course. With a hoped-for production rate of 100 cars a day (which equates to about 20,000 a year, if holidays and other stoppages are considered), it was initially required for launch before the end of 1968—neither the production rate, nor the launch date were, in fact, achieved.

In the meantime, the size of the 130 gradually increased, and the styling changed. The definitive car stood on a wheelbase of 8 ft 11.1 in./272 cm, which was only 2.7 in./7 cm longer than that of the 2300 saloon, which was discontinued to make way for it, but the tracks were considerably wider, and the whole car was 10.5 in./27 cm longer overall. (If an in-line six-cylinder engine had been retained, the wheelbase and length increases would have been more pronounced.) In 1963 the car had looked like an overgrown 124, but it gradually became more and more grand, and ended up with massively square (and, some say, dowdy) lines with a distinct family resemblance to the new square-rig 128 saloon.

All the signs are that Fiat were rushed into showing the 130 to the public before they were really ready to do so, for it was launched at the Geneva Show in March 1969 with the barest of information and display, but did not go into production until mid-summer. Indeed, at Geneva, a complete car on the stand was always locked, and the sectioned 'chassis' was not accompanied by any detail press briefing.

By any standards, however, the running gear of the 130 was advanced, and technically interesting. Lampredi's all-new vee-6 engine was presented as a 2866 cc unit, with light-alloy cylinder heads, internally cogged-belt drives to the camshafts, and with all the necessary 'executive' fittings for power-assisted steering pumps, and air-conditioning compressors. The power output was quoted as 140 bhp (DIN) at 5600 rpm, and the peak torque as 159 lb ft at 3200 rpm—both of which showed that *this* was to be a smooth, torquey, engine rather than a

Fiat Sports Cars

high-revving de-tuned racer like the Dino vee-6. Naturally there was a fully-counter-balanced four-bearing crankshaft, and carburation was by a single twin-choke Weber instrument, though beautifully fabricated tubular stainless steel exhaust manifolds were provided.

There was to be a choice of transmissions. Most 130s, it was suggested, would be built with automatic transmission, this being the latest version of the British-built Borg Warner Type 35 transmission, which had three forward speeds, and was working near the limit of its torque capacity (it had recently been adopted for the 2.8-litre Jaguar XJ6, and for the 3.5-litre vee-8 Rovers, so no-one was worrying too much about this), but there was also to be a five-speed manual gearbox.

The manual alternative was not an existing Fiat transmission (the 2300 had had a four-speed box, with steering column change), but was a new design bought in from ZF of West Germany. As fitted to the 130, it featured a direct fourth gear ratio, and a geared-up 'overdrive' (0.87:1) fifth, and unlike previous Fiat five-speeders, all the gears were incorporated in the one main casing. Naturally, there was a floor gear change, with remote control mechanism.

As I have already mentioned in the Dino chapter, this gearbox was also fitted to the 2.4-litre Dinos, and was a sporty but rather 'truck-like' transmission. In the world of rallying versions of this same transmission became even more famous as optional fitments to the Ford Escort Twin-Cam/RS1600/RS1800 'homologation' specials, to the Talbot Sunbeam-Lotus, the Vauxhall Chevette H5, and the Opel Kadett GT/E, not to mention its use on several other rally cars and limited production machines.

There was a single piece propeller shaft to the body-mounted final drive housing, which incorporated a long torque tube, and which was bolted up to the bodyshell by two rubber-mounted pressed-steel bridges.

Because of the width of the vee-6 engine, and the bulk added by all the accessories (such as pumps and compressors), the front suspension layout used the MacPherson strut linkage, though not the coil springs which normally feature. The advantage of a MacPherson strut layout is that there is no top wishbone to intrude into the engine bay at a critical height, as a long slim damper tube is fixed to the body shell at its top, and direct to the wheel hub at the bottom. However, on the 130, as on the

130 Coupé—speed with dignity

superseded 2300, the actual springing medium was a longitudinal torsion bar, anchored to a body cross-member under the front seats.

The rear suspension, as finalized for production, was neither live axle nor De Dion (as proposed in 1967), but was a fully-independent layout, of the type originally being developed (and standardized) for the 2.4-litre Dinos. This system featured semi-trailing arms and MacPherson strut-type dampers, but with separate coil springs bearing on the arms ahead of the drive shaft line.

As on most current modern Fiats, there was worm and roller steering, available with or without power assistance, and four-wheel disc brakes with power assistance were like those fitted to the Dinos.

All in all, the 130 had a very advanced 'chassis' which was quite hidden away, and muffled, by the big, heavy, and frankly uninspired, four-door saloon body style. The car weighed nearly 3300 lb at the kerb side, which was about 400 lb more than the 2300 had done, and those who drove the early cars found that it was neither fast, economical, nor possessed of good roadholding.

One wondered if Fiat's large-car 'jinx' had struck again, and for the first two seasons there was no indication that the car could ever be acceptable. There was, however, an historic precedent to show that it might. Ghia had made a very acceptable coupé on the basis of the lack-lustre 2300 saloon, and in the 1970s the master craftsmen at Pininfarina were to do a similar transformation job on the 130. The 130 Coupé, launched in March 1971, was one of the most delicately detailed large cars so far offered by any company, and it immediately made many friends.

Pininfarina, of course, was already a distinguished and resourceful builder of sporty and striking bodyshells—and it seemed to grow larger and more important every year. By the time the 130 saloon was announced, the Turin-based company was building 124 Spiders and Dino Spiders in some numbers for Fiat, the Alfa Romeo Spider for the Milan-based company, and a variety of special coachwork for Lancia. Equally as important was the consultancy work they carried out on behalf of many large concerns, and the styles they completed for Ferrari, which were usually built on their behalf by Scaglietti.

Ghia could not repeat their success with the obsolete 2300, as they had recently been taken over by Rowan Industries, in which Alejandro De Tomaso was a major influence, and who had no links with Fiat, so Pininfarina had the field to themselves. They were helped along by the fact that Fiat were already improving the 130's specification (changes introduced at the Geneva Show of 1970 boosted peak power to 160 bhp, from the original 140 bhp), and because Fiat not only liked what they produced, but they were more than happy to do business with such a business-like concern.

The 130 Coupé, as evolved by Pininfarina, was quite amazingly smooth, elegant and specious, not

LEFT *The smart interior of the 130 Coupé, here seen in automatic transmission form*

BELOW RIGHT *A manual 130 Coupé with not much special about the facia*

BELOW *Real luxury in the back of the 130 Coupé. Rear seat legroom was really quite reasonable*

Fiat Sports Cars

ABOVE *Heart and soul of the Fiat 130 series was the vee-6 engine, also designed by Aurelio Lampredi, but completely different from the Fiat Dino vee-6. The 130 design, for instance, had a 60 degree vee and cogged-belt drive to single overhead camshaft heads, whereas the Dino was 65 degrees, had chain drive, and twin overhead cams. Automatic transmission is fitted to this particular engine*

RIGHT *Head-on view of a display-standard 130 Coupé engine with the air conditioning pump at bottom left, the alternator at bottom right, and the power steering pump at upper left, not forgetting the cogged-belt drive to the single-overhead-camshaft per bank. By the early 1970s, engines were becoming complicated!*

least because it took shape on the standard-length wheelbase of the normal four-door saloon. It was, at one and the same time, quite unique, and possessed of a definite family resemblance to the saloon car. At the time, in 1971, it was quite unlike any previous Fiat, but it is perhaps significant that in later years it seems to have inspired not only the (Fiat-owned) Lancia Gamma Coupé, but also the Ferrari 365GT4 2+2 two-door models.

Basically, the style was so simple, that it is difficult to write down the recognition points of what is really an unforgettable shape. (In a way, I suppose, this is something like the old teaser: How do you describe the figure of a sensationally beautiful girl if your hands are tied behind your back. . .?) The 130 Coupé, naturally, had only two doors, but was nevertheless still a full four-seater with a permanent four-window coupé top. The side view featured one continuous and only slightly curving wing line linking the front grille to the tail, with an indentation on the crown line that Pininfarina's own staff referred to as a 'scoop that runs along the side at waist level.'

The front grille was full width and letter-box shaped, incorporating four shallow rectangular headlamps, and there were sculptured 'five-spoke' road wheels to complete the ensemble. The fascia and instrument layout was entirely different from that of the original saloon, and very completely equipped, with a two-spoke steering wheel, and a centre console seemingly crammed full of heater controls and switchgear.

Although the 130 Coupé was mechanically the same as the saloon, both cars benefitted considerably from one of Fiat's 'second-guess' engineering face-lifts, introduced less than two years after the original car went into production. Principally, this involved enlarging the engine, by a bore increase, from 96 mm to a whopping 102 mm, an increase

128

130 Coupé—speed with dignity

which had the effect of raising the capacity to 3235 cc. Peak power was not increased much—it was only up by five bhp, to 165 bhp at 5600 rpm, though the torque improvement (to 185 lb ft at 3300 rpm) was more noticeable.

Clearly, too, there had been second thoughts about the torque capacity of the Borg Warner Type 35 automatic transmission, for when the new 3.2-litre engine was introduced, it was matched to the larger American-built Borg Warner Model 12 transmission, as fitted to the large-engined Jaguars, and one penalty of this was that it added 66 lb to the weight of the car. It was to upgrade the car in all respects, too, that power-assisted steering was standardized.

Fiat themselves professed not to like the ZF manual gearbox, but continued to make it available as a no-cost option. They lost no opportunity, however, in suggesting that the automatic transmission was more suited to the character of the car, and the vast majority of 130 Coupés were built like that. As many rallying enthusiasts later found, the ZF gearbox was very strong, but it also had a very notchy change quality, and was by no means silent in its operation. The Coupé had a final drive ratio of 4.1:1 (that of the saloon was a more relaxed 3.73:1), and a limited-slip differential was standard—this meaning that maximum speed was attained in fifth gear, whereas on the saloon it came up in fourth gear.

Incidentally, even though the Pininfarina-syled coupé had only two doors, and perhaps a touch less accommodation, it was still a very large car, with an overall length of nearly 16 ft, and it weighed more than 3550 lb. Nor was it a very aerodynamic shape (in fairness, Pininfarina's brief had not included making the car very wind-cheating, for we were still in that happy pre-Suez era of cheap fuel)—and this may help to explain why top speed of the automatic transmission model was about 116 mph, and a reasonable average fuel consumption was about 20/22 mpg.

It was, however, exactly right for the customers, and once it had gone into production in September 1971 it was immediately in demand. To summarize its attractions, I can do no more than quote from *Motor*'s distinguished editor, Charles Bulmer, when he assessed the car in 1971: 'Bigger 3.2-litre engine and numerous other changes put Fiat's hitherto disappointing luxury saloon firmly in Jaguar, BMW and Mercedes territory.'

Production and assembly of the 130 Coupé was carried out in what might be described as the 'conventional' Italian manner. Fiat pressed and assembled the underpan and inner structural panels of the 130 saloon in the normal way, and shipped off

Fiat Sports Cars

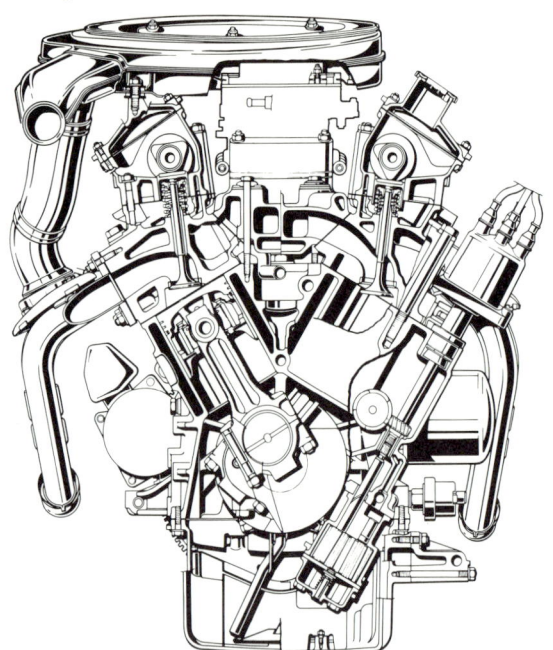

LEFT Cross-section of the Lampredi-designed 130 model's vee-6 engine. A comparison with the Ferrari-type Dino vee-6 proves that they were completely different, for the 130 engine had a 60 degree vee angle, dry liners, single overhead camshaft cylinder heads, and cogged-belt drive to the cams

RIGHT This was the five-speed all-synchromesh ZF gearbox fitted to manual transmission versions of the 130 Coupé—built in West Germany, and shared with the 2.4-litre Dino sports cars of 1969–73

BELOW A real bonnet-full of engine—the 130 installation

130

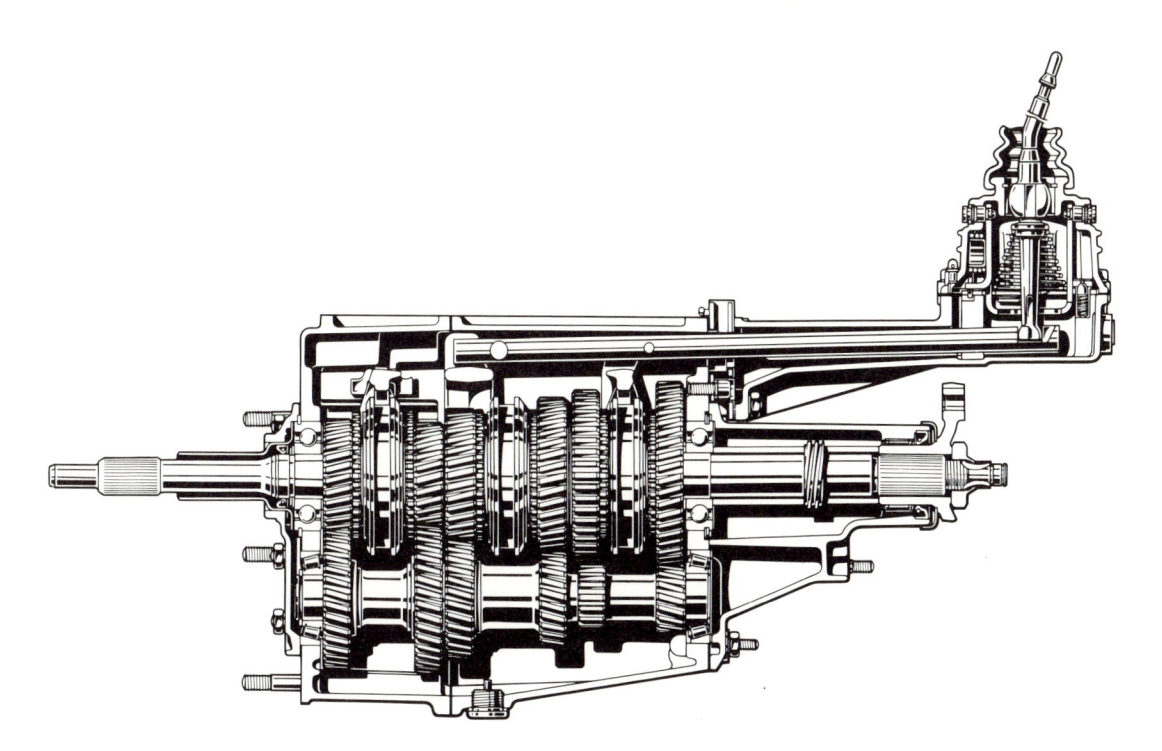

this 'chassis' to Pininfarina's factory. The coachbuilders then completed their own two-door coachwork on this basis, painted and trimmed them, then redelivered them to the new Fiat Rivalta factory, where final assembly took place on the same production line as the normal 130 saloons.

One could summarize the 130 Coupé relatively easily, as being good, but not perfect, upper class but not top class. The lack of a high top speed was disappointing, of course (particularly when compared with the pace of cars like the 3.0-litre BMWs and the new vee-8 engined Mercedes-Benz coupés), and the 130 was by no means as silent or as refined as some of its opposition, but it was still, nevertheless, the most stylish Fiat yet built. All would have been forgiven, I'm sure, if the 130 Coupé had not been such a bulky and heavy machine—*Autocar*'s road test of December 1972 made the point that it was no less than four hundredweight (nearly 450 lb) heavier than the equivalent BMW coupé. On the other hand, they summed it up as follows: 'This very pleasant Fiat, perhaps the most pleasant we have met, is delightful to look at and mostly delightful to drive; we were reluctant to give it back to its owners.'

Motor were even more complimentary about the looks, though they qualified this with considerable criticism of the lack of performance. Of the style, they said: 'the 130 Coupé has an elegance of proportion seldom seen in production, created by attention to detail and careful integration of planes. . . . Pininfarina's straight-cut three-box coachwork—surely the studio's best exercise for years in an otherwise mediocre collection—is so beautifully proportioned that it effectively disguises the car's considerable girth. . . .' It was the sheer style, balance, and elegance of this car which attracted enough praise to make the lack of sheer 'go' almost bearable. The problem was, however, that it was always a costly machine—in 1969 the original 130 saloon had been priced at 3,150,000 lire (about £2100), whereas the first 130 Coupés of 1971 sold for no less than 4,950,000 lire in automatic transmission guise.

While the combination of price, engine size, and running costs meant that it could never be one of Fiat's best sellers, it was nonetheless a success by any standards. Even though the 130 saloon was dropped in 1976, when sales had dropped considerably in the wake of the Suez war, and the hefty rise in fuel prices, production of the Pininfarina-bodied coupé continued for another year. The last of the coupés was built in mid-1977, after a total of 4491 cars had been assembled. Amazingly enough, no fewer than 850 of these cars had right-hand-drive.

Although Fiat made no attempt to carry on using this unique single-cam vee-6 engine, nor the chassis components of the 130 itself, Pininfarina found time to produce two outstanding development studies on the original theme. Neither of these cars were ever put on sale but both, without doubt, would have been a credit to Fiat if they had been.

In 1974 the two new derivatives were the four-door Opera saloon, which was as sleek and attractive as the Fiat-styled saloon had been plain

131

Fiat Sports Cars

and dumpy, and the Maremma, which was a square-back three-door estate car in the Reliant Scimitar GTE/Volvo 1800ES mould. Photographs of both these cars are in this book, and both show just how delicately and successfully the 130 Coupé bodyshell had been altered to suit.

The Opera was quite simply a four-door saloon version of the coupé, the only changes being between the windscreen bulkhead and the rear parcel shelf areas, with unchanged front and rear styling and construction, and for that reason it could very easily have been put into even limited production. The Maremma 'square back' coupé was identical to the coupé ahead of the front seats, and retained the same doors, and rear wings, but had a spacious estate-car style of back grafted on. There was an upward-opening hatchback, of course, and a vestigial flip-up spoiler at the rear of the roof, all of which not only added to the elegance of the concept, but provided a particularly self-cleaning rear window feature.

Not to produce these derivatives, I am sure, was a marketing mistake—or, rather, it would have been a mistake if Fiat had still been a highly profitable company. Pre-Suez, for sure, I can quite see the wisdom of putting such sumptuous fast 'flagships' on sale—but post-Suez, with Fiat worrying even about their survival, let alone being able to consider indulgencies, it was not practical.

A pity, for this line of Fiats was as smart as any made before, or since. Even so, times were changing rapidly, and the mid-engined X1/9s, described in the next chapter, were far more important to Fiat.

130 Coupé

PRODUCED March 1971 to 1977
NUMBER BUILT 4491
GENERAL LAYOUT Front-engined four-seater fixed-head coupé, with unit-construction pressed steel body/chassis unit. V6-cylinder engine driving rear wheels, and all-independent suspension
ENGINE Especially developed for 130 saloon/coupé series, never used on other Fiat/Lancia models, *not* relative to Ferrari/Dino engines. V6-cylinder, 60 degrees between cylinder banks, cast iron cylinder block, light-alloy cylinder heads. Four crankshaft main bearings. Two valves per cylinder, operation by single overhead camshaft per bank, driven by cog-toothed belt from nose of crankshaft. Bore, stroke and capacity 102 × 66 mm, 3235 cc (4.02 × 2.60 in., 197.5 cu. in.). CR 9.0:1. One downdraught dual-choke Weber carburettor. Maximum power 165 bhp (DIN) at 5600 rpm. Peak torque 184 lb ft at 3400 rpm
TRANSMISSION In unit with engine, choice of five-speed all-synchromesh manual or three-speed fully-automatic gearboxes. Final drive ratio 4.1:1. Overall gear ratios (manual) 3.58, 4.10, 5.70, 8.53, 15.88, reverse 15.01:1. Overall gear ratios (automatic—Borg Warner Type 12) 4.1, 6.03, 9.84, reverse 8.2:1. 20.4 mph/1000 rpm in top gear
CHASSIS AND SUSPENSION Front engine, rear drive. Unit construction, pressed-steel, body/chassis unit. Independent front suspension by torsion struts, MacPherson struts and anti-roll bar. Worm and roller steering with power assistance. Independent rear suspension by coil springs, MacPherson struts, and anti-roll bar. 10.8 in. front disc brakes, 10.3 in. rear disc brakes with servo assistance. 205/70VR 14 in. tyres on 6.5 in. wheel rims. Bolt-on cast-alloy road wheels
BODYWORK Pressed-steel shell, in unit with 'chassis', using 130 saloon floor pan and some inner panels, produced for Fiat by Pininfarina. Two-door, four-seater fixed-head coupé style. Length 15 ft 10.6 in.; width 5 ft 9.3 in.; height 4 ft, 4 ft 6.3 in. Wheelbase 8 ft 11 in.; front track 4 ft 9.9 in.; rear track 4 ft 9.7 in. Unladen weight 3530 lb
PERFORMANCE SUMMARY (*Autocar*, 21 December 1972) (Automatic transmission) Maximum speed 116 mph, 0–60 mph 10.6 sec., standing-start ¼-mile 17.7 sec., overall fuel consumption 20.6 mpg (Imperial)

The big 130 Coupé was given independent rear suspension of this type, where semi-trailing arms and transverse radius rods located the wheels, and where a stout anti-roll bar connected the main arms. This layout was also adopted for the 2.4-litre Dino sports cars as well

132

10 X1/9—mid-engined elegance

By courtesy of Bertone . . .

As I have already made clear, in relation to front-wheel-drive Fiats, it takes time to get things right. Good ideas have to be refined, and made practical, which explains why the delicious little X1/9 was so good when it was finally put on sale. The idea of building mid-engined sporting Fiats had been around for some years, and the advent of transverse-engine-transmission power packs made it all possible in the 1960s.

Through the research arm of Fiat, SIRA, Dr Giacosa first considered using the Type 109 (Autobianchi Primula) transverse engine/gearbox to drive the rear wheels of a sporting car in 1964, and the provisional layout was prophetic. The power pack was placed ahead of the line of the rear wheels, so that the same type of drive shafts, and a bascially unaltered transmission, could be retained.

This project was coded G31, and the design was completed in 1966, with prototype construction completed in 1967. Fiat then decided to cut corners, and indulge in a typical 'smoke-screening' operation, by having OSI make up the coachwork for such a car, and exhibit it as their own brilliant idea. Since OSI had partly been set up by Luigi Segre of Ghia, it was perhaps not surprising that the finished mock-up was superficially like some Ghia cars of the day.

The original style had been proposed by Pio Manzu of Fiat (Manzu was one of the young men who produced the startling body style on an Austin-Healey 3000 in 1962, which influenced the eventual shape of the MGB GT), though it was OSI who produced a fibreglass reinforced plastic bodyshell, itself. Even so, there are definite, if not close, similarities, between the looks of the G31 and of the Ghia-styled De Tomaso Mangusta of the day.

Even before the prototype was completed, Fiat were dabbling with a similar transverse installation

In 1969, Bertone produced this Runabout Barchetta as a show car for Turin, which everyone thought very amusing, but no-one realised that the makings of the original X1/9 chassis were under the skin. Although the Runabout was not at all practical—nor ever intended to be—it had the transverse mid-engine layout. This observer (left) is peering underneath to see if an engine is actually fitted. It was!

133

Fiat Sports Cars

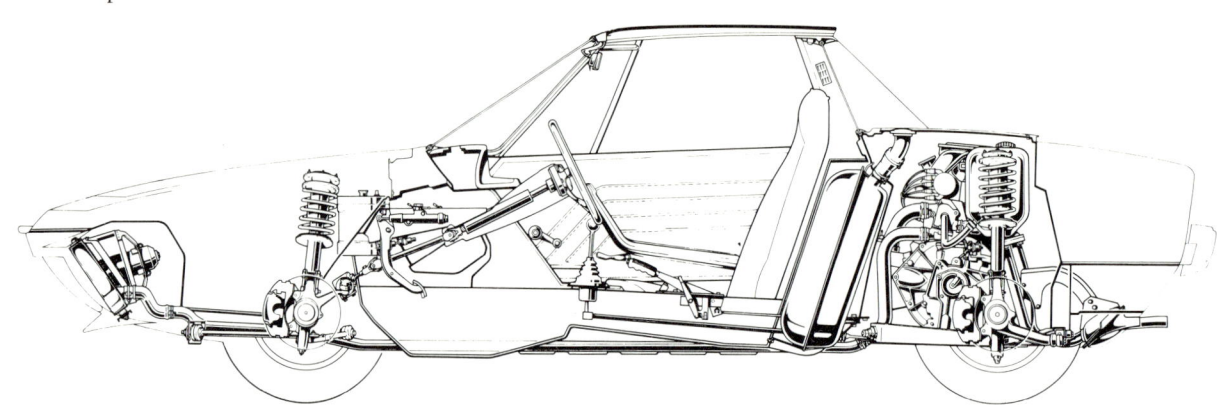

featuring the twin-cam 124 Sport/125 engine, the reason being that Fiat had just become associated with Citroen, and were tentatively looking at ideas for a common medium-sized front-wheel-drive car (see Appendix C, regarding the Fiat-owned Lancia company in the 1970s). Accordingly, the car made its public debut with a transversely-mounted Type 124AC engine of 1608 cc behind the seats.

The 'smoke-screen' approach rather lost its purpose when Fiat decided to show the G31 prototype on the Autobianchi stand at the Turin Show in November 1968. Since the whole motoring world knew they owned Autobianchi, the pundits decided this was an important move, and said so, in print. As Geoffrey Howard commented in *Autocar*, at the time 'It is a mid-engined GT car with no real mechanicals under the skin (he cannot have scrambled underneath to take a peek...), but a clean shape with Lamborghini Miura-type horizontal slats over the fastback rear window. Unconfirmed rumours claim that this car was originally built by OSI with a Fiat 124S twin-cam engine mounted transversely behind the driver on an Autobianchi transmission, and that Fiat took over the design when they found out how good it was. Its presence on the Autobianchi stand is logical, as Autobianchi is really the specialist car division of Fiat anyway, and it seems likely that the car will be marketed in limited quantities to test customer reaction.'

In fact, this speculation was completely unfounded, for Fiat had already decided to drop the project, or rather to suspend its development. In a way, it inspired the development of the X1/20, or Lancia Monte Carlo, of the 1970s, and this car is analysed in more detail in Appendix C. Dr Giacosa, however, makes this comment, backing up the heritage of the X1/9 'The Fiat X1/9 which came out at the start of 1973 can be considered the translation into concrete terms of the concept that had led me in 1964 to design the G31 at SIRA.'

By 1968, of course, plans were already well advanced for the launch of the new front-wheel-drive 128 saloon, and the new family would soon include 'hot' saloons, and coupés all developed from the same mechanical layout, and pressed-steel floor pan. However, in the long term scheme of things, Fiat wanted to see their own 850 Sport Coupé replaced by a 128 Coupé, and the Bertone-styled 850 Spider replaced by a new spider.

Naturally enough, Bertone were very anxious to build the new 128-based spider, as the existing car was such wonderful business for them. Accordingly, at Fiat's urging, in 1968/1969 they began to develop the shape of a new car, which I will call '128 Spider', though they immediately ran into all sorts of artistic problems.

To produce a shapely little coupé on the basis of the rear-engined 850 floorpan had been simple enough, but to produce something equally as stylish on the basis of the front-engine/front-drive 128 floor pan and running gear, was much more difficult. As BMC found when they tried to produce a new 'MG Midget' from the transverse-engined Mini layout, so

ABOVE *Technical profile of the X1/9 of 1972, showing the engine neatly tucked away behind the seats, the fuel tank mounted ahead of it, behind the left-hand seat, and with plenty of space allocated for stowage at front and rear*

OPPOSITE LEFT *The MacPherson strut independent rear suspension of the X1/9 used some elements of the 128's front suspension, so that the expensive-to-build transmission could all be used without change*

OPPOSITE RIGHT *Overhead view of the X1/9's rear suspension, showing the semi-trailing link geometry, and the way that a redundant steering arm from the 128's front suspension had been used to provide additional location as well. It was the tie rod attached to this which allowed rear toe-in/toe-out to be adjusted*

Bertone discovered that such an engine layout was too high, and too wide, to make any kind of sleek front-end style look right.

The new project did not meet their own requirements, and standards, though as dutiful suppliers they carried on refining the style for Fiat to view. Nuccio Bertone, and his chief stylist Marcello Gandini, were so unhappy about this that they decided to branch out on their own. With the lessons of G31 still fresh in their mind, they started to evolve a mid-engined style, also based on the use of the 128's engine/gearbox assembly.

Bertone already knew a lot about transverse mid-engined cars, for they had produced the startling one-off Marzal for Lamborghini and—more important—they were building significant numbers of bodies for the magnificent Lamborghini Miura. If they could produce such a gorgeous body for the Miura, and wrap it round a 4.0-litre, four-cam, vee-12 engine, the little Fiat engine should present no problems!

Right away, it seems, they produced a sensationally beautiful style, though it was not an out-and-out convertible 'spider' this time. Most European manufacturers stood aghast at the flood of new safety legislation which was being produced in North America at this time, among which were draft laws suggesting that full convertibles would soon be banned from North American roads. Since any new sporting Fiat would be announced early in the 1970s, and (if the 850 Spider was any guide) could be expected to stay in production for seven to ten years, the new design had to take note of this.

The new 'spider', therefore, soon became anything but, for it not only needed a fixed windscreen, but a stout roll-over bar behind the seats as well. The style, as it evolved soon came to look like a coupé, but it had a roof panel which could completely be removed if necessary.

During 1969, just about at the time the 128 saloon was revealed to the public, Fiat held a series of important styling 'viewings'. At one of these, Bertone not only showed their interpretation of a front-engined/front-drive 'spider' style, but they also produced their own private-venture mid-engined style. At first, however, Fiat management was rather sniffy about the mid-engined car—after all, *they* had asked for a front-engined car, Bertone had produced one, and *they* were going to have what they wanted. In any case, front-wheel-drive was the coming thing in the European world of motoring, so there were good philosophical and publicity reasons for building a sporting car like that.

Bertone, however, had other ideas. Using the Turin Motor Show of November 1969 as a platform, to get an impression of public reaction, (and given 'under the counter' help by Fiat's designers, who supplied the bare bones of a chassis layout), they hastily produced a one-off show car, with an open two-seater body style, and called it a Runabout.

Under the skin of this bizarre machine there was something approaching the layout of the future mid-engined Fiat, for there was a transversely-mounted engine, and integral gearbox of front-drive

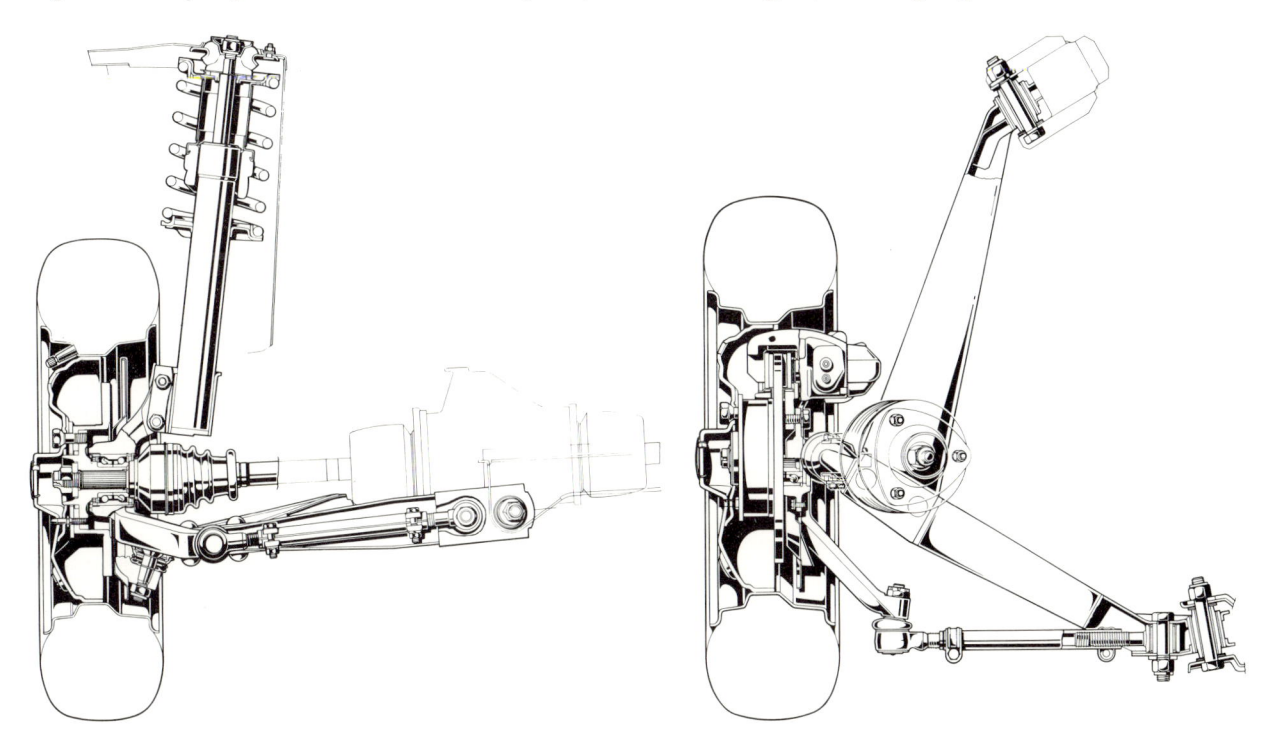

Fiat Sports Cars

type, but for Turin it was, in fact, the old-type pushrod 903 cc engine, in the Autobianchi A112 installation. The A112 was a new Fiat-designed miniature four-seater saloon (originally X1/2) making its debut at the same motor show.

Incidentally, it was the same year, 1969, that not only the mid-engined VW-Porsche 914, but the sensationally-engineered Mercedes-Benz C111 coupé, complete with mid-mounted three-rotor Wankel engine, both made their bows. The time was ripe for the mid-engined fashion to take root, and Bertone were ideally placed to take advantage of it.

The Runabout, in fairness, was a strange and somewhat impractical design, for it had a long sloping nose, a roll-over protection bar steeply forward-inclined over the seats, a very short and stumpy tail, and no windscreen or other weather protection. At Turin, Bertone described it as 'a car for the young, designed for no specific purpose save to give pleasure.'

Even so, the Runabout was very well received, though Bertone made no attempt to convince anyone that there could be any type of production car lurking underneath. Britain's authoritative weekly magazine, *Autocar*, incidentally, quite missed the fact that the engine was mounted behind

ABOVE *Is this an X1/9? No—it's a DeTomaso 'copy', done even before the X1/9 was ready for release! DeTomaso saw sneak pictures of X1/9 prototypes in the Italian press, and commanded Ghia to produce a similar style on a Ford 16 valve BDA-engined chassis of his own. The result appeared in 1971, a year before the X1/9, and was uncannily similar. Which do you prefer?*

RIGHT *The Bertone-styled X1/9 of 1972 was the most practical mid-engined sports car layout yet devised, for it provided front and rear luggage boots. The roof panel could be removed, and stowed in the front boot if required*

the seats. It was generally agreed that it was, and would remain, a totally impractical 'dream car'—a machine which was not a runner when shown, and not likely to be made into a runner in the future. In other words, it was not thought to be significant, or serious.

It was not until well into 1970 that the project began to gain momentum, and approval. After Turin, Bertone made the car look like a practical sporting car, reinstalled the overhead-camshaft Fiat 128-type engine it had originally had at private styling viewings, and turned the car into a running prototype. Personal contact between Nuccio Bertone himself, and Giovanni Agnelli, Fiat's president, eventually resulted in the project being taken up by Fiat in preference to a front-engined Spider—and Project X1/9 was born.

As with the 850 Spider, which was to remain in production until 1973, the new car was to be built as a co-operative effort between Bertone and Fiat. Naturally, Fiat would be responsible for the mechanical and structural design, but Bertone, whose factories had massive presses, and assembly and welding facilities, were contracted to press, assemble, paint and trim the complete body/chassis units, before delivering them to Fiat's old factory in Turin, the Lingotto Plant. From then on, the cars were to be built, and distributed, in the usual Fiat manner.

The design of the new X1/9—which is, so far, the only Fiat ever to have retained its 'X1 . . .' code name when badged for the showrooms—was naturally centred around the transverse engine, transmission, and final drive of the existing 128 saloon (and, soon, the Fiat-styled coupé). However, whereas the 128 Coupés were built in 1100 and 1300 guise, there was never any intention of producing an 1100-engined X1/9. At one jump, therefore, Bertone would progress from the 903 cc Spider to the 1290 cc X1/9.

It was not, however, an entirely simple matter to move the engine/transmission power pack a few feet—from ahead of the driver's toes to behind his ears—at, least, not if the optimum use of space was to be achieved. There was no problem with the width, but to make the engine bay as short (from front to rear) as possible, the complete engine/transmission installation was rotated around the crankshaft, so that the cylinder axes were in a slightly more upright position, just 11 degrees forward of vertical. At the same time this also made access to plugs a bit easier, though Fiat relocated the distributor.

Compared with the 128 Rally and the 128 Coupé 1300, there was one change. The internal gearbox top (fourth) gear ratio was raised slightly, from 1.037:1 to 0.959:1, though the final drive ratio was left undisturbed. The most important change to the transmission was that a new remote control gear change linkage had to be designed. On the X1/9, an unmodified 128 gear linkage would have placed the gear lever somewhere near the rear bumper, so a new linkage was devised, to locate the lever between the seats.

At first, Fiat were worried that access to, and around, the engine would be restricted, but Bertone provided a sizeable, lift-up, 'bonnet' on the rear decking, and there have never been any serious problems in this respect.

Fiat Sports Cars

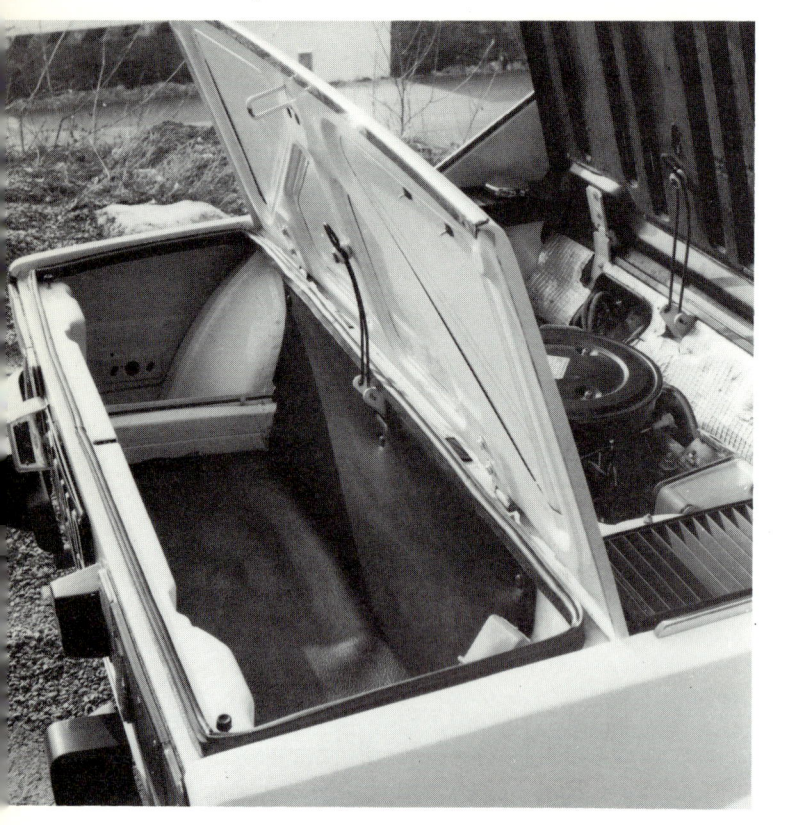

Because of the entirely new engine location, there could be no question of using an existing Fiat floor pan or 'structure', so Fiat had to design a new structure, and to take into account that Bertone would like to have it kept as simple as possible. Fiat also had to take account of new and proposed North American crash and safety legislation, for the new X1/9 would have to sell well in that affluent continent for it to be profitable.

LEFT *Behind the seats of the X1/9, the transverse engine took up surprisingly little space, and there was a sizeable boot behind that.*

RIGHT *Ingenious spare wheel stowage in the X1/9—a well was provided behind the right-hand seat, normally the passenger's seat as nearly all X1/9s were left-hand-drive*

BELOW *The engine bay of the X1/9, behind the seat but ahead of the rear wheels, was well insulated to protect the passengers. MacPherson strut suspension took up very little space, and most engine components were surprisingly accessible*

138

Because the transmission and final drive was all lumped together with the engine, it meant that there were only two choices of rear suspension—independent or De Dion. Accordingly, Fiat chose a simple, yet advanced, layout, with independent front and rear suspension. At the front, there was a conventional MacPherson strut layout, the height of those struts being limited in the interests of keeping the bonnet line low. At the rear, too, a basic MacPherson strut layout was used, utilizing the original front-drive 128 drive shafts and hubs, along with a few other details, but with a wide-based semi-trailing lower wishbone; there was an extra locating link between hub and bodyshell which, at first sight looked as if it was a steering connection but in this context was only used to trim the toe-in/toe-out to close limits. To trim the handling to the exact requirements, Fiat also specified anti-roll bars at the front and at the rear.

The rest of the 'chassis' running gear was completed by rack and pinion steering, front and rear disc brakes, both of the 128 front brake variety, and there were pressed-steel wheels with 4.5 in. rims and small-section (145-13 in.) radial ply tyres.

Although the car, as finalized, was much more rigid than the Spider, mainly due to the use of more thoughtfully designed stiffening panels, it could not gain from a fixed roof, as one of the attractive Bertone-inspired features was a completely removable roof panel. Much of the beam strength, therefore, was in the floor, where there were massive box-section sills under the doors, and a central 'services tunnel' to hide water pipes, and the gear change linkage.

The little car was made torsionally strong by the use of several transverse steel bulkheads, of which that including the toeboard ahead of the seats, and that forming the bulkhead behind the seats were the most important. In addition there was a diaphragm at the front, supporting the water radiator, a further bulkhead behind the engine (and separating it from the rear luggage boot), and a final diaphragm, doubling as the rear skin, at the tail. Is it any wonder, therefore, that according to Fiat's official figures, an early X1/9 weighed 1941 lb/880 kg, compared with a mere 1808 lb/820 kg for the four-seater 120 Coupé with the same engine and 75 bhp power output?

But if the engineering, and the chassis layout, of the X1/9 was clever, the styling, and the accommodation, was quite sensational. For this Bertone takes all the credit, for it had been their project in the first place. Even though the X1/9 was purely a two seater (few designers find any way of improving on this for a mid-engined car, unless they provide an excessively long wheelbase), and looked tiny from most view points, it not only looked sleek and fashionable, but packed a great deal of useful space under its skin.

Naturally, because of current fashions, it had to have a wedge-nose and a high tail, and almost by definition (to meet certain legal requirements) pop-up headlamps had to be used. By comparison, the tail was relatively high, and abruptly cut off behind the rear wheels. Glass area was generous, and there were neat engine bay air intakes in styling scallops behind the doors. There was a big under-bumper spoiler at the front, not exclusively to keep the nose down, as some have suggested, but to help channel air into the water radiator, mounted immediately under the bumper.

Inside, all was modern and integrated, with individual bucket seats, an informative instrument panel, a four-spoke steering wheel, and a centre console ahead of the gear lever. There was no space of any nature behind the seats, and precious little anywhere else inside the cockpit—perhaps the one significant criticism to be made about this little car.

Perhaps the most significant of all features was the way the space had been used to good effect. Apart from the passenger compartment itself, and the engine bay, which was full-width but relatively short, almost all of the rest of the car was given over

Fiat Sports Cars

TOP Back to front. Two early X1/9s at a press launch in Italy. Slim, light and well balanced

ABOVE Few could resist the style of the X1/9. In 1973 Zagato produced this Fiat 132 Coupé—they have nearly disguised that the engine is in the front

RIGHT *Although compact, the two-seater layout of the X1/9's cockpit was not cramped. In this view, the metal roof panel has been removed—a job which only takes seconds*

BELOW *Quite unmistakeable rear end of the X1/9, which does not betray the location of its engine. These were the original-style bumpers, discarded later when USA-market regulations demanded it*

Fiat Sports Cars

ABOVE *Dallara designed this 'street' racing X1/9 in 1974. It did actually influence the style in which real racing X1/9s built . . . a number of which did actually hit the track, some were quite successful*

LEFT *This overhead show of the X1/9 shows what a brilliantly conceived package it was. Note familiar deck chair seat coverings*

to stowage of one type or another, for the X1/9 had not one, but two, luggage compartments.

The front 'boot' was wide and shallow, but rather lost its usefulness if the detachable roof panel was stowed there, in the clips especially provided. The rear boot, deep, square and full-width, was behind the engine, in the extreme tail, with a lift-up flap on the tail.

Behind the seats, however, there was more evidence of careful space utilization, for the 10.6 Imperial gallon fuel tank lived behind the left bulkhead, ahead of the engine (the filler being immediately behind the coupé roof pillar), while the spare wheel was stowed near-vertically behind the right-hand seat. Access to the wheel was by a flap from the passenger compartment, which meant opening up the right-hand door, folding the seat forward, and heaving. There were worries about this at first, but Bertone's nubile secretaries were pressed into service to make sure that it was not going to be too much effort even for a slip of a girl.

Detail design was complete before the end of 1970, but tooling was going to take time, and Fiat therefore planned on having the new car ready for launch in the autumn of 1972. In the meantime, however, there would be a complication, directly caused by Alejandro DeTomaso, and indirectly by Ghia coachbuilders.

DeTomaso had started building cars at Modena in the 1960s, some reaching production, but most being one-offs and follies. He had also taken control of Ghia through Rowan Industries. At Turin in 1970 (by the time the X1/9 was designed, but not yet ready for launch) DeTomaso showed a new chassis project—the frame itself was a folded-steel backbone, like other cars in his stable at the time, and there was 16-valve 1.6-litre Ford BDA engine (and mock-up De Tomaso gearbox) transversely-mounted behind the seats, in the now classic mid-engine position.

The press noted it all down, but thought little of it—De Tomaso prototypes, after all, had been appearing with predictable regularity, and equally predictably disappearing into oblivion. But not this time—on this occasion DeTomaso decided to have it clothed with a bodyshell. This car, which appeared at Turin in November 1971 as the 'new' DeTomaso 1600 Spider-Coupé, caused much more of a furore at Fiat and Bertone than ever it did among the paying customers at the show. Very simply, it was an X1/9 lookalike, shown a full year *before* the real X1/9 was ready to go on sale!

It happened like this. DeTomaso himself saw sneak sketches of what the new X1/9 was going to

Fiat Sports Cars

look like, when they were published in Italian magazines in 1971, liked what he saw, realised that his own BDA-engined prototype was about the same size, and resolved to steal a march on his rivals; in this case, the rival was really Bertone, who could be considered as direct competitors of Ghia.

Accordingly, DeTomaso called up Tom Tjaarda, Ghia's American-born chief stylist, who had produced cars like the Fiat 2300S and the massive Ford-powered Pantera, drew his attention to the X1/9 sketches, and commanded him to produce a Ghia style to match it.

It was not, perhaps, the brief that a renowned stylist like Tjaarda would have liked, but he was a dutiful employee, and drew up a very smart little body on the required lines. The DeTomaso 1600, therefore, looked similar to, but not the same as, the still-secret X1/9. According to DeTomaso in *DeTomaso Automobiles* (Osprey), 'The styling of Tjaarda's proposal was actually aesthetically superior to that of the X1/9, especially in the cleanliness of the rear panel, which was not burdened with a heavy looking engine hatch cover. . . . The side air intake panels of the DeTomaso 1600 were also neater because they didn't protrude as much. . . .'

Incidentally, although nothing came of this car, it caused a real stir at Turin, as author Wyss makes clear 'What happened to the yellow DeTomaso

RIGHT *In 1978, Fiat UK marketed an X1/9 'Limited Edition' called the Lido. Because there is a famous night-club of that name in Paris, it was only natural that the Arc de Triomphe should be used as a backdrop for publicity stills. Lidos were all black*

BELOW *When the X1/9 was launched in the UK in 1977, the original cars were sold in specially equipped form, complete with cast-alloy road wheels, side-striping, and fitted luggage, plus the famous 'Bertone signature' panel on the left-side front wing*

144

prototype isn't known, but DeTomaso's sudden 'inspiration' certainly did nothing to endear him either to Fiat or Bertone, both of whom had many millions already wrapped up in the forthcoming X1/9. Even Italians do not have a sense of humour about such things.'

Fortunately for Fiat's peace of mind, there was little reaction to the DeTomaso car, which faded away unsung, as most of his cars tended to do, and the X1/9 was at last ready for announcement in 1972. In most other years, no doubt, the X1/9 would have been launched with a flourish at the Turin Show of November, but on this occasion it was actually held back by three weeks until the show had closed. The reason was not that Fiat had had delays, or other industrial problems, but that they had even more important (in commercial terms) new models to launch at the same show. In terms of numbers of cars to be built, and profits to be made, it was thought essential to let the world concentrate on the new rear-engined 126 baby saloon, the recently-announced 132 saloons, and of course the re-engined and upgraded 124 Sport Coupés and Spiders.

When introduced, and initially for sale only in Italy, the X1/9 was priced at 1,800,000 lire (about £1250), which made an interesting comparison with the 1,450,000 lire asked for the front-drive, front-engined 128 Coupé 1300. It sounded as if it was going to be something of a bargain, and the North Americans began to rub their hands.

The X1/9 was not ready to go on sale in the USA yet, however, for a great deal of legislative and homologation work still had to be done. Perhaps wisely, too, Fiat and Bertone were happy to have the X1/9 work out its teething troubles close to home at first, and in the event the old 850 Spider remained in production until the middle of 1973. The 'pipe-line' effect meant that Spiders were available in the United States until the end of that year.

It was one of those cars which everyone seemed to love. The styling without the roadholding, or the

Fiat Sports Cars

roadholding without good looks, would still have allowed the car to make friends, but the combination of the two, allied to the obvious sporting zest, and the sheer practicality of the machine, made it truly attractive. The only problem, it seemed, would be to make enough cars to satisfy the demand.

The X1/9, in any case, was not only a thoroughly modern little sports car, but it was launched when the majority of Fiat's competitors were either becoming pessimistic about the future of sports car motoring, or were soldiering on with old designs. Not only was the X1/9 the first well-thought-out mid-engine design, but it was the *only* mid-engine design. In Britain, BL had the MG Midget, first seen as the Austin-Healey Sprite in 1958, and the Triumph Spitfire, dating from 1962, while in Italy there was the Lancia Fulvai (1965) and the 1.3-litre Alfa Romeo Giulia GT Junior of 1966 vintage. It was no wonder that *Road & Track* of the USA were moved to suggest that: 'Anyone who would buy an MG Midget when the X1/9 was available for only $1000 more would have to be a complete masochist.'

Because the X1/9's reputation in North America was going to be of vital importance to its prospects, that sort of response in the enthusiast press was very gratifying. Bertone only produced 247 body/chassis units in 1972 (assembly was only actually beginning when the X1/9 was revealed to the world), but they increased this to 9480 in 1973, the year in which the old 850 Spider finally died. The following year, 1974, was that chosen for the car's launch into the United States, and in spite of the marketing gloom cast by the Suez 'Yom Kippur' war, and the energy crisis which followed it, X1/9 production rocketed to 20,207 units. For the rest of the decade, production stayed at this sort of level, though it is a fact that the car was never again built in such high numbers (the nearest approach was in 1979, when 20,082 of the newly re-engined X1/9 1500s were produced).

The X1/9 not only looked good, but its on-the-road behaviour was splendid as well. One might even have been able to accept a mediocre car if it looked as sensational as the X1/9, but with appointments and roadholding to match the looks it was quite irresistible. It was, perhaps, Giacosa's final masterpiece—for no Fiat designed in the 1970s has yet approached the excellence, and feline grace, of those 1960s creations. Even cars produced years later by Fiat's opposition, like the Triumph TR7, for instance, have not been as good—the TR7 came and went, unloved by many, unprofitable to its owners, while the X1/9 soldiered on.

It was so far ahead of its competition (and that competition gradually fell by the wayside as the 1970s progressed in any case) that there was no need for Fiat or Bertone to start developing a major restyle as soon as the original car had been put on sale. The original car, with its 1290 cc engine, continued virtually unchanged, for six years, during which time about 100,000 examples were built. The only complaints coming back to Fiat were that there was no official right-hand-drive version until the spring of 1977, though in Britain the Fiat specialists, Radbourne Racing (and others), carried out a few conversions from left-hand to right-hand at a considerable price premium.

By 1977, however, the marketing strategy was complete, and in case I am accused of getting my details wrong, I should say that some countries took their X1/9s with steel wheels and original section tyres, some (like Great Britain) originally took them with cast alloy wheels and fatter tyres, while Bertone 'special editions' (including signature plates, numbered individually, on the wings) were also to be found in several territories. The US market cars, of course, had to have de-toxed engines, which clipped some of their performance, and the same cars needed bigger bumpers to meet the latest crash regulations.

But none of this could stifle the X1/9's appeal—an appeal which was beautifully summarized by *Autocar*'s Grand Prix specialist, Peter Windsor, who was, and remains, a Ferrari fanatic. First, there was the running battle, in the magazine's pages, between him, an X1/9 owner, and a colleague who had inherited the Triumph TR7 which Windsor had disliked so much. Next, there was his original 12,000 mile test report, in which he headlined the car a 'baby Ferrari' and had actually acquired a couple of authentic metal Ferrari badges to fix to the front wings of the lime green Fiat. There was also his comment on the roadholding: 'The X1/9's roadholding is in the Dino/Elan class. If you really try hard, if you really decide that this is it, that even if you do go off you're not going to hit anything, then you might get the front Michelins to chirp. You might even notice a trace of understeer. But at that stage you are effectively so far away from the car's ultimate cornering potential that you can make virtually any error you like and the Fiat will forgive,' and the fact that: 'The good news is that Colin Chapman (chairman of Lotus) had bought his daughter an X1/9 for her 21st birthday. And, for me, that is some kind of endorsement. Sports cars don't come any nearer the truth than does the Elan; and yet here was Chapman, surveying the low-price-bracket sports car field, looking at a TR7, a Spitfire, even a Midget, and choosing an X1/9. I am wholly impressed. Not only do I own an Elan . . . I have also been busily forming the opinion that, if you needed an Elan replacement, then the Fiat is it. . . . No other car since the Elan allows its cornering potential to be so fully exploited'.

There was, however, the other side of the coin. Before Windsor's car had reached 24,000 miles, the point at which it would be sold, it had already suffered several trivial faults and one not-so-trivial—a blown cylinder head gasket. There was also the question of the rust. . . .

The rust. Ah, yes. Here was the problem which afflicted all Fiats in the 1970s, and one which helped destroy their reputation in North America. As Windsor commented 'By far the worst feature has been the car's rust. The X1/9 has corroded badly around the headlamps, on the front and on the inside of the front compartment. Fiat's undersealing programme is now working well; their overall weather protection is still dreadful, however.'

In many ways, therefore, *Autocar*'s experience with their 1977 model encapsulated everything known about the X1/9—its appeal, its great character, its splendid roadholding and handling, and its speedy deterioration.

At first, however, none of this deterred the customers, or Fiat themselves. Even while the X1/9 was being put into production, they were beginning to develop a larger version of the same basic layout of components—X1/20, which became the Lancia

The Lido came with striking, if impractical, white seats. The choice of charming model was inspired!

Fiat Sports Cars

Monte Carlo. This car is analysed in more detail in Appendix C.

There was no doubt, however, that the original X1/9 was not as fast as it looked, particularly in US-market tune where the exhaust emission regulations meant that the engine had to be de-tuned to give only 66 bhp. The development of another new Fiat saloon, the Ritmo (or Strada, as it was known in the USA, and in Great Britain), allowed something to be done about this.

This Ritmo/Strada, otherwise known as the X1/38 or Type 138 when it was still a secret project, was intended to be a slightly larger and more versatile replacement for the 128 saloon, although the two cars ran on, side-by-side for some time, and although it had an entirely new hatchback bodyshell of somewhat controversial style, it used the same basic engine/transmission layout as that of the older car.

Right away, the Ritmo was equipped with 1116 cc, 1301 cc and 1498 cc engines, all being developments of the overhead-cam unit already to be found in the 128 and the X1/9. The 1498 cc engine was effectively a long-stroke version of the unit, and was no larger, physically, than before. In addition, the transmission was reworked, and the 1498 cc engine was mated with a five-speed gearbox cluster, in which fifth was a geared-up 'overdrive'.

Since the Ritmo was announced in April 1978, and it was freely admitted that one of its engines would eventually be fitted to the X1/9, we did not have to wait very long for this to happen. Fiat, in fact, took the very unusual step of launching their new derivative, called the X1/9 1500 five-speed, at the British NEC Motor Show of October 1978, rather than first showing it at Turin, or Geneva, as would have been usual.

The X1/9 1500, therefore, had the long-stroke 1498 cc engine, and the five-speed gearbox. Power output was up from 75 bhp to 85 bhp (the Ritmo had 75 bhp at first, but it would eventually pick up the X1/9's engine too, as an option), and peak torque was also increased from 72 lb ft to 87 lb ft. Because of the use of the high fifth gear ratio, the X1/9 at last lost its special fourth gear ratio, reverting to that already made common in 128 and Ritmo transmissions. Overall gearing rose from 16.3 mph/1,000 rpm to 18.1 mph/1000 rpm.

More important than the improvements made to the home-market X1/9s was that made for US-market cars. In this case the peak power rose from 66 bhp at a very peaky 6200 rpm, to 67 bhp at 5250 rpm, while torque went up from 68 lb ft at 3600 rpm to 76 lb ft at 3000 rpm. In bald figures that might not sound dramatic, but the result was that the latest X1/9 was not only lustier and easier to drive at lower engine speeds, but it had higher overall gearing to encourage better fuel economy and more fuss-free motoring.

At the same time, for the 1500 five-speed there were style changes, both externally, and in the cockpit, though none of the basic layout was

Fiat prototype X1/9 Group 4 rally car on display. It was used as a mobile test-bed for many engines and a number of other components. Its style is not that of the Dallara car

X1/9—mid-engined elegance

changed. Because most X1/9s were sold in the United States, Fiat decided to build all cars, for all markets, with a new type of '5 mph' bumper, which was by no means universally popular, and which increased the overall length by several inches. Apart from these bumpers, and the new badging, the most obvious difference was to the black engine compartment cover, which was raised and altogether more prominent. The common assumption was that it was taller so that clearance could be provided for the new long-stroke engine, which was nonsense, for the same cylinder block and head castings were retained. The fact of the matter was that there was a more bulky carburettor air cleaner, and *that* was the item which had to be cleared.

Inside the car there was a new fascia, with completely circular dials, and relocated minor controls, while the stripe style of the 1300's seat covering was abandoned in favour of monochrome shades.

The result was that when *Road & Track* got their hands on a 1979 model they headlined their report 'There's no substitute for cubic centimetres', and commented happily that 'trade-offs for this increased performance are minimal.', and, 'A comment from our X1/9 test notebook sums it up well:

Visually, the X1/9 1500 was different from the earlier car because of its larger energy-absorbing bumpers, and because of a higher engine compartment cover. The engine had been enlarged to 1.5-litres, with a five-speed gearbox, the power pack coming from the Fiat Ritmo/Strada. The wheel centres are missing

"Before people sample this car, they should spend time with a traditional roadster so they'll appreciate just how good the X1/9 really is."' The price, of course, had risen considerably—from $5700 in 1978 to $7115 in 1979—but the customers did not seem to mind this.

With a top speed now well over 100 mph, even in US-tune, the X1/9 was now at the peak of its development. It could only have been made better if the engine had been tuned, or enlarged, even further, but neither of these alternatives was practical. On the other hand, although it would have been possible to shoe-horn the larger Fiat twin-cam engine and front-drive transmission into place (as was made available in the Strada 105 and 125 models at the beginning of the 1980s) this would have made the X1/9 a more or less direct competitor to the Lancia Monte Carlo/Scorpion, which already used this power pack, and which was already fighting for its corporate life.

In the end, although Fiat certainly toyed with the idea of using the twin-cam engines in the X1/9 (a tentative competitions programme was also explored for it, incidentally), by using a 1.6-litre in this car, compared with use of 1.8/2.0-litre engines in the Monte Carlo/Scorpion models, nothing came of it.

There were no further changes to European-market X1/9s until 1982, though the US-market models received a Bosch fuel-injected engine for 1981, in which the power and torque both rose again—to 75 bhp and 79 lb ft respectively.

By the beginning of the 1980s, however, the X1/9, like other sporting Fiats, was in trouble. There had been no major new models introduced in North America since the mid-1970s, and the fickle American public was getting bored with the same cars, season after season. Worse than this, there was the fact that Fiat's corrosion record was poor—and there was also the problem that the entire market for new cars was plunging as the world-wide recession deepened, the price of gasoline soared, and as further legislation began to bite hard.

It must have been at about this time that Fiat ostensibly decided gradually to get out of the sports car business completely. We do not know—we may never know—if replacements for the X1/9, the 124 Spider and the Monte Carlo/Scorpion were ever proposed, but we certainly do know that each of these three ranges were being phased out by 1983/1984. For the X1/9, Fiat adopted the same policy as that propounded for the 124 Spider (and described more fully in Chapter 6)—they would not actually drop the car completely, but they would hand over production entirely to the coachbuilders building the bodywork.

Accordingly, and without publicity, they arranged for Bertone not only to build painted and trimmed body/chassis units, but to take on completion of the complete cars as well. The first of these, destined for the United States, were built in September 1981, but by the beginning of 1982 the transition was complete.

Strictly speaking, at this point the X1/9 stopped

being a 'Fiat' and became a 'Bertone', but this is such a ticklish change that I propose to ignore it. Bertone's own press release, put out in March 1982 at the Geneva Show, was headed 'The X1/9 now carries the Bertone emblem on the front', and in the text there was the comment that 'As part of the new Fiat-Bertone agreement, the X1/9, like the Cabrio Bertone on the Ritmo Super 85, will now be marketed directly by Bertone. . . . Bertone has now taken over fully assembly of these models, including mounting of the engine and final testing of the completed cars.'

It was a brave move, but one not nearly as significant as Fiat would have us believe. USA sales plummeted from 10,817 cars in 1978 to 7628 in 1980, and to 6343 in 1981, and stocks of unsold cars piled up. Production (not sales, please note) at Bertone dropped abruptly from 20,082 in 1979 to 14,993 in 1980, and to a mere 4619 in 1981.

The 1982 'Bertones' were given a new title, becoming X1/9 IN, where the 'IN' might mean Injection (now adopted for all markets), or 'In Vogue', meaning, I suppose, high fashion, with new colour schemes, red leather seating and carpets, electric window lifts, and a brushed copper name plate on the dashboard carrying individual numbers and Nuccio Bertone's signature. It was the old way of dressing up an existing car to make it rather special, and it had all the hallmarks of a limited edition.

There was, I had hoped, time for a revival, but when I visited the Bertone factory in October 1982, the X1/9 production lines, and all the body assembly jigs, were not only at a standstill, and deserted, but were actually completely empty of cars or body structures. I drew the conclusion, then, that the X1/9 had not merely been withdrawn for a period to balance stocks, but had already died, and nothing I have seen since makes me change my mind. In spite of the fact that X1/9s were still listed as 1983 models, it could only be a matter of time before Fiat and Bertone gave into the inevitable, and let a great little car die away.

And so it was that, in 1983, the last Fiat sports car was built—which makes a tidy, but disheartening, end to this narrative. It is sad to compare the Fiat scene in 1983 with that of 1973, only a decade earlier. In 1973, not only were Fiat building 124 Coupés and spiders, Dino Coupés and spiders, 128 Coupés and 130 Coupés, but the X1/9 was building up as the 850 Spider faded away, and plans were afoot to build X1/20 as another Fiat as well.

Two oil price shocks, industrial disruption on a massive scale in Italy, a gathering world recession, a complete change in the North American market, and policy shifts at Fiat, all conspired to kill off the Fiat sports car. Fiat, like BL and Alfa Romeo, have found that a sporting image does not pay the rent— and all three have chosen survival instead of glory.

How sad. But of Fiat perhaps we can say—*They don't make them like that anymore.*

X1/9—1300

PRODUCED November 1972 to October 1978
NUMBER BUILT Approximately 100,000 (see text, and X1/9 1500)
GENERAL LAYOUT Mid-engined two-seater coupé, with unit-construction pressed-steel body/chassis unit. Four-cylinder engine, transversely mounted behind seats, in unit with transmission and final drive. All-independent suspension. Removable roof panel
ENGINE Developed from Fiat 128 Coupé 1300 unit. Four-cylinder in-line unit, cast iron cylinder block, light-alloy cylinder head. Five crankshaft main bearings. Valve operation by single overhead camshaft, driven by cogged belt from crankshaft. Bore, stroke and capacity 86 × 55.5 mm, 1290 cc (3.38 × 2.19 in., 78.7 cu. in.). CR 8.9:1. One downdraught dual-choke Weber carburettor. Maximum power 75 bhp (DIN) at 6000 rpm. Peak torque 72 lb ft (DIN) at 3400 rpm. From 1977, CR 9.2:1, and 73 bhp (DIN) at 6000 rpm.
TRANSMISSION In unit with transversely mounted engine, and final drive. Final drive ratio 4.077:1. Overall gear ratios 3.91, 5.93, 9.11, 14.61, reverse 15.14:1. Synchromesh on all forward gears. 16.68 mph/1000 rpm in top gear
CHASSIS AND SUSPENSION Transverse mid-engine, rear drive. Unit construction, pressed steel, body/chassis unit. Independent front suspension by coil springs and MacPherson struts. Rack and pinion steering. Independent rear suspension by coil springs, MacPherson struts, and lower wishbones. 8.9 in. front disc brakes, 9.0 in. rear disc brakes, no servo assistance. 165/70SR 13 in. radial ply tyres on 5.0 in. rims. Bolt-on cast-alloy road wheels
BODYWORK Pressed-steel shell, in unit with 'chassis', produced by Bertone. Two-door, two-seater style, with removable roof panel (stowed, if required, in luggage compartment) Length 12 ft 6.75 in.; width 5 ft 1.75 in.; height 3 ft 10 in. Wheelbase 7 ft 2.75 in.; front track 4 ft 4.5 in.; rear track 4 ft 5 in. Unladen weight 2010 lb. (USA) length 12 ft 9.5 in.; weight 2156 lb
PERFORMANCE SUMMARY (*Autocar*, 19 March 1977) Maximum speed 99 mph, 0–60 mph 12.7 sec., standing start ¼-mile 18.8 sec., overall fuel consumption 30.7 mpg (Imperial)

X1/9—1500

PRODUCED October 1978 (replacing 1300) to 1982/83 (see text)
NUMBER BUILT Approximately 50,000 (see text)—150,000+ of all.
TECHNICAL SPECIFICATION As for original X1/9–1300 except for
ENGINE Developed version of original, and basically as used in Ritmo saloon model. Bore, stroke and capacity 86.4 × 63.9 mm., 1498 cc (3.40 × 2.51 in., 91.4 cu. in.). CR 9.2:1. Maximum power 85 bhp (DIN) at 6000 rpm. Peak torque 87 lb ft at 3200 rpm. (USA version) CR 8.5:1. 67 bhp (net) at 5250 rpm. Peak torque 76 lb ft at 3000 rpm.
TRANSMISSION Five-speed, in place of four-speed. Overall gear ratios 3.52, 4.25, 5.93, 9.11, 14.61, reverse 15.14:1. Synchromesh on all forward gears. 18.27 mph/1000 rpm in top gear.
BODYWORK Length 13 ft 0.3 in. Tracks now quoted as (front) 4 ft 5.4 in., (rear) 4 ft 5.2 in. Unladen weight 2010 lb
PERFORMANCE SUMMARY (*Autocar*, 14 April 1979) Maximum speed 106 mph, 0–60 mph 11.0 sec., standing start ¼-mile 17.8 sec., overall fuel consumption 26.1 mpg (Imperial)
NOTE Fiat X1/9 officially known as Bertone X1/9 from March 1982. Engine with Bosch injection. (USA) max. power 75 bhp (net) at 5500 rpm. Peak torque 79 lb ft at 3000 rpm.

Appendices
1   124 Abarth Rallye Homologation special

Carlo Abarth, though born in Austria in 1908, found fame in Italy in the 1950s and 1960s. He had arrived in Turin after World War 2, to set up in business with Rudolph Hrushka, who was a long-time friend of Dr Ferdinand Porsche. Since Porsche were commissioned to work up a design for a four-wheel-drive Grand Prix car for Piero Dusio, it was almost inevitable that Abarth would eventually become involved with him, at Cisitalia. Cisitalia, too, were building Fiat-engined single-seaters and sports cars, and after the company had collapsed into financial ruin, Abarth eventually set up his own business in Turin, which came to concentrate on the modification and super-tuning of Fiat models.

In the 1950s and 1960s, therefore, one could not only buy lightly-modified Fiat Abarths, but one could buy Fiats with completely special Abarth twin-cam engines, special bodied coupés hiding more or less mundane Fiat components and chassis platforms, and even entirely special Abarth sports-racing machines. Almost all of them were noisy, flamboyant, and extremely fast.

By the late 1960s the Fiat-Abarths based on the Fiat 600 saloons were so fast, and so numerous, that they could, and often did, win major touring car races, for sufficient had been built to have them homologated as series-production machines. It was inevitable, therefore, that Carlo Abarth's firm, Abarth & Cie, should move closer and closer to Fiat itself, and on 1 August 1971 it was actually taken over by the Torinese giant.

From this point, the fortunes of Abarth, and of Fiat, began to become inextricably mixed up. Soon after the merger, the official Fiat competitions department was moved into one of the Abarth factories in Turin, in Corso Marche. It was inevitable, too, that more and more Abarth ideas, and modifications, should find themselves incorporated in the 'works' rally cars. By the end of 1972, the team which had started out so modestly, with lightly-modified Fiat 125s, and 124 Sport Spiders, was producing purposeful machines which could, under some circumstances, be outright winners.

Just before the Turin Show of 1970 (when, incidentally, the Bertone Stratos 'concept car' was shown...), Fiat's Giovanni Agnelli announced that factory-prepared Fiats would henceforth be entering the tough and competitive world of international rallies. At the time he suggested that Fiats *or* Lancias might be used (though, in truth, Lancia had been in motor sport, and winning for many years), and some of us even speculated that the latest all-independent suspension 2.4-litre Fiat Dinos would be used.

For the record, Fiat's first entry of all was of two 124 Sport Spiders in the 1970 RAC Rally, where they achieved no worthwhile results, though within months the world of rallying realised that they were serious, after all. Right from the start, the 124 Sport Spiders were competitive, for in January 1971 Hakan Lindberg took seventh place overall in the Monte Carlo Rally, while later in the year Ceccato's car took fourth place in the Acropolis behind two Alpine-Renaults and a Lancia Fulvia.

The first outright victory came in May 1972, only 18 months after the team had officially been formed, when Hakan Lindberg triumphantly took a 124 Sport Spider to win in the Acropolis. For such a new team, and with such a relatively conventional and underpowered car, it was a remarkable result. Fiat's competitors, however, were somewhat complacent about this, as Fiat clearly had a serious power deficiency with their 1.6-litre engines, and they lacked the services of top-line, world-class, Scandinavian drivers.

In 1972, Fiat produced their first true 'homologation special'—the 124 Abarth Rallye—which was basically a 124 Spider with more power, less weight, and independent rear suspension. This is the overhead view of the running gear, with a five-speed gearbox being a standard fitting

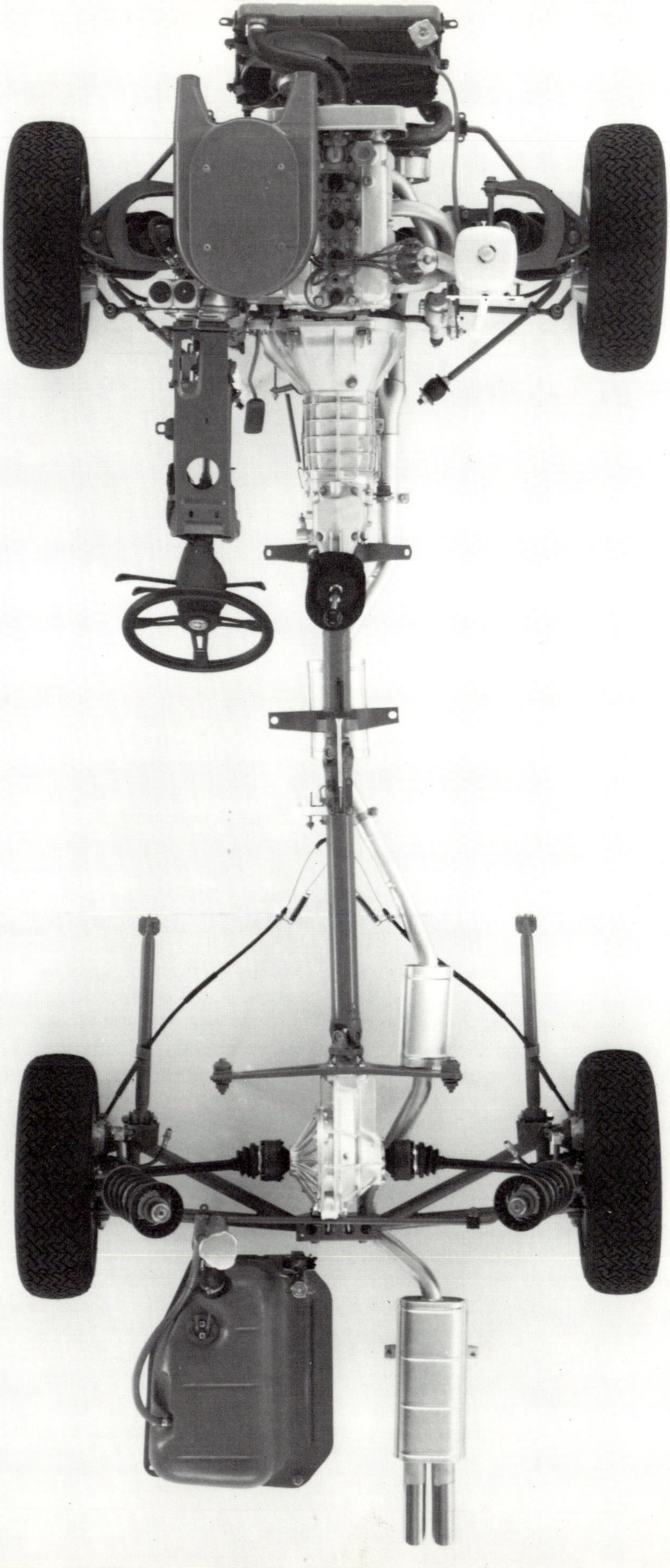

Fiat Sports Cars

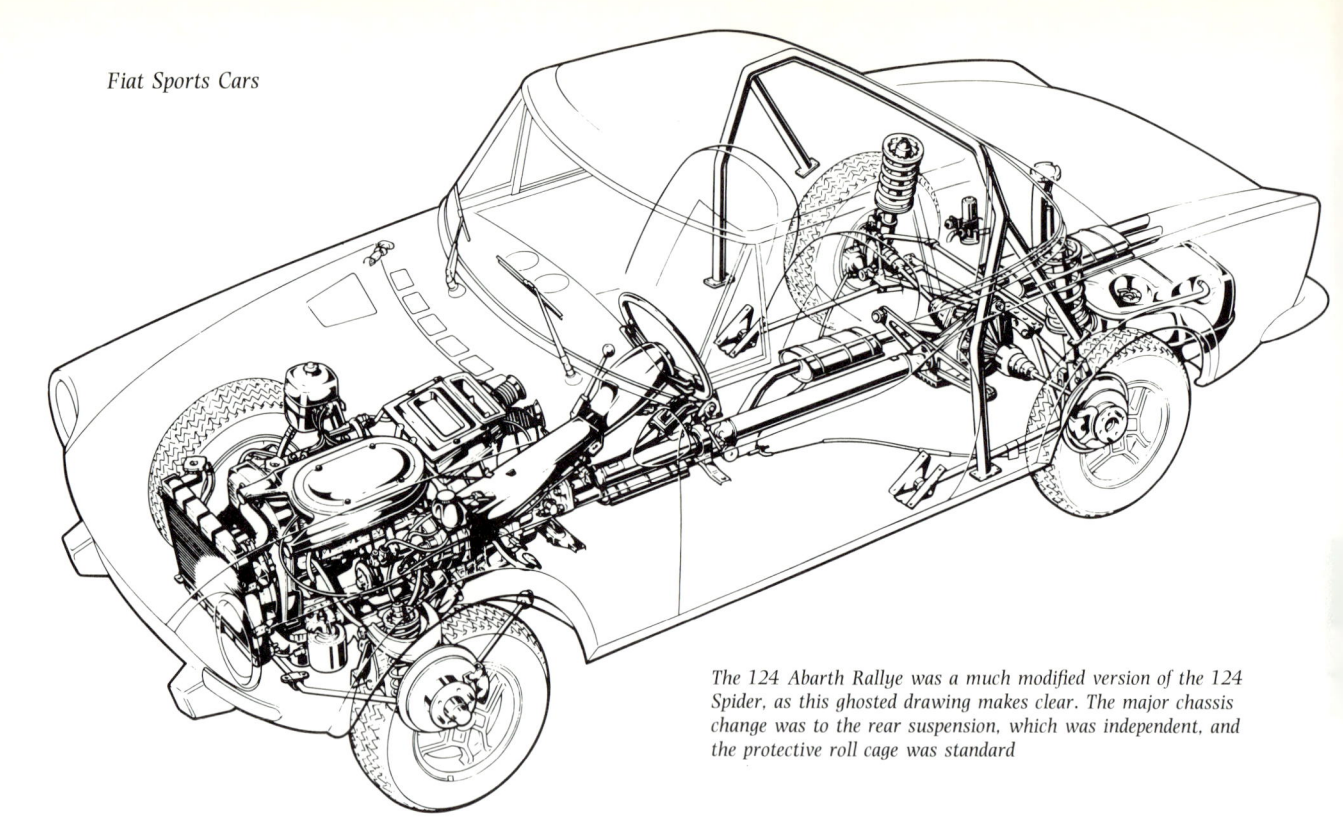

The 124 Abarth Rallye was a much modified version of the 124 Spider, as this ghosted drawing makes clear. The major chassis change was to the rear suspension, which was independent, and the protective roll cage was standard

For Fiat, however, problems were only there to be overcome, and one way to overcome them was by spending lots of money in the right places. Top drivers could be hired, if the inducements were high enough, and this led to stars like Bjorn Waldegard and Rauno Aaltonen joining the team on a freelance basis for 1973. The car problem, however, was more serious.

Ideally, Fiat would have liked to use a mid-engined or rear-engined car with a power/weight ratio to match, or beat, the Porsches and the Alpine-Renaults, but there were no such possibilities in the existing range of cars. They wanted a better car *now*, for 1973, not in two or three years after a long and costly design and development programme. During 1972, therefore, Fiat turned to Abarth, for assistance and inspiration. Abarth's brief was to take the 124 Sport Spider which, all in all, was the most versatile and rugged of the current Fiat models, and to modify it as much as necessary (and possible) to turn it into a truly competitive rally car.

Thus it was that the 124 Abarth Rallye, to give the car its full and formal title, came into existence. It was launched in the autumn of 1972, hololgated in January 1973, and achieved one win and a couple of second places in World Championship events in 1973. By almost any standards the 124 Abarth made astonishingly rapid progress from concept, to production, to approval for competition use. The homologation documents stated that production began in September 1972 (well before the car was revealed at the end of November 1972), and that the first 500 cars had been completed by the end of November! By the standards of the day, this was stretching the truth no more than any other rallying company was attempting to do, but the truth of the matter is that very few cars indeed were built before the end of 1972, and almost all of them went straight into use with the Fiat 'works' team.

Abarth looked at every aspect of the car, and managed to make changes to almost every aspect of it, even to the body itself. The 124 Abarth was lighter, more powerful, and had different rear suspension from the standard production car, and was designed purely with an eye to competitions; function was everything, and refinement, comfort, and silence all took a back seat.

The 124 Sport Spider, of course, had been revised in the autumn of 1972 (along with the 124 Sport Coupé), when the 1.6-litre and 1.8-litre twin-overhead-camshaft engines of the 132 saloon had been specified in place of the rather different 1.4-litre and 1.6-litre 124/125-based units. The larger of the two new engines actually had a bore and stroke of 84 × 79.2 mm, and a swept volume of 1756 cc, and it was this unit which was taken as the basis of the new 124 Abarth.

Abarth started by modifying the bodywork, although apart from the removal of the bumpers it still looked just like that of the normal steel-bodied 124 Sport Spider. For the new car, Abarth retained the same basic monocoque, apart from changes

124 Abarth Rallye

LEFT *Abarth designed a new independent rear suspension for the 124 Abarth Rallye. The new differential was bolted up to the bodyshell with the aid of a front beam around the axis of the pinion, while the forward radius arms used the existing live axle radius arm mountings. MacPherson strut coil spring suspension units were a feature, as was the anti-roll bar*

BELOW LEFT *The 124 Abarth Rallye used the same basic bodyshell as the ordinary spider, but bumpers were removed, wheel arch 'eyebrows' standardized, a permanent hardtop was specified, and lightweight bonnet, boot lid and other panels were all used*

BELOW *On the highway, the 124 Abarth Rallye looked purposeful—all the cars having matt black bonnets and hardtops to match the little black wheel arch 'eyebrows'. The front was clean and uncluttered—but normal rallying extras like lamps and sump guards soon ruined that!*

needed to accommodate the different rear suspension, such that Pininfarina supplied bodyshells with light-alloy scuttle and door skin panels, fibreglass bonnets and boots, and a permanently fixed fibreglass hardtop which concealed a stout tubular roll-over bar. In addition, front and rear wheel spats were also fitted, so as to allow wider-rim wheels to be fitted without breaking the 'coverage' regulations. Every car, not only the team cars, was supplied with the bonnet, the boot lid, and the hardtop, all painted anti-reflective matt black. Inside the car, the centre console of the production car was omitted, and the standard seats were high-backed buckets, facing the virtually standard fascia panel, and a small, thick-rimmed, leather-padded steering wheel. Recaro seats were optional.

Apart from the roll cage, which was triangulated to give the maximum possible rigidity, the main 'chassis' change was to the rear suspension. In place of the rigid 'live' axle always previously used on 124 Sport Spiders (and inherited from the 124 saloons), the new car was given a new design of independent rear suspension, in which a type of MacPherson strut (combined coil-spring/damper unit) was used, along with reversed lower wishbones, GP-car style, radius arms, and an anti-roll bar. The final drive featured an alloy casing with a long nose, and was fixed to the bodyshell at three widely spaced points. Ing. Gianfranco Sqvazzini, who was not only managing director of the fast-expanding Abarth organisation, but also technical director of Fiat's automobile division, had clearly done a radical job around very tightly-drawn parameters.

Although the brakes, cooling system, and other 'chassis' items were little changed, quite a lot of attention had been directed at the engine and transmission. The engine itself remained at 1756 cc with a modified version of the latest 124 Sport

Fiat Sports Cars

ABOVE Inside the 124 Abarth Rallye, a modified instrument panel was used, along with body-hugging bucket seats

RIGHT All 124 Abarths had special light-alloy wide-rim road wheels

Spider's eight-valve twin-cam cylinder head, but there were larger valves, new camshaft profiles, a fabricated steel-tube exhaust manifold, and twin downdraught dual-choke Weber 44IDF carburettors (instead of a single dual-choke instrument as used in normal 124 Sport Spiders). The result was that the 'customer' peak power output was 128 bhp (DIN) at 6200 rpm, and at the same time it was stated that there was potential for 165/170 bhp in fully-tuned competition cars.

The gearbox was standard Fiat, but five speeds (with a 0.881 'overdrive' fifth gear) were standard, whereas this cluster was only optional on the normal 124 Sport Spider. There was also an optional close-ratio gearbox, for competition purposes. The homologation form quotes the two sets as follows:

Standard: 3.667, 2.10, 1.361, 1.00, 0.881, reverse 3.526:1
Optional: 2.724, 1.857, 1.351, 1.00, 0.84, reverse 2.806:1

—and in addition to the standard final drive ratio of 4.3:1, a low 5.375:1 ratio was also homologated.

Even in standard form, the 124 Abarth Rallye could rush up to around 120 mph, at which time the engine was buzzing over at something like 7000 rpm. With 0–60 mph acceleration in no more than nine seconds, and a price tag in Italy of around £2250, it was both quicker and vastly more costly than the £1540 124 Sport Spider, but this did not matter. Here, at last, was an 'homologation special' which Fiat could use as the springboard to even greater sporting achievements.

The 124 Abarth Rallye was always thought to be more important as a competition car, than as a showroom machine, and it started to repay its investment costs straight away. With a larger, and more star-studded team of drivers, Fiat were more competitive than ever before. In Italy, and in many European championship events, the cars could be winners, and even at World Championship level, where Alpine-Renault were dominant, they were usually among the leaders.

In the World championship of 1973, Achim

Warmbold won the Polish Rally outright, while Rauno Aaltonen came second in the Acropolis, and Maurizio Verini took second place in the San Remo event. Apart from this, there were a couple of fourth placings, while in the San Remo (the Fiat 'home' event, don't forget), the 'works' 124 Abarth Rallye cars were also fourth, fifth and sixth.

For 1974, with the cars still in small-scale production at Abarth and Fiat, the car was re-homologated yet again, this time into Group 3, which is to say that the CSI had become convinced that 1000 examples had been built in a 12-month period. This figure would have been remarkable enough, for an 'homologation special', even if it had been built in a logical manner, but in the case of the 124 Abarth it was not. As *Motor*'s Michael Bowler pointed out after he had driven an early production car at the end of 1972 'The method of assembly is rather long-winded as Abarth do the non-standard bits. Fiat send engines and transmissions to Abarth; he modifies the engines and sends them back to Fiat together with rear suspensions. The body arrives at Fiat from Farina. Fiat bolt it all together, take it to Abarth for individual testing, and it then returns to Fiat for sale.'

However, in sporting terms, it was all worth it in 1974. Although Bjorn Waldegard and Rauno Aaltonen both moved on, the youthful Markku Alen became the resident Scandinavian superstar. The cars, in 'works' tune, were getting quicker all the time, and the season started well, in spite of repercussions from the energy crisis, with a 1-2-3 result in the Portugese TAP rally, Raffaele Pinto driving the winning car.

Fiat even felt bold enough to send three cars to compete in the Safari rally, which was (like most first-time Safari efforts) not very successful, for only one car finished (driven by Robin Ulyate) in tenth place. Things bucked up later in the season, though, for Alen was third in the 1000 Lakes (behind the rapid Ford Escort RS1600s of Hannu Mikkola and Timo Makinen), Giulio Bisulli was second on San Remo (behind Munari's remarkable new Lancia Stratos), and Markku Alen was second in the Press-on-Regardless rally (in the USA).

Things improved even more in 1975, even though actual production of the 124 Abarth Rallye had virtually come to an end, for an optional 16-valve cylinder head had now been homologated and the cars were back in Group 4 again. The 16-valve head

Fiat Sports Cars

was by Abarth, rather than Fiat, was also used on the Lancia Beta 'works' rally cars, and was destined for use in the saloon to replace the Rallye in 1976. It gave the 1.8-litre cars more than 180 bhp, even more torque, and a fighting chance of keeping up with everyone except the rampaging and seemingly unstoppable Lancia Stratos.

Markku Alen stayed with the team and, from time to time, was joined by Hannu Mikkola. Bjorn Waldegard, and Bernard Darniche. During the year Maurizio Verini became European Rally Champion, with no fewer than five outright victories, while at World Championship level Markku Alen won the TAP Rally in Portugal, Hannu Mikkola finished second in Monte Carlo and Portugal, and Verini second in the San Remo (once again, behind a Lancia Stratos, this time with Waldegard at the wheel).

By the end of 1975, however, Fiat had rather lost interest in the car, not only because it was becoming outclassed and outpaced, but because it was soon to be replaced by another Fiat-Abarth model. Accordingly, after a mere 1013 124 Abarth Rallye spiders had been built in rather more than two years (which puts the homologation claims into more clear perspective), the model was dropped.

Its replacement was the 131 Abarth Rallye, a new type of 'homologation special' which began winning rallies outright in 1976, and was still good enough for Markku Alen to win a World Championship rally (Portugal) in 1981, and for Adartico Vudafieri to win five events on the way to the European Rally championship of the same year. Along the way Fiat also won the World Rally Championship for Makes in 1977, 1978 and 1980 (they were beaten by Ford in 1979), and provided cars for the individual World Champion drivers Markku Alen (1978) and Walter Rohrl (1980). The 131 Abarth won so many important events that Fiat could almost sit back and let their private owners do the job for them in some countries. It was such an impressive list that British-language adverts for 1982 Fiats used success tables—and almost ran out of space in which to use them. But all that's for another book.

The definitive 124 Abarth Rallye of 1975, complete with final 'works' modifications including four-valve cylinder heads, extra air outlets in the front wings, cooling slots to the rear brakes, and extra headlamps built in to the bonnet top

124 Abarth Rallye

Swedish Rally 1975, with Hannu Mikkola driving the 'works' 124 Abarth, and Jean Todt co-driving

124 Abarth Rallye

PRODUCED November 1972 to mid-1975
NUMBER BUILT 1013
GENERAL LAYOUT Front-engined two-seater sports car, with unit-construction pressed-steel body/chassis unit. Four-cylinder engine driving rear wheels, and all-independent suspension. Lightweight body skin panels
ENGINE Developed from 124 Sport Coupé/Spider twin-cam. Four-cylinder, in-line unit, cast iron cylinder block, light-alloy cylinder head. Five crankshaft main bearings. Two valves per cylinder, operation by twin overhead camshafts, driven by cog-toothed belt from nose of crankshaft. Bore, stroke and capacity 84 × 79.2 mm, 1756 cc (3.31 × 3.12 in., 107.2 cu. in.). CR 9.8:1. Two downdraught dual-choke Weber carburettors. Maximum power 128 bhp (DIN) at 6200 rpm. Peak torque 117 lb ft at 5200 rpm
TRANSMISSION In unit with engine, five-speed all-synchromesh gearbox. Final drive ratio 4.3:1 (many competitions options). Overall gear ratios 3.78, 4.30, 5.85, 9.03, 15.77, reverse 15.16:1. 17.28 mph/1000 rpm in top gear

CHASSIS AND SUSPENSION Front engine, rear drive. Unit construction pressed-steel, body/chassis unit. Independent front suspension by coil springs, wishbones and anti-roll bar. Worm and sector steering. Independent rear suspension by coil springs, MacPherson struts, longitudinal and lateral links, anti-roll bar. 8.9 in. front disc brakes, 8.9 in. rear disc brakes. 185/70VR 13 in. radial ply tyres on 5.5 in. wheel rims. Bolt-on cast-alloy road wheels
BODYWORK Pressed steel shell, in unit with 'chassis', but with fibreglass and light-alloy skin panels, and fibreglass hardtop, produced for Fiat by Pininfarina. Two-door, two-seater style. Length 12 ft 10 in.; width 5 ft 4.2 in.; height 4 ft 0.8 in. Wheelbase 7 ft 5.8 in.; front track 4 ft 7.5 in.; rear track 4 ft 7.1 in. Unladen weight 2070 lb
PERFORMANCE SUMMARY (Factory claim) Maximum speed 118 mph, 30 mpg (Imperial). No other details

2 Ferrari and Fiat co-operation
Engines, assembly lines, technology

Ferrari's links with Fiat go back a long way—much further, if you understand my meaning, than Fiat's links with Ferrari. Enzo Ferrari himself, in company with a million other young Italians, was looking for a job at the end of World War 2, and applied to Fiat, who could not help him.

By the mid-1920s, Ferrari was a successful racing driver for Alfa Romeo, and in 1923 he effectively 'raided' Fiat, first by persuading his friend Luigi Bazzi to join Alfa Romeo in Milan, and then by urging the distinguished designer Vittorio Jano to join him. Fiat's reaction to this is not recorded. . . .

Ferrari eventually rose to run quasi-works racing teams for Alfa Romeo, under the banner of Scuderia Ferrari, but before the end of the 1930s Alfa took over the running of their teams again and, following a row with the company's new chief engineer (Wilfredo Ricart), Ferrari left to start up again on his own.

The very first 'Ferrari'—which was only ever known as an '815'—was a 1500 cc sports-racing two-seater based largely on Fiat components, and was completed in 1940, for use in the Brescia-Mantua-Verona Mille Miglia race. This was the first (and, until 1967, the last time) that Ferrari was to use Fiat-made parts in his cars.

There was no further Fiat connection for many years, although Ferrari concluded a sensational deal with Lancia in 1955, whereby he took over their D50 Grand Prix cars, the parts, and all the designs, when that other Turin-based company withdrew from Grand Prix racing.

In Chapter 7 I have already detailed the way in which Ferrari finally got back into business with Fiat, through the Dino engine production deal, and I have also mentioned the way in which Fiat came to acquire a half of Ferrari's production business. To round it all off, however, I should bring matters up to date.

When Fiat took 50 per cent of the share-capital of SEFC-Ferrari in June 1969, they confirmed that Enzo Ferrari would stay on as chairman, and they also confirmed that they would not interfere with the Maranello company's racing activities. This was an arrangement which was ideal for Ferrari, in that it gave the firm access to large quantities of capital, if necessary, and it also underpinned their racing future by making large budgets possible, and by opening up the vast store of Fiat technological expertise for Ferrari research.

Apart from the fact that Ferrari's assembly buildings were expanded and, for a time, the Fiat Dino cars were assembled at Maranello rather than in Turin, the Fiat involvement had little obvious effect on the running of Ferrari. On reflection, however, it might not have been possible for Ferrari, on its own, to entertain the thought of introducing new flat-12 (Boxer) and vee-8 (308 GTB-type) engines in the same year, and building them in considerable quantities, without a great deal of cash to back the schemes, and in these economy-conscious years is it not likely that an independent Ferrari might have suffered, if not as terminally, in the same way that Maserati, Lamborghini and Iso all did during the 1970s?

I should also make it clear, if it has not already been spelt out properly in Chapter 9, that the Fiat 130 engine was *not* a Ferrari-designed engine, nor was it a direct descendant of the smaller Dino unit. However, even in this case it is quite easy to spot the Maranello connection, for the large Type 130 engine was laid down in Turin by Aurelio Lampredi, who had been back at Fiat for some years, after a fruitful and famous period at Ferrari in the 1940s and 1950s when several famous Ferrari engines *including* the original 65-degree vee-6 Dino unit, had been conceived. Lampredi, in fact, left Ferrari before the Dino engine actually ran for the first time, and has been a well-respected member of Fiat's design staff ever since. The fact that he, or his department, were also responsible for engines like the twin-overhead-camshaft units used in the 124 Sport Coupés and

Ferrari and Fiat co-operation

Spiders, and the single-overhead-cam units used in the front-drive 128 Sport Coupés, and the mid-engined X1/9s, really means that there is a little bit of Ferrari in almost every modern Fiat.

By the end of the 1970s, the Fiat-Ferrari situation had moved forward one stage further. In 1977 Enzo Ferrari himself resigned as chairman of the company which builds the cars, though he still retained absolute control over the SEFAC (racing) side of the operation. From this moment, therefore, the design and production of Ferrari road cars became a complete Fiat responsibility. Perhaps, one day, we will see this as the event which signalled the birth of a whole new generation of road-going Ferraris, more closely linked with the Fiat company which own them. Perhaps. Who knows?

Fiat took courage in late 1976 and decided that it was about time they labelled the Ferrari Grand Prix cars with their own decal. This is Carlos Reutemann's 312 T2 in the 1977 Argentine GP, one of, if not the first time, the decal appeared

3 Lancia in the 1970s
Monte Carlo, Beta Coupé and HPE—all powered by Fiat

Three famous Italian car-making concerns survived World War 2, and expanded mightily in the years which followed—Fiat, Alfa Romeo and Lancia. For Fiat, whose resources were enormous, expansion was easy enough to arrange. For Alfa Romeo, which had become a state-owned concern (through the Istituto Ricostruzione Industriale, IRI) in 1933, finance was no problem, for expansion was a matter of national policy. For Lancia, it was all very different.

Lancia had come into existence in 1906, founded by Vincenzo Lancia, who had once been chief inspector at Fiat, after an apprenticeship at Ceirano. Between the wars, the Lancia concern which, like Fiat, was based in Turin, built a series of splendid machines in limited numbers, of which the most famous were probably the Lambda and the Aprilia. In postwar years the first successful new model was the Ardea, then the Aurelia and, soon, the Appia. Such projects, allied to an ambitious competitions programme culminating in the D50 Grand Prix cars of 1954, eventually led Gianni Lancia to sell out to Carlo Pesenti, a cement and financial tycoon.

During the 1960s, Lancia, controlled by Pesenti, grew larger and larger, introducing new multi-derivative models like the Flaminias, Flavias, and Fulvias, each with its own type of unique engine and (in some cases) transmission and suspension components. In general, the press and public admired the idiosyncracies of the cars' design, and equipment, but it was sad to note that the company was not selling enough of these machines, and was not profitable. By 1968 Lancia's financial situation was becoming somewhat desperate, and it was generally assumed that they would either have to close down their business, or offer themselves for takeover by a larger business.

The end came quickly. Immediately before the opening of the Turin Motor Show, at the end of October 1969, Fiat held a large press conference where Giovanni Agnelli announced that he was taking Lancia into the fold. There was little surprise at this news—but there was astonishment at the financial terms which had been agreed. Fiat contracted to pay a mere one lira per share for Lancia (which meant that the entire million-share company was valued at a mere £670, or $1608!), but they then sugared the pill by also guaranteeing to become responsible for all of Lancia's existing debts and liabilities, which totalled a massive £67 millions ($161 millions).

In his statement, Giovanni Agnelli gave assurances that Lancia would continue as a small specialist concern (small, that is, by Fiat's gargantuan standards), but that he thought that annual production would eventually have to be raised from 40,000 to 100,000 vehicles a year. He also hinted that there were no new Lancia cars in preparation (the company, after all, had been without a technical director for more than a year), and that the company's revival could only be assured by an all-new, and flourishing, model.

The problem at Lancia was that, by 1969, major financial problems had put paid to all schemes demanding a lot of capital investment. The new-model cupboard was bare. For the next three years, therefore, there was little obvious effect at Lancia, of new ownership by Fiat, except that the existing

ABOVE *When the press were shown this car, it was the Abarth 030 prototype, and was assumed to be a future 'big brother' for the Fiat X1/9. How wrong we were even though the styling was by Pininfarina, and the car was built by Abarth in 1974, it would eventually be badged as a Lancia*

RIGHT *The prototype Abarth 030, from which the future Lancia Monte Carlo was evolved, had a 3.5-litre much-modified Fiat 130 vee-6 engine behind the driver, and was entered in the Giro d'Italia for Georgio Pianta to drive in 1974*

Lancia in the 1970s

Fiat Sports Cars

The 030 prototype, with the modified Type 130 vee-6 engine almost buried, and well forward in the chassis. The bottom of the unmistakeable snorkel cold-air inlet is also obvious

ranges of cars, the Fulvias and Flavias, were updated, and that car assembly began to be concentrated on the newest Lancia factory at Chivasso, to the north-east of Turin.

At this point I should also mention that Fiat had already signed an arms-length agreement with Citroën of France in 1968, which was to involve the two technical teams rather more closely on future products, and to allow common components to be developed. (This was, incidentally, rather a short-lived initiative, complicated by the fact that Citroën was owned by the Michelin tyre organisation, and obstructed from time to time by a French government acting in their usual nationalistic way. It was finally unscrambled in 1973, when Fiat got their investment back, and were left with the rather untangible fruits of the exercise. That doyen of the French motoring press, Edouard Seidler, later commented that 'for five years, Fiat had been no more than Citroën's bankers'.)

However, one of the very first joint projects to be studied by Fiat and Citroën was a new type of medium-sized saloon car range for the 1970s. Citroën's current offering was the DS range, with front-wheel-drive, an in-line engine installation, great length *and* great complication, while Fiat's was the strictly conventional Fiat 125 model, complete with front engine, rear drive, and live axle rear suspension.

Both firms agreed that such a new car should have front-wheel-drive, and a transversely mounted engine, allied to wedge-nosed, fastback styling. They were not able to agree on a common design, for Citroën wanted to keep their own engine, and their own complex hydro-pneumatic suspension, while Fiat wanted to keep their own twin-cam engine (which, privately, they thought to be much superior to that of the DS Citroën), and have rather more simple suspension and structural arrangements.

They were, however, able to agree on the need for a new front-wheel-drive transmission. The same basic design of all-indirect, two-shaft, all-synchromesh gearbox, complete with a spur-gear final drive, was to be detailed by Citroën, and was to be supplied in five-speed form to Fiat, and in four-speed form to Citroën.

Perhaps this explains why Fiat were able to bring forward a major new model at Lancia so quickly (a mere three years after the merger had been agreed), for work on what became the Lancia Beta had already begun. It also explains the apparent but obvious coincidence that there are definite similarities in the general layout of the new Lancia Beta of 1972 and the Citroën CX of 1974.

Even so, the arrival of the Lancia Beta, in November 1972, caused something of a stir, for it was only three years since the Fiat takeover of Lancia had been announced. Normally it takes at

Lancia in the 1970s

least four years to produce an all-new model, to get it through from the concept stage to being in series production. Although the new car was badged as Lancia, and bore some signs of Lancia design influence, it was demonstrably influenced by Fiat, and used a Fiat engine. Its layout was to influence the sporting Lancias of the 1970s, and these cars were, to all intents and purposes, 'badge-engineered' Fiats.

The Beta, which took its model name from the Greek alphabet, and repeated the name of second early-production Lancia (of 1909), was a four-door saloon, although its fastback styling suggested that it ought really to be a five-door hatchback. Under its newly-fashionable wedge-nose styling there was all-independent suspension by coil springs, MacPherson struts, and wishbones, along with rack and pinion steering, but the main technical interest was in the arrangement of the engine/transmission assembly.

Like so many new models of the early 1970s the Beta had its engine mounted transversely, just ahead of the line of the front wheels, and drove those wheels through an all-indirect, all-synchromesh five-speed gearbox and helical spur final drive gear. At first there were to be three different sizes of engine—1438 cc, 1592 cc and 1756 cc—all being specially developed versions of the Fiat twin-cam unit, which was itself descended from the conventional overhead valve unit first found in the Fiat 124 of 1966. By using these engines, therefore, Fiat established direct links between the new Betas and the 124/125/132 Fiat models of recent years.

As installed in the Beta, however, the Fiat engine was considerably modified. Not only were the camshaft profiles new, and various castings modified, but the entire engine was inclined towards the rear of the car at an angle of 20 degrees. Belt

The Lancia Monte Carlo, as revealed in March 1975, still with solid sail panels at the rear quarters, and those smart wheels. Pininfarina were proud of their work which originally had carried a Fiat project number, and was once dubbed the 'X1/20' when still in secret prototype guise. The transverse engine and transmission, behind the seats, was from the front-drive Lancia Beta saloon. This is a British market version in 1977

Fiat Sports Cars

drive was, however, retained to drive the twin overhead camshafts, and carburation was of course by a downdraught twin-choke Weber, mounted ahead of the transverse unit, in the nose of the car, and close to the water radiator. That the engines were similar to, but not identical with, the Fiat 124 Spider/Coupé units is shown by a study of peak output figures:

Lancia Beta 1800	110 bhp (DIN) at 6000 rpm
	106 lb ft torque at 3000 rpm
Fiat 124 Coupé/Spider	118 bhp (DIN) at 6000 rpm
	113 lb ft torque at 4000 rpm
Fiat 132 saloon	105 bhp (DIN) at 6000 rpm
	104 lb ft torque at 4200 rpm

—production of engines, however, took place at the main Fiat Mirafiori plant in Turin, but final assembly of Betas took place at the modern Lancia factory of Chivasso.

The five-speed gearbox, too, was all-new, and was mounted in line with the crankshaft of the engine. Looked at from above, therefore, the twin-cam engine was mounted over to the right hand side of the engine bay (to the kerb side in Italy and North America, towards the middle of the road in right-hand-drive countries like Great Britain), while the gearbox itself was mounted over to the left side of the bay. As the box was a two-shaft all-indirect layout, it was possible to arrange for the final drive assembly to be behind the gearbox, as installed in the car, but still in the same overall light-alloy casting which housed the gearbox, and the clutch itself. A central floor gear change lever was provided, with remote actuation via an idler lever mounted on the engine/transmission subframe.

Production of Beta saloons was already under way, at the rate of 350 cars a day, when the new

RIGHT *Two versions of the production-type Monte Carlo, now with glass in the quarter 'sail' panels. One car has the steel roof in place, one has the roll-back feature displayed*

BELOW *The stylish interior of the Lancia Monte Carlo of 1975, with the seats hard back against the engine bulkhead, or firewall, and with nicely laid out facia and controls. The roof panel could be removed on some versions*

model was announced at the end of 1972. However, in spite of the modern layout, and the spirited performance of the 1.8-litre version, the Beta saloon could certainly not be called sporting. Its importance in the scheme of things, however, was that it formed the very important foundation to a complete range of cars which included three major derivatives—the Beta Coupé and Spider, the HPE, and Monte Carlo, of which the one most closely linked with Fiat was the Monte Carlo.

My coverage of the other derivatives, therefore, will be brief. The first of these derivatives to appear was the Beta Coupé, in June 1973 (the open-top spider version followed rather later), which was a factory-styled 2+2 model, built on a shortened wheelbase, floorpan, and running gear of the Beta saloon itself; the saloon's wheelbase was 254 cm/100 in., while that of the Coupé was 235 cm/92.5 in. The Spider, in fact, was styled by Pininfarina, following the lines of the factory coupé, but was actually built up by Zagato in Milan.

The HPE was—as its initials suggest—really a High Performance Estate hatchback in three-door form. The cocktail of mechanical equipment, dimensions, and layouts was stirred up even further, for the HPE used the standard-length Beta saloon wheelbase, underpan and running gear, allied to the frontal styling, and doors of the Beta Coupé, but an entirely new fastback/hatchback bodystyle which combined a four-seater layout with a large load-carrying capability. It made its debut at the Geneva Show in March 1975, and has been part of the Lancia line-up ever since.

The Monte Carlo was entirely different. Its roots go back to Fiat, the early 1970s, and to the mid-engined X1/9 sports car. Fiat had no modern medium-sized model to replace the 124 Spider at first, but as soon as they saw the enthusiastic public reaction to the elegant and nimble Bertone-styled X1/9 they decided to repeat the exercise on the basis of a larger-engined car. Whereas the X1/9 was a mid-engined car based on the engine/transmission assembly of the 128 saloon, the new Fiat project, coded X1/20, was to be designed around the latest Beta engine and transmission, which is to say that a Fiat engine and a new Lancia transmission was to be used. There is no doubt that it was intended to be a Fiat when first conceived, as its alternative project code was 'Fiat 137' (following on the famous sequence which, as every Fiat enthusiast knows, includes 124, 128, 131, and 132), and because its production engine and chassis numbers carry Fiat, rather than Lancia, designations, on the production cars.

The X1/20's styling, and the construction of the bodyshell, was entrusted to Pininfarina. This legendary styling house had retained links with Fiat for many years, but it had gradually taken on more

Fiat Sports Cars

LEFT *Monte Carlo road cars might have been a touch lacking in performance, but no-one ever complained about the turbocharged Martini-sponsored racing cars. This vividly liveried example is being checked out in the Pininfarina wind tunnel in Turin*

RIGHT *For 1982, Fiat-Lancia further developed the Monte Carlo theme for a new Group B rally car. This was the Lancia Rallye, here seen in road car form. Front and rear panels are in fibreglass.*

and more series-production manufacturing facilities, and was now able to tackle the building of a complete, pressed-steel, unit-construction body/chassis unit of its own.

In the beginning, however, the X1/20 (as leaked to the press) was looked on as something of an enlarged X1/9, which was always really a fallacy, since the wheelbase was 4.1 in. longer, the tracks three to four inches wider, and construction by Pininfarina instead of Bertone! In philosophy, for sure, in general layout (transverse mid-engine, all MacPherson strut suspension, demountable roof panel, mid-mounted fuel tank, and general lines) and in 'image', the two cars were similar, but in detail they were very different indeed.

Perhaps the X1/20 could, one day, have replaced one of the sporting 124s, if it had kept its Fiat badges, or perhaps it could have had the magic (in Italy) name of 'Abarth' in its title. Certainly, in the early days, it was a Fiat project, for production in a Fiat factory. Only at a very late stage did it take on Lancia badging and a Lancia identity.

The public got its first sneak previews of the new car in the spring of 1973, when sketches published in the Italian motoring press showed an early rendering of a new mid-engined car, tentatively identified as a Fiat 132 X20, though the choice of Pininfarina as stylists was correctly identified. Things then went very quiet for a time (as I have already pointed out, there was something of a hiatus in Fiat new-model launches for a time after the onset of the Suez crisis and the oil price shortages which followed), but the X1/20 project surfaced again in the autumn of 1974 when Abarth let it be known that they were developing a competitions successor to the 124 Abarth Rallye, and that the X1/20 could be it. For the Giro d'Italia (Tour of Italy) rally-cum-race of October 1974, they were preparing an X1/20 fitted with a race-tuned 3.5-litre Fiat 130 vee-6 engine!

Thus equipped, and dubbed the Abarth-Pininfarina SE 030 for the occasion, the X1/20 took a remarkable second place overall in Giro d'Italia, where (driven by Fiat's competitions test driver Giorgio Pianta, and co-driven by Christine Beckers) it was only beaten by the turbocharged Ferrari-engined Lancia Stratos of Jean-Claude Andruet and his lady co-driver 'Biche'.

This Abarth-prepared car, however, was a real red herring as far as genealogy and the future production car was concerned, for not only did it carry an Abarth badge, and a big 'horn' air intake above the engine bay, but its vee-6 engine was mounted longitudinally behind the seats, rather than transversely. Abarth's further complication, at the time, was that they had also shoe-horned a four-valves-per-cylinder Beta engine and transmission into an X1/9 for development purposes—yet another hybrid to confuse the issue, and to keep Italian enthusiasts happy.

All this was thoroughly confusing, and most Fiat/Lancia enthusiasts were amazed to see the X1/20 revealed at the 1975 Geneva Motor Show, in March—as a Lancia! The name 'Monte Carlo' had been chosen because of Lancia's recent successes in the world-famous rally of that name (Sandro Munari had won the event in a Fulvia Coupé HF in 1972, and in a mid-engined Stratos in 1975), but Lancia were soon to run into trouble with that name in North America, where the bulk of production was aimed. In those markets, General Motors already held the 'Monte Carlo' trademark, and so the new Lancia had to be renamed 'Scorpion' (using the Abarth trademark) instead.

The Monte Carlo revealed at Geneva (ex-Fiat 137, ex-Fiat X1/20, ex-Abarth model as shown at Turin in November 1974...) was seen to be very similar in general layout to the smaller X1/9, except of course that it was entirely styled, and the monocoques built by the Pininfarina factory. Like the X1/9, the Monte Carlo had a pressed and fabricated steel body/chassis monocoque, a wedge-style nose, and a short and stubby tail. Unlike the X1/9, the roof panel could not be removed altogether, but one version had a clever flexible fold-back top panel which achieved much the same sort of effect. To meet current (and threatened) North American safety legislation, the Monte Carlo could not have a completely convertible body style, and this 'opening-top' variety was the nearest equivalent which could be supplied. Even with the top folded back, there was still impressive strength in the windscreen pillars, the roll-over hoop behind the seats, and in the rails above the door openings. Unlike the X1/9, however, the Monte Carlo had headlamps of roughly rectangular shape permanently on view, and it also had permanent 'flying buttresses' down the rear quarters, linking the roll hoop with the corners of the car.

In spite of its larger engine/transmission pack, the Monte Carlo was almost exactly the same length as the X1/9—12 ft 6 in.—though it was a full five inches wider, with wider wheel tracks and larger wheels. Suspension was all-independent, by coil springs and MacPherson struts (with very similar geometry and details to the X1/9 in both cases), and there was rack and pinion steering. As with the X1/9, the Monte Carlo used a complete saloon car engine/transmission pack, mounted behind the two seats. In fact it was the front-wheel-drive transverse-engine installation of the Beta saloon, mounted ahead of the line of the rear wheels, with the normal alignment of drive shafts driving the rear wheels of the Monte Carlo, rather than the front wheels of a Beta saloon. For the Monte Carlo installation, the engine was a new long-stroke 1995 cc version of the well-known Fiat twin-cam unit; this, in fact, was the first Fiat/Lancia model of all to be put on sale with the 2.0-litre engine, though it spread rapidly throughout the corporation in the next year or so. Naturally this was not only powerful, but it was very torquey as well. In European-tune, the maximum power output was 120 bhp (DIN) at 6000 rpm, and peak torque was 121 lb ft at 3500 rpm.

Apart from the use of a lowered first gear ratio, and a slightly raised final drive ratio (3.71:1 instead of 3.929:1 for the 1.8-litre Beta), the five-speed transmission was the same as that used in Betas,

169

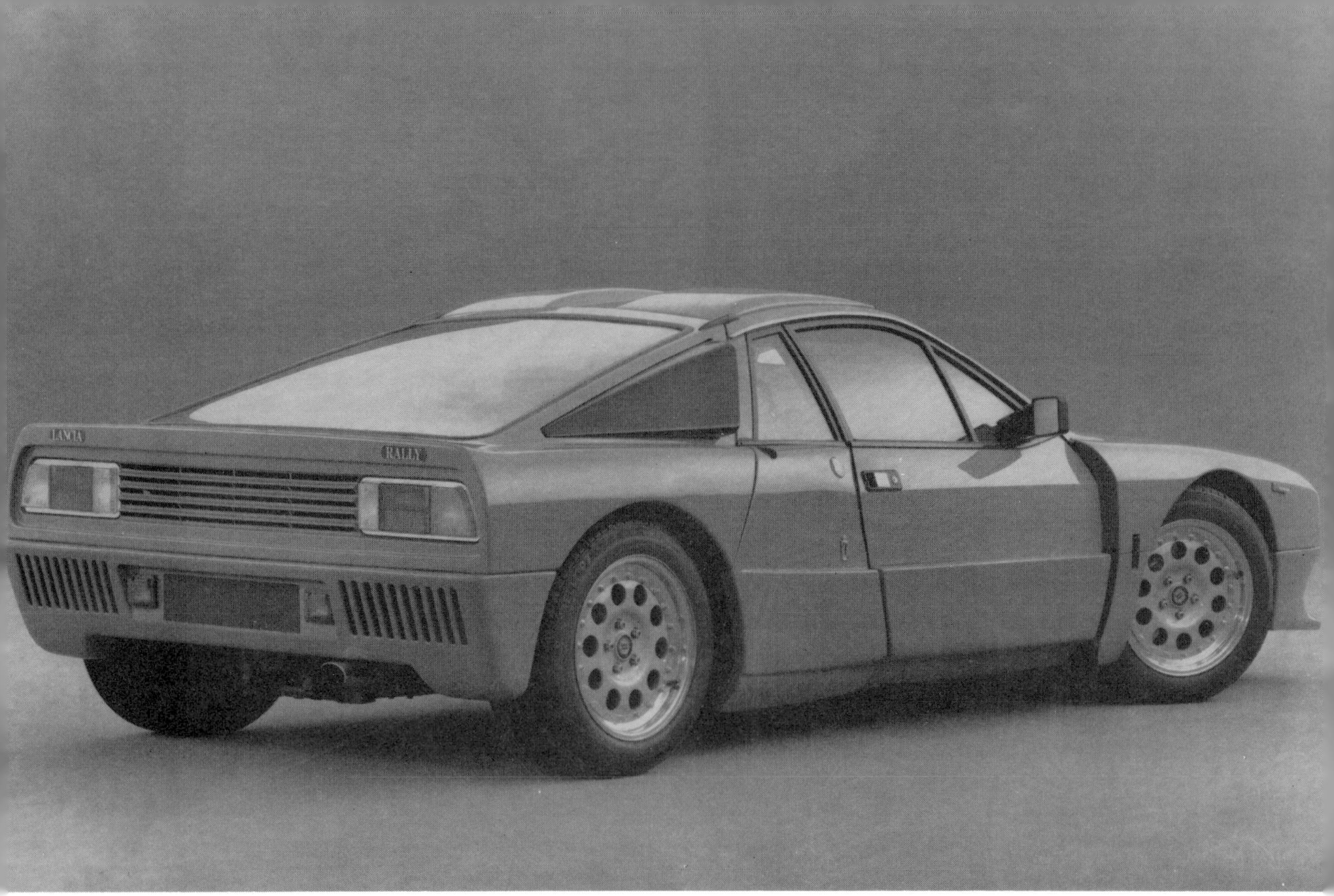
LANCIA
RALLY

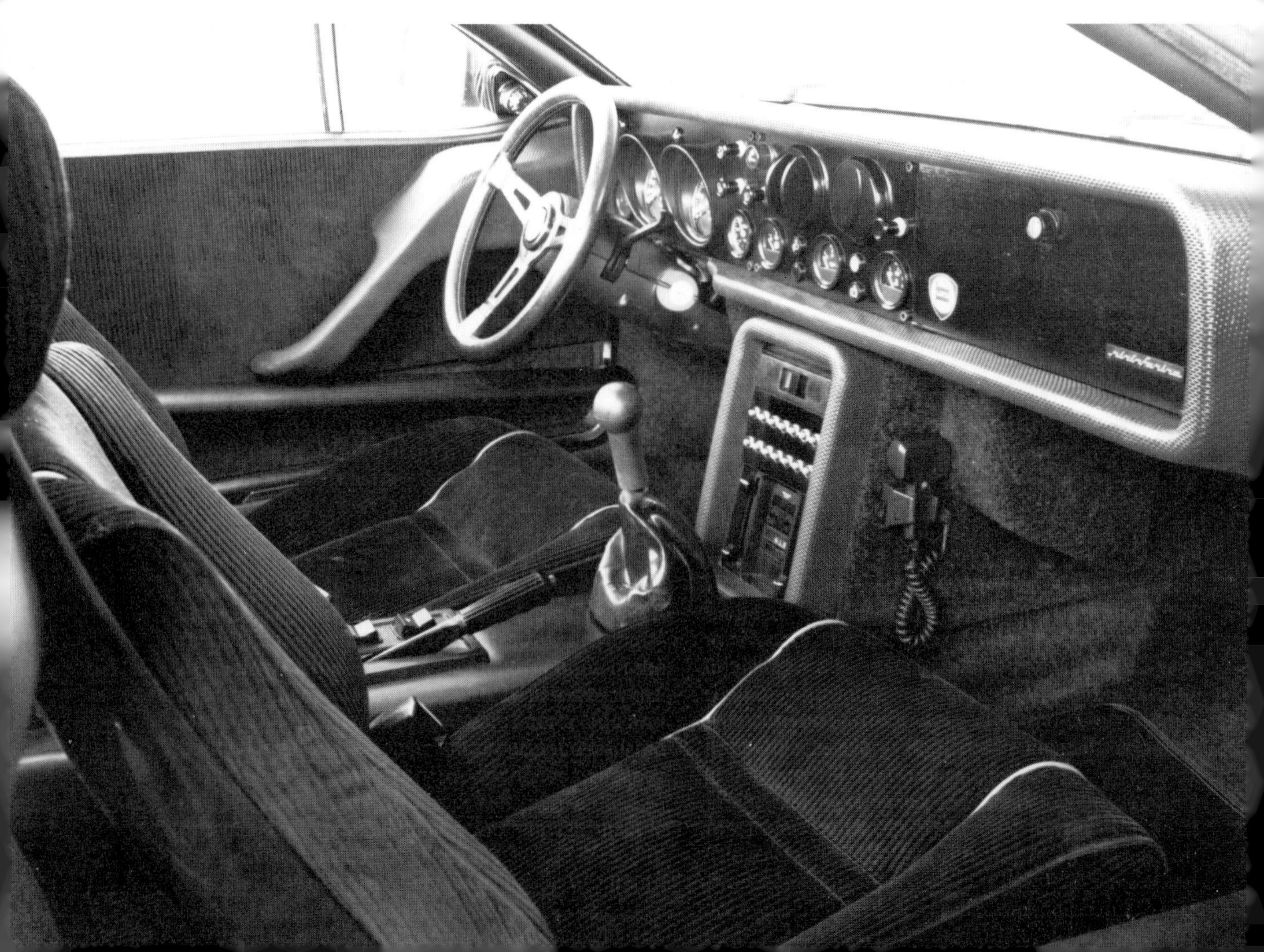

though a modified gear change linkage had to be provided. 13 in. instead of 14 in. wheels were used, to keep the car as squat as possible, though tyre sections were widened a little to help the roadholding; servo-assisted Beta-sized four-wheel disc brakes were standardized.

It had not been easy to optimize the front/rear weight distribution of this 2315 lb car, but early road tests showed that there was 41 per cent of that weight over the front wheels, and 59 per cent over the rear; this rather tail-heavy characteristic was to lead to problems when the car had to build up its reputation.

As with any two-seater mid-engined car, stowage space was at a premium, and in many ways the Monte Carlo was less efficiently laid out than its smaller relative, the X1/9. For the Monte Carlo there was only rather small (7 cu. ft) locker in the nose between the front wheels, but the tail was so short and stubby (and, in any case, filled with spare wheel) that nothing could be stowed behind the engine/transmission installation.

No matter. The Monte Carlo looked sensational—almost Ferrari-like—in European tune it was fast, and seemed to be everything that a proper sports car should be. Even fuel economy promised to be good, for early road test cars recorded over 25 mpg in day-in/day-out conditions. Lancia's problem, however, was that such cars were not likely to sell in large numbers. Like almost every other sporting car being built in Europe, for the new mid-engined Lancia to be profitable, it would *have* to sell well in the United States.

This, however, was where everything started to go wrong for Lancia. The minor irritation was that the car needed a new name, and the major problem was its performance. The 'Monte Carlo' name could not be used in North America, where Chevrolet, of all people, were already using that title on a singularly uninspiring five-seater monster; accordingly, Lancia decided to call the car 'Scorpion', which linked its ancestry back to the Abarth connection.

The major drawback was the Scorpion's lack of performance. To meet all current USA exhaust emission regulations, and to allow the engine to run on lead-free fuel, *and* to keep the expense of certification within bounds, Fiat-Lancia were obliged to rationalize, and to de-tune the engine severely. Whereas the European-style Monte Carlo had 1995 cc, 120 bhp, and 121 lb ft or torque, the Scorpion had to get by with a 1756 cc engine, a miserable 81 bhp, and 89 lb ft of torque. The smaller engine was chosen because it was the same as that used in other Betas, and it made the legislative burden somewhat less complex. In addition, the Scorpion had larger '5 mph' bumpers and other extra reinforcements, and was almost 100 lb heavier than the Monte Carlo.

The result, therefore, was that the Pininfarina-styled machine was really little more than a Los Angeles *poseur*'s car in North America. Although *Motor Trend*, testing the car in September 1976, called it: 'Almost, but not quite, superb'; *Road & Track*, who published their findings in the same month, pulled no punches at all; their test was merely headlined: 'So lovely, so agile, so ingenious, so slow.'

'The car tantailizes you with its looks, leading you to the cockpit and promising you an excellent drive down the first twisty road you can find. So you settle in, start up and head out only to find the Scorpion is slow, no faster than the Fiat and Lancia sedans that use the same engine.' *Road & Track* said: '... In its American form, it is merely a show piece, albeit the best such creature on the market today.... Yet, like Ulysses' Sirens it keeps drawing us back for one more ride, just as surely as it turns most every head on the freeway.'

This, incidentally, was the conclusion of a test of a car costing $11,027 (Porsche 924, Datsun 280Z or Chevrolet Corvette levels), with a 104 mph top speed, but with 0–60 mph acceleration of 13.4 seconds. However, *Road & Track* also complained of severe front brake locking, and fade in severe use, and they appeared to be distinctly disappointed by that high price tag, even allowing for the fact that the test car was loaded up with extras.

European performance—a 120 mph top speed, 0–60 mph in 9.8 sec and a standing start quarter mile in 16.0 sec were about typical—was much more acceptable, though customers were soon to be found complaining about the braking, and there were disturbing reports about low quality of finish, and an early onset of corrosion.

The net result was demand for Scorpions slumped badly in 1977, and broke no records in Europe either, such that production dropped way below the levels Lancia and Pininfarina had planned for in the early stages. In May 1978 Sergio

ABOVE *On road-going versions of the 200-off Lancia Rallye 'homologation special' there was no big rear spoiler. The visual similarity to the Fiat-designed Monte Carlo is obvious, though everything is different underneath*

LEFT *The facia of the road-going Lancia Rallye of 1982—rally cars were considerably more stark!*

Fiat Sports Cars

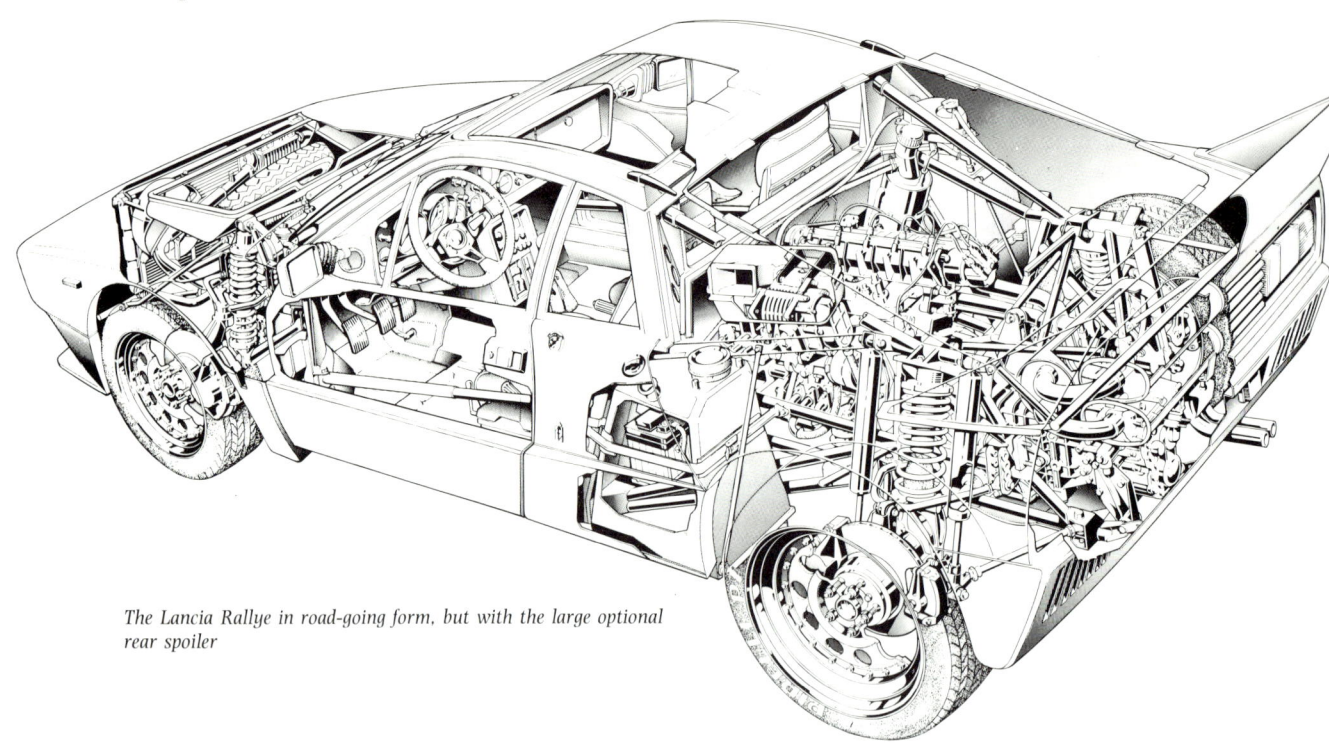

The Lancia Rallye in road-going form, but with the large optional rear spoiler

Pininfarina announced that Monte Carlo/Scorpion production 'had been suspended', while Lancia made reassuring noises and said that this was because his factories were completely occupied by the building of Gamma Coupés on their behalf. It was a transparent untruth, which fooled no-one, and many of us did not expect the car to be revived.

Happily, we were wrong, for the revised Monte Carlo, distinguished by the use of glass in the rear quarter 'sail panels', by the use of larger, 14 in., road wheels, the new Lancia 'corporate' front grille, and a redeveloped brake system, plus new instruments and fittings, made its comeback at the Geneva Show in March 1980. Unfortunately, however, no attempt was ever made to relaunch the car in North America, and as a result sales and production were well down on the heights of 1976. Cars were still being made in 1982 and 1983, but it may be that by the time this book is published, the Monte Carlo, like the Fiat X1/9, may be no more.

In the meantime, however, the inventive Cesare Fiorio, Lancia's competitions team chief, had been at it again. With a new set of rallying regulations to be introduced in 1982 (where the old Group 4, for 400-off cars, was to be replaced by Group B, for 200-off machines), and with Fiat-Lancia being as committed as ever to the sporting scene, a new car was needed. The Stratos was effectively dead (but would not lie down, in the hands of private owners), and the Fiat 131 Abarth saloon obsolete. So—what next?

When Abarth, who had been responsible for all of Fiat-Lancia's competitions activities since 1977, started work on a new car in the spring of 1980, they considered three approaches—the 'mid-engined' conversion of a front-wheel-drive car (Renault 5 Turbo-style) on the Fiat Ritmo, or the Lancia Delta, or the extensive modification of the Monte Carlo. After a great deal of discussion, where company politics played almost as important a part as technical considerations, the Monte Carlo was chosen for development.

Of course, Group 5 Monte Carlos, with turbo-charged engines, had been racing with success since 1978, and outside observers who did not know what Fiat-Lancia were up to thought that this radical solution would merely be productionized. But it wasn't—the end result was even more way out than that!

Design work began in the spring of 1980, and the very first prototype was ready at Christmas 1980. During 1981, and still working in great secrecy, a total of six cars were built. Although pictures of prototype road cars were officially 'leaked' by Lancia, there were no clues about the mechanical layout, until the new machine, quite simply called the Lancia Rallye, was unveiled in December 1981.

If the Monte Carlo had, at least, been a Fiat design which turned into a Lancia, the new car was something else again. It certainly wasn't a Fiat any more, and not really a Lancia. It would have been

172

Lancia in the 1970s

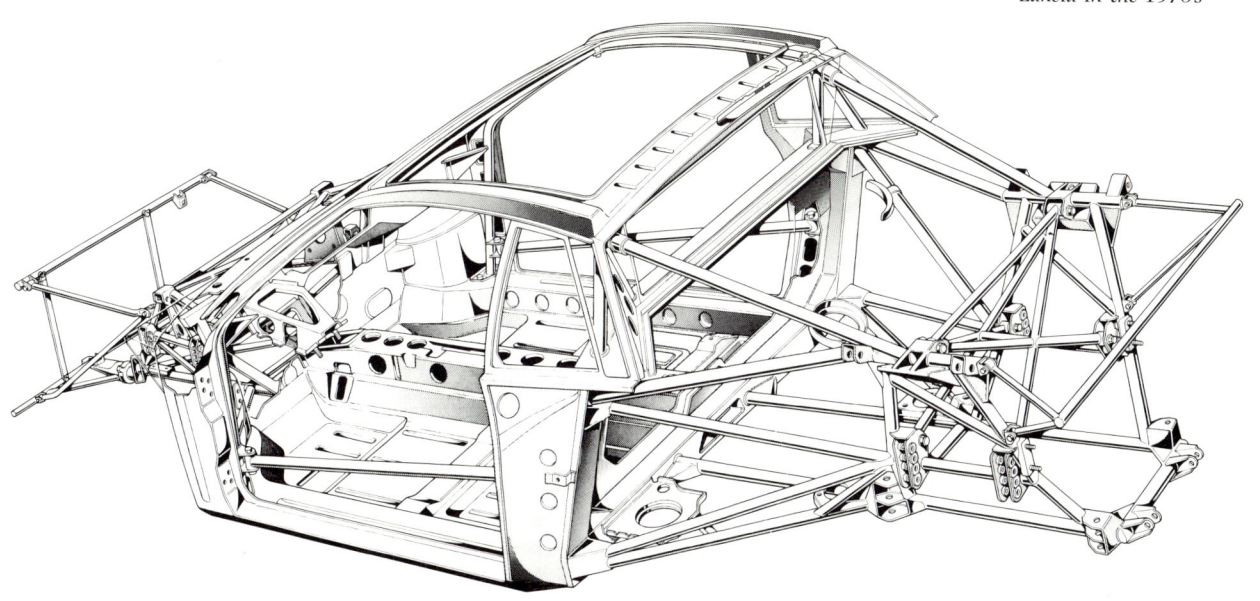

The basic structure of the 1982 Lancia Rallye is a far cry from that of the Fiat-designed Monte Carlo, of which only the basic shape, and the passenger cabin, really remains. In almost every way, the Rallye is a throw back to successful sports racing cars of the 1960s

more just if it had been named an Abarth, because it was that company, led by Ing. Sergio Limone, who had done all the design work.

Visually, at least, the new Rallye looked superficially like the Monte Carlo, which is to say that the same basic lines as that car were retained, but that was almost as far as the resemblance went. In particular, the structure was entirely different. The central section of the Monte Carlo's monocoque—the passenger compartment, comprising floor, roof rails, front and rear bulkheads—was retained, but the one-piece front and rear hinge-up body sections, and the doors themselves, were in thin fibreglass, the side windows were perspex, and there were no bumpers.

The layout under the skin was even more remarkable. Instead of the pressed steel front and rear sections of the Monte Carlo, which normally supported the suspension systems, and the engine/transmission power pack, there were multi-tube 'chassis' sub-frames bolting up to the central tub. Front *and* rear suspension was by double wishbones with coil spring/damper units at the front, separate coils at the rear, with anti-roll bars, and almost every setting—caster, camber, toe-in, toe-out, and ride heights—was adjustable. In short, this was a racing sports car in the 1960s pre-monocoque tradition.

However, the engine/transmission layout was also completely different. The Monte Carlo's transversely positioned installation had been abandoned, and in its place the 1995 cc Fiat engine was mounted in a fore-and-aft position, driving a proprietary ZF five-speed and transaxle. The engine, naturally, was of the 131 Abarth/16-valve twin-cam variety, but for the rally it was supercharged—not turbocharged, mind you, but supercharged, in the age-old tradition. When questioned at a later date, Cesare Fiorio confirmed that Fiat-Lancia had plumped for supercharging for this car (and for the Trevi Volumex production saloon) because of the more instant response it offered from low speeds, though he also admitted that the ultimate power and torque potential might not be as high as that of a turbocharged unit. (Paradoxically, the Group 6 racing car unveiled at the same press conference was seen to use a turbocharged 1.4-litre derivative of the same basic engine.)

When we first saw the car, it was in rally tuned form, complete with large tail spoiler, a denuded interior, and two large dual-choke Weber carburettors, but we were assured that the road car would appear in a matter of weeks, and that the necessary 200 cars would be built by the end of March 1982. Even the most generously-disposed among us smiled kindly at that boast, and put it down to Latin optimism.

But it was, in fact, achieved. Ten cars, all prototypes, had been built before the car was shown, and series production of the multi-tubular frames,

173

Fiat Sports Cars

and glass-fibre sections, had been started in September 1981. Abarth constructed the tubular frames, Lancia contracted Pininfarina to assemble the special frame/monocoque assemblies, and to provide fibreglass body sections, and the cars were all built in a batch, at one of the Lancia factories in Turin, before the end of March 1982. FISA inspection was made before the end of the month, and the car was duly homologated into Group B on 1 April. In road car form, the Rallye had 205 bhp at 7000 rpm, peak torque of 166 lb ft at 5000 rpm, and weighed 2580 lb. Top speed, it was claimed, was 137 mph.

'Works' cars started the Costa Smeralda Rally literally on the day of homologation, 1 April 1982, but no success was achieved in the first few events. Indeed, there were several disturbing accidents, including one in which Attilio Bettega was badly injured when his car hit a stout stone wall, and concertina'd around him, and another where a driver came out of his seat belts in a high speed roll, and literally was punched out through the lightweight roof of the machine.

Success, however, followed before the end of 1982. The first cars had only boasted 255 bhp in rally trim, and were not fast enough, but the 'evolution cars' allowed under Group B were more competitive, with Markku Alen's 1000 Lakes car having fuel injection and about 305 bhp, though 290 bhp was more normal in events which followed that. The car led the San Remo rally for a time, then won its first national event, the British Pace rally in October 1982. Lancia sent just one car over to tackle the Lombard-RAC Rally, where Markku Alen finished third, a splendid result in a really gruelling rally, for he was only beaten by the two invincible factory-built four-wheel-drive Audi Quattros.

For 1983, notonly was a full World Championship programme promised, but Markku Alen was joined for the season by twice World Champion Walter Rohrl, and by Attilio Bettega, who made a remarkable recovery from his injuries. In spite of the massive and expensive attack mounted by Audi, with their four-wheel-drive Quattros, Lancia beat them on several occasions, and clinched the series well before the end of the year.

ABOVE *On the Monte Carlo the engine/transmission was transversely mounted, but on the Lancia Rallye of 1982 the engine was fore-aft, and the gearbox behind the line of the rear wheels. Power was boosted by supercharging, not by the more fashionable turbocharging of the early 1980s*

LEFT *In December 1981, Lancia showed off the Lancia Rallye Abarth Martini, as their 1982 contender for Group B rally honours. Before the development team got at it, it looked very smart in its white, red and blue livery*

There were outright wins for Lancia on the Monte Carlo (for Rohrl), Tour de Corse (Alen), Acropolis (Rohrl), Sanyo New Zealand (Rohrl), and Sanremo (Alen), with many other near-misses, including third in Portugal (Rohrl), fifth in Argentina (Alen), and third in the 1000 Lakes (Alen). The only real controversy throughout the season was that the team opted not to enter for the Lombard-RAC Rally, the last of the World Championship season, on the grounds that since they had already won the Championship (and vastly overspent their budget!), there was no point in turning up.

Even so, for 1984 Fiorio and Lancia did not intend to rest on their laurels, for they were hoping to win the rallying World Championship for the sixth time. Although Rohrl had left the team again, Bettega was expected to play a bigger part, and Henri Toivonen also joined the team for several events.

For 1984 the Rallye became the 'E2' evolution type, 20 new cars having to be built for this specification to be approved. Visually the car was seen to have an even sharper tail cut-off than before, though the basic Monte Carlo centre section and the multi-tubular frames were not changed. The Fiat-Abarth 16-valve engine was modified, however, with a longer (95.25 mm) stroke, and a capacity of 2111 cc, and the claimed power had risen to 325 bhp.

By this time, of course, there was very little 'Fiat' left in the Lancia Rallye, but in the end the successes, and benefits, of such specialized cars will surely rub off on future Fiat designs. If, that is, Fiat ever get back into the sports car business themselves.

Lancia Monte Carlo (Scorpion in US market)

PRODUCED March 1975 to 1978, 1980 to date
NUMBER BUILT Still in production
GENERAL LAYOUT Mid-engined two-seater fixed-head coupé, with unit-construction pressed-steel body/chassis unit. Four-cylinder engine, transversely mounted behind seats, in unit with transmission and final drive. All-independent suspension. Roll-back roof panel
ENGINE Basically that of 124 Sport Coupé/Spider models, and used in many other 124/131 and 132 saloons. Four-cylinder in-line layout, with cast-iron cylinder block, and light-alloy cylinder head. Five crankshaft main bearings. Two valves per cylinder, opposed in part-spherical combustion chamber, operated by twin overhead camshafts, driven by cogged belt from nose of crankshaft. Bore, stroke and capacity 84 × 90 mm, 1995 cc (3.31 × 3.54 in., 121.8 cu. in.). CR 8.9:1. One downdraught dual-choke Weber carburettor. Maximum power 120 bhp (DIN) at 6000 rpm. Peak torque 121 lb ft at 3500 rpm
TRANSMISSION In unit with transversely-mounted engine, and final drive. Final drive ratio 3.71:1. Overall gear ratios 3.43, 4.27, 5.65, 8.29, 13.91, reverse 11.39:1. Synchromesh on all forward gears. 19.5 mph/1000 rpm in top gear
CHASSIS AND SUSPENSION Transverse mid-engine, rear drive. Unit construction, pressed steel, body/chassis unit. Independent front suspension by coil springs, MacPherson struts and anti-roll bar. Rack and pinion steering. Independent rear suspension by coil springs, lower wishbones, MacPherson struts and anti-roll bar.

175

Fiat Sports Cars

The Lancia Rallye made its first competition appearance in the Costa Smeralda Rally of April 1982, with Markku Alen driving. It failed then, but started winning events before the end of the season

8.9 in. front dis brakes, and 8.9 in.rear disc brakes, with vacuum servo assistance. 185/70HR 13 in. radial ply tyres on 5.5 in. wide rims. 185/65HR 14 in. from 1980 relaunch. Bolt-on cast-alloy road wheels
BODYWORK Pressed-steel shell, in unit with 'chassis', produced by Pininfarina for Fiat-Lancia. Two-door, two-seater fastback coupé style, with roll-back roof panel. Length 12 ft 6.1 in.; width 5 ft 6.8 in.; height 3 ft 10.6 in. Wheelbase 7 ft 6.6 in.; front track 4 ft 7.6 in.; rear track 4 ft 9.6 in. Unladen weight 2290 lb.
PERFORMANCE SUMMARY (*Autocar*, 1 November 1975) Maximum speed 119 mph, 0–60 mph 9.8 sec., standing start ¼-mile 16.0 sec., overall fuel consumption 25.2 mpg (Imperial)
NOTE In US markets, the car was called a Scorpion, and built with the following important mechanical differences:
ENGINE 84 × 79.2 mm, 1756 cc (3.31 × 3.12 in., 107.1 cu. in.). CR 8.0:1. Maximum power 82 bhp (DIN) at 5900 rpm. Peak torque 89 lb ft at 3200 rpm
PERFORMANCE SUMMARY (*Road & Track*, September 1976) Maximum speed 104 mph, 0–60 mph 13.4 sec., standing start ¼-mile 19.1 sec., overall fuel consumption 23.4 mpg (Imperial)

4 Stratos

Lancia design, Bertone construction, Fiat money. Corporate glory

I include an appreciation of the fabulous Lancia Stratos in these pages for one very simple reason—it could not possibly have been built without Fiat's support, and money. Even though the Stratos was badged as a Lancia, and powered by an engine previously fitted to the Ferrari Dino, such a project could never have evolved a few years earlier.

Strictly speaking, the Lancia Stratos was born early in 1971, when Lancia's competitions chief, Cesare Fiorio, began to formulate his plans for a new rally car for the mid-1970s, but its origins are to be found somewhat earlier, in events precipitated by Fiat. Three things directly influenced the Stratos concept—the partial takeover of Ferrari by Fiat in June 1969, the rescue of Lancia from oblivion, also by Fiat, in October 1969, and the sensational exhibition of the Lancia-engined Bertone 'Stratos' at the Turin Motor Show in the autumn of 1970.

As already recounted, Fiat had rescued Lancia towards the end of 1969, by taking them over and honouring all their debts, and instantly set about making changes for the 1970s. They perceived that one of the 'old' Lancia's strong marketing points was its successful competitions image, so Cesare Fiorio and his talented team of drivers and designers were encouraged to build on the success they already enjoyed with the vee-4 engined, front-wheel-drive, Lancia Fulvia coupés.

Fiorio's problem, however, was that by 1970 his Fulvias were already at their peak, and the competition was increasing all the time. The Fulvia HF was as large and powerful as possible (1.6-litres and about 135 bhp was its limit, already reached), and it was exploring the outer limits of front-wheel-drive technology which BMC's Mini-Coopers had already found impossible to break. Rear-engined cars like the Porsche 911s and Alpine-Renaults could beat it in many conditions, while fast conventional cars like the Ford Escort RS1600s could match it in others. To beat such cars, Fiorio would have to find a more advanced rally car—but before the takeover of Lancia by Fiat there were no prospects of this ever happening, for Lancia's new-products cupboard was bare.

In November 1970, Bertone inadvertently suggested a solution, when they exhibited their sensationally styled, wedge-shaped, 'Stratos' at the Turin Show. This car, graced with a dramatically contoured two-seater layout, and a mid-mounted Lancia Fulvia HF engine of 1.6-litres behind the seats, was a non-runner at the time, and was by no means practical, though (as with all such show cars) it suggested ways in which car design might be moved forward. No one, surely, would have considered using a layout which had no doors, but which featured a huge lift-up windscreen (hinged behind the top of the seats) so that the driver and passenger could gain access to their seats? The engine/transmission unit, incidentally, was laid out in precisely the same way as in the Fulvia saloons and coupés, except that it had been moved bodily backwards in the space of the car, and was driving the rear wheels, rather than the front.

It was at about this time that Cesare Fiorio formulated his ideas for the future. Not only did he ask his engineers what was possible, but he also asked his contracted drivers (Sandro Munari, Harry Kallstrom and Simo Lampinen being the most famous) what they would like to drive. All, without exception, requested a new, lightweight, specially-designed machine, with its engine behind the driver, driving the rear wheels.

(Strangely enough, Ford of Britain had come to the same conclusion in 1970, and produced the mid-engined GT70 prototypes, though this car was never put into production.)

With approval from Lancia's new design chief, Piero Gobbato, a Fiat man who had previously been seconded to Ferrari at Maranello when the Fiat/Ferrari Dino project was getting under way, Fiorio therefore began to plan a new competition car, and was encouraged by being allowed to look

Fiat Sports Cars

TOP In 1970 Bertone showed this astonishing Lancia Fulvia-engined 'dream car' at the Turin Show, and called it the 'Stratos'. From such a vision, the Fiat-financed and engined Lancia Stratos project was inspired

ABOVE The original Lancia Stratos prototype of 1971, still not a runner when shown at Turin, used a transversely mounted Ferrari Dino engine/transmission power pack behind the seats. The engine, of course, was manufactured by Fiat

Stratos

TOP Apart from its mock-up tail lamps, the original 1971 Lancia Stratos looks exactly like the production cars which followed

ABOVE An early production example of the Stratos, complete with Italian trade plates. On the original road cars, the rooftop aerofoil section, and the rear spoiler, had not been standardized

Fiat Sports Cars

anywhere in the vast Fiat empire for an engine to power it. In truth, there was no future in considering any Lancia engine, for the flat-four Flavia was too old-fashioned, and the Fulvia vee-4 was already at its limit, and no longer powerful enough. With Porsche disposing of more than 220 bhp, and Alpine-Renault having 160/170 bhp in a very light car, Fiorio needed well over 200 bhp to be sure of having a potentially competitive car.

The story goes that Fiorio consulted Fiat about major changes to the twin-cam four-cylinder Fiat 125/132 unit already intended for a new quantity-produced Lancia (the Beta, to be launched at the end of 1972), and was told that 2-litres, and perhaps 180/200 bhp was possible, if not available 'off-the-shelf' at the moment, but that he was not enamoured by this.

Instead he turned to Ferrari, now owned by Fiat, and found the ideal solution. Not only was there a

ABOVE *Short, unmistakeable, and very purposeful, this Stratos has all the aerodynamic aids found to be necessary by the 'works' rallying team.*

TOP *Like many other cars of its type, with a wedge nose, the Lancia Stratos had flip up headlamps*

ABOVE RIGHT *Mike Parkes (left) had much to do with the successful development of the Stratos into a rally winner, while Daniele Audetto (in cap) was the team manager during the car's most successful period*

RIGHT *Bjorn Waldegard's Stratos splashing through the ford in Sutton Park on the 1975 Lombard-RAC Rally, an event which this car so nearly won*

Fiat-built four-cam 2.4-litre vee-6 engine produced for the Ferrari Dino 246GT, but this car had a well-developed transverse-engine/integral five-speed gearbox/ZF limited-slip final drive unit installation in use. The fact that several thousands of these cars had already been built, or were scheduled, and that Fiorio's boss, Ing. Gobbato had much knowledge of this car, and its components, all helped enormously. Fiorio's engineers even went so far as to test, and assess, a Ferrari Dino 246GT as a potential rally car, but found it both too large (at 13 ft 9 in. long) and too heavy (around 2400 lb) to impress them. When faced with the Alpine-Renault's power/weight ratio of—say—160 bhp in a mere 1400 lb car (about 250 bhp/ton, unladen), the Dino was quite simply too bulky.

In 1971, at Lancia, there was really no time to design a new competition car, for the engineers were up to their ears in work on the still-secret Beta saloons, coupés and estate cars, but Cesare Fiorio persuaded his bosses to allocate a small team to the job, and for ex-Lamborghini, ex-De Tomaso, chief designer Gianpaolo Dallara to bring his Supercar expertise to bear.

There never seemed to be any doubt as to the company which would build the structures—that honour went to Bertone, also of Turin, whose 1970 Turin Show 'Stratos' (so called because the staff at Bertone thought it quite 'out of this world'—in fact, from the stratosphere!) had created such a stir, and inspired Lancia so much, that it was thought they should now style a road-worthy car, and build the result.

The result, dubbed the 'Stratos HF', and looking much more like the car eventually to be put into limited production, was designed during 1971, and the partly-complete first prototype (with paper stuck-on tail lamps!) was shown at the Turin Show of that year. It was not, in fact, to become a runner until the summer of 1972, much to the chagrin of Fiorio and his drivers. There was no doubt, however, that the speedy development of the finished car, and the robust nature of the structure, was partly to the credit of Dallara, who had a distinguished track record which began when he assisted Mauro Forghieri at Ferrari, then Ing. Alfieri at Maserati—by the time he arrived as a contract designer at Lancia, he had been involved in a number of very famous designs, including the sensational transverse vee-12 engined Lamborghini Miura.

The Fiat connection with the Stratos, therefore, when it went into production in the winter of 1973/4, was that it was their commercial acumen which had added Ferrari and Lancia to their group before the end of the 1960s, and their encourage-

181

Fiat Sports Cars

ment of Fiorio which led to the evolution of the world's most successful rally car. The Stratos, indeed was the world's first *purpose-built* rally car, whose design was not compromized by mere marketing considerations. As styled by Bertone, designed by Dallara, and definitely developed by the British ex-Ferrari engineer, Mike Parkes, it was a 2100 lb Ferrari-engined projectile, with monocoque chassis and fibreglass bodyshell wrapped as tightly around the engine/transmission unit, the front and rear suspensions, and two rather cramped occupants, as possible. Compared with the original 1970 Bertone Stratos 'theme' car, it was a less stylish, more stubby, and infinitely more practical machine—but at the same time it had very few obvious uses.

At the development stage, and well before the first of 500 cars necessary for Group 4 homologation had been started, Lancia's sales force tried to add attraction (or compromise—who knows?) to the specification. At Turin 1971, on the occasion of its first appearance, it was suggested that the Ferrari-engined car might also eventually be joined by a rather more tame version fitted with a transversely-mounted 1.6-litre Fulvis vee-4 engine. During 1972, too, once testing had begun, trials were made with a 2-litre Fiat 132/Lancia Beta type of engine, and Beta transmission. Indeed, when the car was shown at Turin in November 1972, Lancia said it was ready to go into production, and that the Fiat/Lancia Beta engine and transmission, with a power output of about 150 bhp at 6000 rpm would be specified on the road cars; the rally team, it was suggested, would use the Ferrari installations, but how this was going to be homologated unless road cars were also to be sold with the same engine was never explained.

Fortunately, nothing ever came of this, and every Stratos ever sold (or raced or rallied) was equipped with the Ferrari/Fiat vee-6 four-cam engine. Cars first competed in races in Italy, as prototypes, in November and December 1972, but the first win came in the Spanish Firestone rally in April 1973.

Even though every manager at Lancia realised that the Stratos was necessary to its competition future, for the Fulvia HF coupés were rapidly becoming outclassed, development of the Stratos dragged on and on, and it was not until the spring of 1974 that the first cars were ready for sale. The sheet steel monocoques were built by Bertone, at their Grugliasco factory in the Turin area, along with the fibreglass body skin panels, whereas final assembly took place at the Lancia factory at Chivasso, some distance out of Turin, alongside the Turin-Milan *autostrada*.

The records show that 492 of a proposed sanction of 500 cars were actually built—all before the end of 1974—but it is also true to say that many of these cars hung around Lancia warehouses, unsold, for some time, for they were really only suitable for use in competitions, and not at all useful for general touring, high-speed business motoring, or for normal road use. Homologation for sporting purposes, into Group 4 (500 cars built) was achieved on 1 October 1974, and as its inspector (to verify numbers built) the CSI chose the noted engineer/motoring writer Paul Frère.

Writing in *Motor* in November 1974, Frère said 'By the beginning of September (1974) well over the required 500 cars had been made (I was commissioned by the CSI to find out about it) and

The Stratos was so versatile that it could be competitive in almost every condition. In the 1977 East African Safari this car, driven by Sandro Munari, finished third overall

182

Stratos

ABOVE *Lombard-RAC Rally action for the Stratos, with Sandro Munari driving a Pirelli-sponsored car in the 1978 event*

LEFT *Markku Alen, the 'Italian Finn' as he is affectionately known, loved the Stratos, and took several famous victories with it. Here, he's urging this Stratos to outright victory in the 1978 San Remo Rally. Slick tyres are being used, for a tarmac test*

production continues until the 1000 mark is reached.' That might once have been Fiat-Lancia's intentions, but it never happened. Only the single, original, batch of Stratos cars were built, and it is not at all certain that some of them were ever completed. In Weernink's history of Lancia, these words appear 'Insiders believe that only 250 Stratos ever went on the road, this poor commercial performance resulting from the oil crisis and tax rates of 18 per cent, then 35 per cent, for larger-capacity cars. The Stratos was not made in American 'safety' form ... even some European countries did not allow it on their roads.' Also '... although it is always officially denied, it seems very unlikely that all of the 500 cars were produced. Even in 1978 [which was actually more than three years after the last Stratos monocoque was built by Bertone—AAGR] one could still buy a new Stratos at the Turin factory for the equivalent of £7500, the 12 million lire asking price representing a tax-free figure.'

Not that any of this really mattered to Fiat-Lancia, who had gained homologation (at a considerable cost) of what was to be a quite outstanding competition car. Between 1972 and the end of 1978, when the Stratos was officially 'retired' from 'works' team use, the Lancia competitions department used no fewer than 28 different cars themselves, and supplied other cars to several other countries, teams or individuals.

Although the Stratos was a space-age machine, which looked as if it should only have been good for scudding up and down tarmac passes, or racing around the circuits of Europe, it was a quite astonishingly versatile rally car. By the time Mike Parkes and the Lancia engineers had developed the short-travel and long-travel suspension, and new aerodynamic aids, the high and low settings, the different gearboxes, and all the other strengthening

Fiat Sports Cars

The Stratos won the Monte Carlo rally four times in the 1970s, but the last occasion was the most famous of all, when Bernard Darniche drove a semi-private entry to defeat the might of Ford in 1979. Chardonnet were the Lancia importers in France

features, the Stratos could, and did, win on tarmac, on gravel, on snow and ice, in the rough, and in extremes of temperature.

It is a measure of its excellence that most enthusiasts willed the Stratos to win the Safari, and the Lombard-RAC rallies, both of which deafeated it; on Safari, in fact, it achieved a second place on its first attempt, and on the Lombard-RAC it finished third, also on its first attempt—in both events it was quick enough and strong enough, but never lucky enough.

Once established, indeed, the Stratos was always *the* car to beat, and it lifted the World Rally Championship for Lancia in 1974, 1975 and 1976. Even in 1977, it was still good enough to win with some ease, but inter-company politics had now turned against Lancia, and towards the Abarth-developed Fiat 131 saloons already described. The wheel, therefore, had turned full circle—Fiat had encouraged the birth of the Stratos, so that their group could have a dominant rally car, but eventually they withdrew it, to allow a Fiat-badged (if not Fiat-engined) car to take the limelight instead.

5 Turbine car project
Dabbling in the jet age

In April 1954, the arrival of *La Turbina* caused a sensation. Without news of its existence ever leaking out in advance, Dr Giacosa's engineers had been working on a gas-turbine powered prototype for some time—the car ran for the very first time on 14 April 1954, and on 23 April it was shown off the press. Immediately after this, it was wheeled in to the recently-opened *Salone dell' Automobile* in Turin, where it instantly became the most significant machine of the hundreds on display.

And yet, in spite of that vast wave of publicity which followed the launch, the Fiat turbine car project started and stopped at that point. It had little significance at the time, and none thereafter. Now it is one of the many curious exhibits in the Biscaretti Museum in Turin, and—like all the world's turbine-car projects—merely an intriguing 'might-have-been' in motoring history. Even so, when it was new, Fiat called it a sports car, so it ought to be described here.

The gas-turbine engine project—Type 8001, in official Fiat language—originated in the mind of Dr Giacosa, at a time when he ought to have been fully occupied with the development of Fiat's new post-war models. Any normal man might not have had time to consider such whimsical diversions, but Giacosa could—he was no ordinary man!

Even in 1948, when Giacosa first began to dabble with the idea, Rover had shown off their pioneering gas-turbine unit to the world, though they were by no means ready to put it into a car. Giacosa, however, was wondering if gas-turbine engines would suddenly become fashionable, and feasible,

La Turbina, Fiat's one-off gas-turbine engined prototype of 1954, carried this dramatic body style, in white and bright red, with two seats. The engine was carried behind the seats in true 1970s mid-engine fashion. Note the way the rear opening doors are curved over into the roof panel

185

Fiat Sports Cars

and if this happened he did not want Fiat to be left behind in the rush. Accordingly, he set Ing. Bellicardi to work in no great rush, to assimilate all available knowledge, and eventually to start the design of Fiat's first automotive gas turbine. The Type 8001 project, effectively, came into existence at that moment, and it was to Fiat's advantage that their aviation division soon began to start building British de Havilland Ghost jet engines under licence.

Developing the engine took a great deal of time (as Rover of Britain, had already found out). The first design work on the definitive engine began in September 1950, but it did not run until January 1953. Work on the actual car itself was delayed yet further, then completed in a glorious, exhilarating, rush. Chassis frame assembly began at the end of

ABOVE *From low down, the Turbina prototype has a superficial resemblance to the 8V sports coupé, no water-cooling radiator to be accommodated for a turbine-engined car*

RIGHT *This was the chassis layout of La Turbina, the gas-turbine powered Fiat prototype of 1954, complete with mid-mounted 300 bhp engine, and all-independent suspension*

Turbine car project

The Turbina's 300 bhp gas-turbine engine was mounted behind the cockpit, with very little insulation for the unfortunate driver. As is obvious from this picture, La Turbina was a research project, rather than a serious prototype with production cars in mind

February 1954, body construction on 1 March, the engine was delivered for installation on 15 March, and completion was on 10 April. Up to this point the very existence of a gas-turbine car project was virtually unknown, and the first-ever test run of the car was carried out on the rooftop test track of the Lingotto factory, in Turin itself!

Even discounting its engine, which would be very foolish, the Turbina prototype was an extremely advanced design for its day. Apart from the fact that it had a mid-mounted turbine driving the rear wheels (and there was also some residual jet thrust to add to the motive power), it also featured a very smooth body style (developed on scale models in a wind tunnel at the Turin Polytechnic) with an extremely low drag coefficient. Incidentally, I refuse to believe the figure of 0.14 quoted in some Fiat sources, for the drag coefficient of this car—something over 0.4 is much more likely to be the true figure.

The chassis of the turbine car was a simply ladder-style affair, featuring two large-diameter tubular longitudinals. Its wheelbase was 7 ft 10.5 in., exactly the same as that of the current 8V sports coupé. As the turbine car also used front and rear suspension assemblies, steering and brakes from the 8V, it has sometimes been said that a complete 8V rolling chassis was employed, but this is not strictly true, even though the same tracks, wheelbase, and major suspension parts were used.

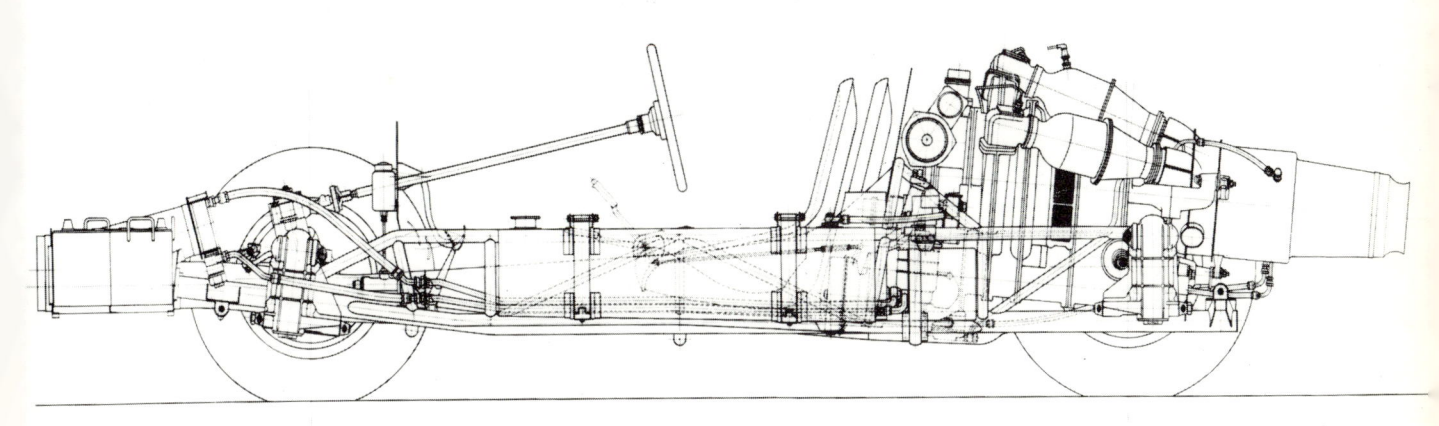

In the manner later to become normal for racing cars, the turbine engine was mounted longitudinally, but behind the seats, though the very simple transmission, such as it was (for a gas-turbine is its own fluid flywheel), was immediately ahead of, and below, the main turbine shafts.

The gas-turbine engine itself was a conventional (for the period) double-concentric-shaft unit, featuring two single-sided centrifugal compressors, with separate combustion chambers above the main shaft, and three axial turbine stages behind the line of the rear wheels. The fuel used, kerosene, was stored in two 11 gallon containers in the body sills beneath the doors, and consumption was never quantified, but known to be very much higher than the equivalent car.

The 'equivalent' car, incidentally, would have had to have a 300 bhp engine (which power, by the way, was developed at 22,000 rpm), and would have had to weigh no more than about 2315 lb unladen.

There was no gear changing to be done, of course, for the gas turbine engine was both extremely powerful, and able to act as its own fluid coupling. From the front of the turbine shaft, driven by the third of the three axial stages, power was dropped through a train of idler gears, taken backwards towards the rear wheels, raised again by another pair of gears, and fed to a simple spiral bevel final drive assembly. Five drop gears were involved in all, all being straight cut and, by definition, being rather noisy.

The technology of the day was not yet advanced enough to exract all the jet thrust as it passed through the turbine stages, so on the Fiat turbine car it was necessary to exhaust the hot gases through a large circular hole in the tail. As *Motor* commented in their analysis of the design 'Fiat do not, of course, claim that it represents a practical vehicle in its present stage, and they have not bothered to provide it with lamps as it is unlikely to be driven at night ... there is a large volume of very hot air coming out of the tail pipe even at idling speeds which would be a great embarrassment in traffic.'

Not only was La Turbina a very striking car, complete with large stabilizing fins, white coachwork, and bright crimson styling 'flames' along the sides, but it was very fast as well. The estimated maximum speed was about 250 km/h/157 mph, though in its demonstration at Turin's Caselle airport it achieved no more than 215 km/h/135 mph; this estimate, incidentally, confirms the drag coefficient as being more than 0.4, good, but by no means sensational.

In the end, however, the gas turbine car was something of a 'so what?'. Fiat made little further use of it, especially when it became clear that the twin bogeys of high cost, and poor fuel economy could not be conquered, and the car was soon consigned to the *Museo dell'Automobile* in Turin, where it can be seen to this day. Perhaps Dr Giacosa, as so often, got it absolutely right when he said, in his autobiography, that 'Fiat got a good deal of benefit in the way of publicity from the turbine auto.'

In 1983, this was the closest to sports car motoring that Fiat could boast. In fact it is the Ritmo Cabrio, produced in toto at Bertone's Grugliasco factory, and it was mechanically the same as the Ritmo saloon, complete with front-wheel-drive and a transversely-mounted engine. But a sports car?

Index

Aaltonen, Rauno 154, 157
Abarth, Carlo 62, 152–159
Abarth & Cie. 6, 55, 56, 64, 67, 89, 152–159, 162, 168, 171, 173
Acropolis Rally 4, 152, 157, 175
Agnelli, Giovanni 66, 115, 137, 152, 162
Alen, Markku 4, 157, 158, 175, 176, 183
Alfa Romeo SpA 41, 50, 76, 95, 151, 160, 162
Alfa Romeo 7, 11
    2000 56
    2600 Sprint 64
    Giulia Sprint 45, 62, 78, 83, 88, 146
    Giulietta 30, 31, 41, 62, 78
    Spider 127
Alifieri, Ing. 181
Allemano 38
Andruet, Jean-Claude 168
Aosta-St Bernard Hillclimb 28
Apruzzi (family) 14
Audetto, Daniele 180
Audi 175
    Quattro 175
Austin A40 31, 39
Austin-Healey 29, 56, 57
    3000 133
    Sprite 29, 51, 146
Autobianchi 67, 113, 115, 134
Autocar (The) 6, 27, 28, 39, 41, 54, 56, 64, 69, 71, 74, 85, 89, 94, 106, 119, 121, 131, 132, 134, 136, 146, 147, 151, 176
Autosport 106, 112

BMC 51, 113, 134, 177
    Mini 134
    Mini-Cooper 177
BMW 50, 129, 131
Barcelona 47
Bari (3 Hours) 28
Bazzi, Luigi 160
Beckers, Christine 168
Bellicardi, Ing. 100, 186
Bertone, Nuccio 6, 57, 58, 60, 62–65, 69, 71, 78, 92, 102, 105, 106, 112, 117, 120, 133–152, 168, 177, 178, 181–183, 188
Bertone
    Cabrio 151
    Runabout Barchetta 133, 135, 136
Bettega, Attilio 175
'Biche' 168
Biondetti, Clemente 11
Biscaretti Museum (Turin) 185
Bishop, Hugh 6
Bisulli, Giulio 157
Boano, Mario Felice 62, 63, 117, 125
Boano (son) 62, 63
Bologna 29
Bolster, John 106
Bowler, Michael 157
Brands Hatch 6
British Leyland 6, 51, 87, 90, 93, 121, 146, 151
British NEC Motor Show 148
British Pace Rally 175
Bulmer, Charles 129

CSI (Commission Sportive Internationale) 95, 157, 182
Capelli, Ovidio 11, 28
Caselle airport (Turin) 188
Ceccato 152
Ceirano 162
Centro Storico (Turin) 6, 26, 28
Chapman, Colin 146
Chardonnet 184

Chevrolet 171
    Corvette 171
    Corvette 'Rondine' 81
Chiti, Carlo 98
Chivasso (factory) 164, 166, 182
Cisitalia 11, 14, 15, 152
Citroën, Automobiles 134, 164
    CX 164
    DS 164
Colombo, Giocchino 95
Corso Marche (factory) 152
Costa Smeralda Rally 175, 176

Dallara, Gianpaolo 143, 148, 181, 182
Darniche, Bernard 158, 184
Datsun
    1600 66
    280Z 171
Dellis, Fred 91
DeTomaso 136, 143, 145, 181
    1600 Spider-Coupé 143, 144
    Deauville 51
    Mangusta 133
    Pantera 51, 144
    Vallelunga 71
DeTomaso, Alejandro 127, 143–145
DeTomaso Automobiles 144
Dino: the little Ferrari 98
Dusio, Piero 11, 152

EEC 120
East African Safari Rally 157, 182, 184
Energy Crisis 112
European Rally Championship 158

FISA 175
Ferrari 14, 27, 56, 146
    250GT 31
    250LM 95
    308GT4 109
    308GTB 160
    330GT 2+2 51
    365GT4 128
    V12 11
    Boxer 160
    Daytona 69
    Dino 95, 96, 100, 105, 109, 112, 125, 130, 146, 160, 177, 178
        206GT 112
        246GT 111, 112, 181
        GTS (Spider) 112
Ferrari, Alfredino ('Dino') 95, 98
Ferrari Dino (AutoHistory) 100
Ferrari, Enzo 95, 98, 99, 160, 161
Ferrari SpA 7, 28, 30, 42, 50, 72, 78, 96, 98–100, 102, 103, 105, 106, 109, 112, 127, 160, 161, 168, 171, 177, 180–182
Fiat
    8V (*Otto Vu*) 22–28
    8V Coupé 10, 15, 24, 27, 28, 63
    8V Sports Coupé 26, 47
    109 72
    120 Coupé 139
    124 Abarth Rallye 4, 89, 105, 152–159, 168
    124 saloon 44–46, 71, 72, 74, 76, 78, 83, 84, 87, 90, 93, 94, 102, 115, 123, 125, 155, 165
    124 Sport 76, 78, 88, 89, 134
    124 Sport Coupé 7, 56, 66, 72–94, 102, 106, 112, 145, 151, 154, 159, 160, 166, 175
    124 Sport Spider 4, 45, 62, 72–94, 102, 105, 106, 127, 145, 150–152, 154–156, 159, 161, 166, 167, 175

189

124 Spider Turbo 91, 94
124S 76, 134
125 saloon 76, 77, 84, 88, 89, 103, 115, 123, 152, 164, 165
125S saloon 84, 89, 134, 154
125 Spider 45
126 saloon 145
127 (Autobianchi A112) 67, 136
128 76, 78, 113–121, 125, 135, 136, 139, 148, 167
128 3P 113–121
128 Coupé Sport 113–121, 134, 137, 145, 151
128 Rally 113, 117, 137
128 Spider 134, 139
130 saloon 76, 105, 109, 116, 129, 131, 162
130 Coupé 112, 122–132
131 90
131 Abarth Rallye 158, 172, 173, 184
132 X20 168
132 Coupé 140
132 saloon 77, 89, 145, 154, 165, 166, 182
137 167, 169
600 and 600D 15, 17, 19, 30, 33, 47, 57–59, 117, 122
850 46, 78, 117, 119
850 Cistilia Spider 58
850 Coupé 17, 57–71, 83, 84, 90, 117, 119, 134
850 saloon 57, 58, 71, 113
850 Spider 17, 57–71, 105, 117, 134, 135, 137, 145, 146, 151
1100 saloon 11, 13–15, 17, 19, 21–23, 45, 47, 78, 115
1100 Gran luce 31
1100 Type 508 20
1100E saloon 15
1100ES Coupé 13–15, 20, 21
1100R 78, 115
1100S 8–21, 119
1100 Coupé 10, 11, 13–15, 20, 21
1100S Sports Coupé 10
1100/103 Coupé 14, 57
1100/103 saloon 14, 15, 19, 25, 42, 72, 74
1200 29–46, 115
1200 Cabriolet 29–46, 57, 62, 72, 74
1200 convertible 21
1200 Gran luce 19, 31, 34, 37, 42
1200 Spider 19
1300 saloon 44, 46, 54, 72, 74, 103, 119, 149
1400 10, 47, 49, 54
1400 saloon 15, 17, 19, 22, 24, 25
1500 Cabriolet 30, 35, 37–39, 42, 44–46, 49, 62, 75, 77, 78, 81
1500 Coupé 38, 45
1500 saloon 33, 40, 42, 44–47, 54, 72, 74, 103
1500S Cabriolet 33–35, 40–42, 45, 46
1600 78, 88
1600 Cabriolet 40
1600S Cabriolet 35, 37, 39–42, 44–46, 62, 75, 77, 78, 81
1600S Coupé 45
1800 Coupé 56
1800 saloon 31, 40, 42, 47, 50, 51, 72
1800B 54
1900 saloon 15, 17, 47, 49, 54
1900B 50
2100 Coupé 56
2100 saloon 31, 40, 42, 47, 50, 51, 72
2100 Special 50, 51, 54
2300 Coupé 49, 54, 56
2300 saloon 42, 47, 55, 56, 72, 123, 125, 127
2300 Special 54
2300B 54
2300S Coupé 47–56, 64, 122, 125, 144
X1/1 115
X1/2 67, 115, 136
X1/3 123
X1/4 115
X1/9 6, 7, 90, 92, 117, 120, 133–151, 161, 162, 167–169, 171, 172
X1/9 IN 151
X1/9 Lido 144
X1/20 90, 134, 147, 165, 167–169
X1/38 148

Abarth-Pininfarina SE030 168
Balilla
    508 9
    508C 9, 10
    508C MM 9–11, 13
    508CS 9
    508S Sport 9
    1100 25
Campagnola 24, 25
Cisitalia 11
    1100 11, 14
    Coupé 11, 15
    Sports 11
Dino 7, 28, 76, 78, 88, 95–112, 126–128
    166P 99
    168 99
    Coupé 56, 62, 78, 96, 97, 105, 106, 109–112, 125–127, 130, 132, 151, 152
    Spider 4, 78, 83, 87, 96–98, 100, 102, 105, 106, 109, 110, 112, 127, 130, 132, 151, 152
FSO (Poland) 42
La Turbina 185–188
Maremma 132
Nuova 500 123
Opera saloon 131, 132
Osca 29–46, 57, 77
Panda 122
Polski (Poland) 42
Project
    030 162, 164
    100 17, 57, 58, 115
    101 17, 24
    102 17
    103 17, 37, 42
    104 24, 27
    105 24, 49
    106 24
    109 113, 133
    111 47
    112 47, 49, 50
    115 42, 44, 54, 88
    116 44, 54, 72
    118 31, 41
    122 58
    123 113
    124 72, 138
    125 88
    130 164
    132 89
    135 102
    137 90
    138 148
    140 17, 123
    8001 185, 186
Ritmo/Strada 6, 116, 121, 148, 150, 172, 188
    105 150
    125 150
    Cabrio 188
    Super 85 151
Seat (Spain) 42
Topolino 30, 33, 47, 57, 106, 122, 123
Trasformabile 8–21, 29
    103E 17
    1100 19
    1100TV 17, 19, 21, 46
    1100/103E 20
    1100/103TV 17, 19, 31
    1200 29, 34
    1200TV 30, 31, 37, 38, 46
Uno 93
Fiat Auto (UK) Limited 6
Fiat Dino Register (UK) 112
Fiat Motors of North America 6, 90, 91, 93
Fiat of Milan 123, 127
Fiat of Turin 6, 15, 20, 26, 28, 30, 40, 49, 54, 58, 63, 67, 92, 100, 127, 143, 144, 152, 160, 162
Fiorio, Cesare 6, 172, 173, 175, 177, 180–182
Florida 93
Ford 143

Index

Capri II 119
Escort 109, 126, 157, 177
Ford Motor Company 51, 116, 119, 158, 177, 184
Forghieri, Mauro 181
Frankfurt Motor Show 40
Frère, Paul 88, 182

Gandini, Marcello 64, 135
Gandolfo, Paola 6
Gauld, Graham 6
General Motors 169
Geneva Motor Show 14, 15, 19, 22, 24, 27, 40, 62, 63, 67, 71, 78, 81, 83, 92, 102, 105, 109, 125, 127, 148, 151, 167–169, 172
Ghia 28, 38, 47, 49–52, 54, 56, 127, 133, 136, 143, 144
    2100S Coupé 51
    2300 Cabriolet 52
    2300 Club 52
    2300 Coupé 52
    2300 estate 52
Ghidella, Vittorio 93
Giacosa, Dr Dante 6, 7, 9–11, 14, 17, 19, 22, 24, 25, 27, 29, 40, 47, 49–51, 57, 58, 67, 72, 89, 100, 103, 109, 113, 115, 117, 123, 125, 134, 146, 185, 188
Giro d'Italia 162, 168
Giugiaro, Giorgetto 63
Gobbato, Piero 177, 181
Goddard, Geoffrey 6
Gregoire 17, 113
Grugliasco (factory) 62, 63, 71, 182, 188

Holmes, Martin 6
Howard, Geoffrey 106, 134
Hrushka, Rudolph 152

Innocenti Spider 950 51
IRI (Instituto Ricostruzione Industriale) 162
Iso Grifo 64, 160
Italian sports car championship 28

Jaguar 7, 76, 129
    E type 69
    XJ6 126
    XK120 27
    XK150 40
Jano, Vittorio 50, 95, 96, 98, 99, 102, 160

Kallstrom, Harry 177

LAT 6
1000 Lakes race 157, 175
Lamborghini 135, 160, 181
    Marzal 135
    Miura 64, 134, 135, 181
Lampinen, Simo 177
Lampredi, Aurelio 30, 42, 50, 54, 72, 75, 76, 95, 96, 98, 100, 102, 103, 109, 115, 116, 125, 128, 130, 160
Lancia (company) 4, 50, 90, 95, 115, 127, 134, 152, 160, 162–184
Lancia, Gianni 162
Lancia, Vincenzo 162, 175
Lancia
    HPR 90, 162, 167, 181
    Appia 162
    Aprilia 162
    Ardea 162
    Aurelia GT Coupé 11, 14, 15, 19, 162
    Aurelia Spider (America) 20, 31
    Beta 90, 91, 158, 162, 164, 165, 166, 167, 169, 171, 180–182
    Delta 172
    Flaminia 162
    Flavia 37, 162, 164, 180
    Floride 31
    Fulvia 146, 152, 162, 164, 169, 177, 178, 180, 182
    Gamma Coupé 128, 172
    Lambda 162
    Monte Carlo/Scorpion 90, 134, 148, 150, 162, 165–169, 171–173, 175

Rallye 4, 171–173, 175, 176
Stratos 6, 96, 109, 112, 152, 157, 158, 168, 169, 172, 177–184
Trevi 173
Langworth, Richard 6
Legend Industries of Detroit and Hauppage 91
Limone, Ing. Sergio 173
Lindberg, Hakan 152
Lingotto (factory) 10, 19, 34, 54, 63, 71, 84, 87, 121, 137, 187
Lloyd, Bill 30
Lombard-RAC Rally 175, 180, 183, 184
Los Angeles 171
Lotus 146
    Elan 64, 146, 147
Lotus-Ford 76
Ludvigsen, Karl 6, 91

MG 7, 29, 40, 57, 87, 88, 90, 93
    MGA 30, 40, 41
    MGB 83, 87, 90, 92, 93, 133
    Midget 64, 121, 134, 146
Makinen, Timo 157
Manzu, Pio 133
Maranello 98, 112, 160, 177
Maserati, Alfieri 29, 30, 35
Maserati, Ernesto 29, 30, 35, 37, 39
Maserati, Ettore 29, 30, 35, 39
Maserati (company) 160, 181
Mercedes-Benz 123, 129, 131
    300 125
    C111 Coupé 136
Mikkola, Hannu 157–159
Milan 41, 88, 123, 160, 167
Mille Miglia 9–11, 27, 160
Mini-Minor 113
Modena 143
Monclavo Fotographie 6
Montabone, Oscar 10, 58, 72, 113, 115, 117
Monte Carlo Rally 152, 158, 169, 175, 184
Monza 56, 99
Moretti 33, 66
Moss, Stirling 30
Motor (The) 6, 27, 54, 55, 88, 129, 131, 157, 182, 188
Motor Sport 6
Motor Trend 46, 171
Munari, Sandro 157, 169, 177, 182, 183
Mundy, Harry 54
Museo dell'Automobile (Turin) 188
Mussolini, Benito 10

Nuvolari, Tazio 11
Nye, Doug 98

OSI 133, 134
Opel Kadett 109, 126
Osca (Officini Specializzata Construzione Automobili) 29–46
Orsi (family) 29, 30

Panico, Gian Beppe 6
Paris Show 19, 72
Parkes, Mike 180, 182, 183
Pesenti, Carlo 162
Pianta, Georgio 162, 168
Pininfarina, Sergio 6, 13–15, 17, 19–21, 24, 27, 28, 31, 34, 37–40, 42, 44–46, 49, 51, 52, 62, 64, 71, 72, 78, 80, 83–85, 87, 89–95, 98, 100, 102, 105, 106, 112, 123, 124, 127–129, 131, 132, 155, 157, 159, 162, 165, 167–169, 171, 172, 175, 176
Pinto, Rafael 157
Plains of Lombardy 10
Polish Rally 157
Pomeroy, Laurence 27
Porsche, Dr Ferdinand 152
Porsche (company) 152, 180
Porsche 59, 154
    911 177
    924 171
    Abarth 71
Press-on-Regardless Rally (USA) 157

Fiat Sports Cars

RAC Rally 152
Radbourne Racing 146
Rapi, Luigi Fabio 19, 24, 25
Reliant Scimitar GTE 132
Renault 50
    Alpine 152, 154, 156, 177, 180, 181
    5 Turbo 172
Ricart, Wilfredo 160
Rivalta (factory) 102, 131
Road & Track 19–21, 41, 46, 65, 66, 87, 89, 93, 94, 146, 149, 171, 176
Rocchi, Franco 96, 98, 99
Rohrl, Walter 4, 158, 175
Rome 10
Rover of Britain 185, 186
Rowan Industries 127, 143

SEFAC racing 160
SIRA 133, 134
Salamano, Carlo 11, 27
Salone dell'Automobile (Turin) 185
San Remo Rally 157, 158, 175, 183
Sanyo New Zealand Rally 175
Sassi 11
Savio, Carrozzeria 9, 11, 21
Scaglietti 127
Scarfiotti, Ludovico 28
Scuderia Ferrari 160
Seat (Barcelona) 47, 59
Sebring 12 hour race 30
Sedgwick, Michael 22, 67
Segre, Luigi 51, 133
Seidler, Edouard 164
Seifert, Dr Eberhard 6
Siata of Turin 27, 28
    208 28
Simca (company) 47, 58, 72, 113
Simca
    1000 58
    1100 117
    1200S Coupé 64
    Aronde 47
    Autobianchi Primula 58, 72, 74, 113, 115, 116, 133
Sloniger, Jerry 6
Spanish Firestone Rally 182
Sqvazzini, Ing. Gianfranco 155
Stella Alpina 28
Suez War 131, 132, 146, 168
Superga 11
Sutton Park 180
Swedish Rally 159

TAP Rally (Portugal) 157, 158, 175
Talbot Sunbeam-Lotus 126
Colin Taylor Productions 6

Thorold-Palmer, Mike 6
Thoroughbred & Classic Cars 6, 56
Tjaarda, Tom 51, 144
Todt, Jean 159
Toivonen, Henri 175
Tonegutti, Cesare 123
Tour de Corse 175
Triumph 7, 29, 40, 57, 84
    TR3 30
    TR7 146
    Spitfire 64, 66, 121, 146
Turin 45, 62, 78, 111, 123, 137, 152, 160, 162, 164, 166, 175, 181–183, 185, 187, 188
Turin-Milan axis 10, 182
Turin Motor Show 28, 38, 51, 78, 83, 85, 88, 89, 100, 102, 105, 109, 118, 127, 133–136, 143, 145, 148, 152, 162, 169, 177, 178, 181, 182
Turin Polytechnic 187
Tutte le Fiat 19

Ulyate, Robin 157

VW Karmann-Ghia 1500 51
VW-Porsche 914 136
Valentini, Fredi 6
Valletta, Vittorio 10, 22, 47, 95, 100, 115, 123
Vauxhall Chevette 126
Verini, Maurizio 157, 157
Vignale 27, 28, 62, 84
Via La Manta (studios) 63
Vitale, Richard 6
Volvo 1800ES 132
Vudafieri, Adartico 158

Waldegard, Bjorn 154, 157, 158, 180
Walton, Jeremy 6
Warmbold, Achim 157
Webb, Ian 100
Weernink, Wim Oude 27, 183
Wilkins, Gordon 27
Windsor, Peter 146, 147
World Championship
    Constructors' 98
    Drivers' 98
    Makes 158
    Rally 4, 154, 156, 158, 175, 184
    Sports Car 6
World War 1 160
World War 2 10, 95, 152, 162
Wyss, Wallace 144

'Yom Kippur' war (Suez) 90, 120, 146

ZF (Germany) 109, 126, 129, 130, 173, 181
Zagato, Elio 27, 28, 140, 167